Lessons of the Pandemic

Also Available

Reading Instruction That Works:
The Case for Balanced Teaching, Fifth Edition

Tim Pressley, Richard L. Allington, and Michael Pressley

Lessons of the Pandemic

Disruption, Innovation, and What Schools Need to Move Forward

David T. Marshall
Tim Pressley

Foreword by
Harry Anthony Patrinos

THE GUILFORD PRESS
New York London

A Division of Guilford Publications, Inc.
370 Seventh Avenue, Suite 1200, New York, NY 10001
www.guilford.com

Printed in the United States of America

This book is printed on acid-free paper.

Last digit is print number: 9 8 7 6 5 4 3 2 1

Library of Congress Cataloging-in-Publication Data is available from the publisher.

ISBN 978-1-4625-5387-7 (paperback) — ISBN 978-1-4625-5388-4 (hardcover)

About the Authors

David T. Marshall, PhD, is Associate Professor of Educational Research in the College of Education at Auburn University. Since 2020, much of his research has focused on the COVID-19 pandemic and its impact on K–12 education. Dr. Marshall edited *COVID-19 and the Classroom: How Schools Navigated the Great Disruption*, one of the first books to share social science research documenting the first 15 months of the crisis. His research interests also include school choice and charter schools. Dr. Marshall's work has been published in leading journals of education research, policy, and practice. Prior to his doctoral studies, he taught middle and high school social studies in both traditional public schools and public charter schools in Philadelphia. He served two terms as chair of the Alabama Public Charter School Commission.

Tim Pressley, PhD, is Associate Professor of Psychology at Christopher Newport University, where he is also a faculty member in the Master of Arts in Teaching program and the Center for Education Research and Policy. Before receiving his doctorate, Dr. Pressley was an elementary school teacher, and giving teachers a voice on issues affecting their lives has been a driving force behind his research. Currently his research focuses on the impact of COVID-19 on teachers, teacher effectiveness, and teacher burnout. His work has been published in leading education journals. Dr. Pressley is coauthor of *Reading Instruction That Works, Fifth Edition*.

Foreword

When schools started to shut down in the spring of 2020, I thought we were in for a few weeks or at most months of closures. Then summer would come, and we would have 3 months or so to help children get back on track. Nevertheless, we educators and policymakers started to think about the implications. It wasn't just schools that shut down; almost whole economies were closed. We knew from past crises that the effects would be significant and long-lasting. We forecast the impact of a few weeks or months of closures on school attendance and likely learning losses. We made conservative estimates and assumed that losses could be minimized with online learning and recovered soon after the (short) lockdown.

As we know now all too well, the shutdowns lasted a lot longer. In some developing countries the school closures were for more than 2 years. Those initial forecasts of learning loss turned out to be very conservative. Actual losses around the world are on average about a year's worth of learning. They are even higher in low-income countries and in populations that were already struggling academically even before the pandemic. The learning losses will be difficult to recover. The future earnings losses of today's students will be huge. Their impact on productivity and national income are historical losses of enormous proportion.

In 2020, most countries closed schools and universities, affecting more than 90% of the world's learners. The evidence strongly indicates that school closures result in learning loss, and the longer the school closure the more significant the loss. In most countries, with very few exceptions, the losses were typically proportionally higher for students who were already disadvantaged. In other words, losses were not distributed uniformly. The worst affected students belong to the high-risk groups—the students who had fallen behind and children from low-income families. The main reason for these learning losses was a lack of preparedness for the transition to online education.

All this means that schooling matters. By extension, this proves that teachers matter—which brings us to the subject of this book, *Lessons of the Pandemic: Disruption, Innovation, and What Schools Need to Move Forward.* After the summer of 2020, and by the time of vaccine availability, the prolonged school closures that resulted in these learning losses were a policy choice. This book calls it a policy failure. One of the groups this policy failed most is teachers.

The authors of this book look at the crisis from an interesting perspective: the impact of COVID-19 on teachers. This is important because one of the positive outcomes of the pandemic is the realization that we need teachers, perhaps now more than ever. The school closures reminded us of the importance of in-person instruction with a qualified professional. Emergency remote teaching is no substitute for in-person teaching. Yet, the voice of the teacher has not been given prominence. That makes this book so important and unique. It gives voice to the teachers through research reviewed by the authors and original surveys they implemented.

Unfortunately, the school closures became politicized in many countries. It did not have to be that way. Some countries closed schools for a few weeks in the spring of 2020, then focused on remedial education in the summer and were back to normal in 2020–2021. Learning losses were minimal in those countries.

The abrupt closures in the spring of 2020 caught us all off guard. But they were especially difficult for teachers, who suddenly had to organize remote learning. As this book documents, teachers were often not supported for this transition. The prolonged closures, which were ineffective in terms of disease management, made it even more difficult for teachers who, in most cases, continued to work without adequate support.

The other positive outcome of the pandemic is that we learned something about technology in education. While emergency remote teaching is not an adequate solution, blended learning might nevertheless be useful as an aid to teachers. Online tutoring increased exponentially during the pandemic and continues to be used in the recovery efforts in many countries. Artificial intelligence is being used in conjunction with traditional teaching methods, thus giving us a glimpse of the future of education and personalized learning. Going forward, during crises and otherwise, a blended learning model that empowers teachers and provides state-of-the-art support to students could be implemented. This will give teachers the autonomy they want and provide the tools needed to make teaching and learning more effective.

It's not too late to adjust. We must reach out to teachers with the support they need. This book allows us to hear the voices of teachers—what they need and what they desire to do. Without support for teachers—from administrators, policymakers, parents, and the public—the problems will persist. However, if teachers are supported and given the autonomy and resources they need, then something can be done about learning loss, and we will have a fair chance at recovery. If not, the students and their teachers will continue to suffer. Worse, they may turn away from schools altogether. Students will drop out, and teachers will leave the profession.

The authors of this book call prolonged school closures the biggest education policy mistake of the past century. It's time to make the subsequent reopening of schools a time of promise, progress, and achievement. Going forward, teachers and technology will be important for a speedy recovery. Tutoring, especially online, has proven effective in mitigating learning loss. It should be part of any serious implementation of a national learning recovery program. At the same time, it is important to protect the education budget. Learning recovery is costly, even if online tutoring is cost-effective. As schools struggle to help students recover, teachers need support and professional development. Education systems need to be rebuilt and prepared for future shocks. Most important, before doing any of these things, it is imperative that schools measure learning outcomes. School systems that addressed learning loss quickly did this first by measuring losses and using assessment to gauge the results of their efforts. This will enable educators to identify gaps and make remedial learning plans. In most countries, we also need more effective teaching. This means adequately funded and equipped training programs and courses for teachers. During the recovery, additional learning time is needed, which could occur through remedial classes, shortened vacations, after-school programs, and tutoring—including online.

Practically all these policies require an increase in education spending in the budget. Most countries reduced their spending during the pandemic. Three years later the budgets are yet to recover. It is most important, however, that money is well spent on the most pertinent aspects: teachers, professional development, information systems, and assessment.

It would have been prudent, as this book says, to have followed the science. Hopefully, the next time such a crisis occurs, we will have the confidence to do so. Keeping schools open—safely—should be a priority, along with supporting teachers and students. And this should be done in a way that empowers teachers by giving them the resources they need and the autonomy to carry out their mission.

HARRY ANTHONY PATRINOS, PHD
Senior Advisor, Education
The World Bank

Preface

In 2020, we both started exploring the impact of the COVID-19 pandemic for different reasons. Ultimately, we both wanted to understand the effects it would have on teachers. Since 2020, we have spent countless hours surveying and interviewing teachers across the United States to learn about their experiences during this global pandemic. As former classroom teachers, we have great respect for teachers and their work. Even though we had the same goal with our research, our initial motivations to begin exploring the impact of COVID-19 had different origins.

David Marshall

There are moments in life that are inflection points, moments for which you'll always remember where you were and the surrounding context. One such moment in my life was the Al-Qaeda terrorist attack on the World Trade Center and the Pentagon in 2001. The COVID-19 pandemic was also such a moment in time. Admittedly, I did not initially believe the pandemic would amount to much. Previous pandemics during my lifetime—including the outbreaks of SARS-CoV-1 (better known simply as "SARS") between 2002 and 2004 and the swine flu in 2009—certainly affected some individuals; however, life as we knew it was not altered in any meaningful way. As such, when I first began seeing news of a pandemic emerging from China in late 2019 and early 2020, I simply wrote it off as an event similar to what I had seen before. To say I was wrong would be quite an understatement.

I recall having a conversation with my colleague David Shannon the Friday before schools shut down. We were getting ready to go into spring break and were discussing something mundane such as department scheduling when the conversation shifted to the topic du jour in the news—COVID-19. By this point, we were both concerned enough about the looming crisis that we had gone out and purchased groceries, including toilet paper (Fisher, 2020). Rumors had been going around campus that we might move to online instruction for the week following spring break. It was beginning to seem like this time was going to be different. But would they really close K–12 schools? That seemed extreme and far-fetched. We mused that, if policymakers did indeed close schools, someone should check in with teachers to see how they were making sense of all of this.

Prior to working at Auburn University, I played multiple roles at a teacher residency program in my home state of Virginia, and I was connected with several of the teachers I helped prepare via social media. When they announced that schools would close for 2 weeks in Virginia, I saw these teachers' reactions to the news. After scrolling through Facebook and reading some of what these teachers had to say, I picked up the phone and called David Shannon again. I recall saying something along the lines of, "Hey, remember when we said someone needed to check in with teachers if they closed schools? Well, they've closed schools. I think we have to do this." We spent the next 36 hours putting together the survey and institutional review board (IRB) protocol with my colleague Savanna Love from Randolph-Macon College. (Students—this is *not* best practice; we didn't have time for that.) Our IRB was approved within the next 36 hours, and the rest is history. As former teachers (Savanna and me) and as someone who has worked with STEM-based programs in Alabama's Black Belt region for years (David), it mattered to us that we accurately captured what the pandemic was like for stakeholders in K–12 schools, including teachers. I hope we've done them justice.

Tim Pressley

My wife, Stephanie, who is now in her 15th year of teaching, has taught in elementary and middle schools throughout her career and has significantly influenced my desire to learn more about the impact of COVID-19 on teachers. In 2020, Stephanie was a reading intervention teacher at an elementary school and worked with small groups of students to improve their reading skills. When schools moved online in March 2020, I had a front-row seat for the virtual classroom experience. I saw my wife set up at our dining-room table for her reading groups and hoped her students would log on for their daily small groups. I saw Stephanie work to engage her students virtually for every lesson and check in with her students to learn how they were coping throughout this new and challenging time. I heard stories of parents sitting to the side of the camera telling students answers or talking on the phone, disrupting the lessons. I also saw firsthand my wife getting online at all hours of the day and night just to make sure she connected with students who had missed their group time for any number of reasons—say, because they had to share tablets with brothers or sisters or because their parents or guardians were not available to help them log on to the virtual system. Throughout this time, I also saw former teachers I had worked with and former students who had become teachers making comments on social media about the challenges they faced because of the move to remote learning. This continued through the summer of 2020, as I watched the local school board meetings that included hours of public comment regarding the reopening of schools and the constant media coverage of districts weighing decisions on how and when to return to in-person instruction.

In the fall of 2020, I began researching how teachers felt during the pandemic. My first survey of teachers aimed to hear their perspectives on the different instructional approaches, to know how they were affected, and, most important, to allow them to share their opinions and concerns. Some of the most powerful moments during the data collection came when teachers thanked me for conducting this research—even though I was the one thankful for the many teachers who even took the time to complete my survey. It had never occurred to me that this was the first time anyone had asked some of these teachers how they felt about teaching during the pandemic. Because of this, I continued to explore the effect of the COVID-19 pandemic on teachers throughout the subsequent years.

* * *

This book draws on our own research efforts over the past few years to understand the impact of the pandemic on teachers, with a specific focus on including teacher perspectives. Marshall surveyed teachers at three time points (March/April 2020, January/February 2021, and May 2021). He also conducted interviews at two time points (January/February 2021 and May/June 2021) and focus groups in 2021. Pressley conducted surveys with teachers at two time points (October 2020 and May

2021). We crossed paths as we were both wrapping up our May 2021 surveys and have been collaborators in this work ever since then.

Our most recent and final two surveys were a collaboration between the two of us. In addition to drawing on the existing academic literature on COVID-19 and K–12 education, our insights include our interactions with almost 3,500 teachers and stakeholders involved in education. See Table P.1 for a list of our collective data collection efforts. All individuals we highlight in this book are identified using pseudonyms. Any personally identifiable details about them, including their names, have been altered to protect their identities. The Appendix at the end of this book offers a more detailed overview of our methodology.

TABLE P.1. Our Research Efforts Exploring the Pandemic's Impact on Schools, 2020–2023

Primary author(s)	Time period	Study participants	Data collection
Marshall, Shannon, Love	March–April 2020	Teachers (n = 249)	Survey
Marshall, Neugebauer	Summer 2020	Charter school leaders (n = 33)	Interviews, surveys
Marshall, Trammell	Fall 2020; Fall 2021	Teacher preparation staff/ participants (n = 37)	Interviews, survey
Pressley	Oct. 2020	Teachers (n = 361)	Survey
Marshall, Shannon, Love	Jan.–Feb. 2021	Teachers (n = 335)	Survey
Marshall, Love	Jan.–June 2021/ Feb. 2023	Teachers (n = 12)	Interviews
Pressley	May 2021	Teachers (n = 316)	Survey
Marshall, Shannon, Love	May 2021	Teachers (n = 302)	Survey
Marshall, Neugebauer, Smith	Fall 2021	Teachers (n = 20)	Focus groups
Marshall, Pressley	May 2022	Teachers (n = 830)	Survey
Marshall, Pressley, Smith, Trammell, Neugebauer	Aug.–Sept. 2022	Teachers (n = 40)	Focus groups
Marshall, Pressley	Apr.–May 2023	Teachers (n = 927)	Survey

As we told our participants when we were conducting the studies, *we aim to be their voice*. We hope this book sheds light on the impact of the COVID-19 pandemic on students and teachers. We also hope this book provides school leaders a chance to reflect on the decisions made during the pandemic and how we move beyond it.

Acknowledgments

We would both like to thank our families for their patience and support during the process of writing this book.

We would also like to offer our gratitude to the colleagues who collaborated with us between 2020 and 2023, as we have tried to make sense of the impact that the COVID-19 pandemic has had on schools. We would also like to thank Nat Malkus and John Kristof for sharing data with us.

Our gratitude goes out to the team at The Guilford Press, and especially to Senior Editor Craig Thomas: He saw something in our project, and we're grateful for the effort he put forth to ensure its success. Our book is a better product because of him.

And last but certainly not least, thank you to every teacher who completed one of our surveys or took the time to speak to us in an interview or focus group. We cannot thank you enough for giving us a window into your world. We would not know half of what we know if not for you.

Contents

Lessons of the Pandemic

Chapter 1

The Great Disruption

The Severe Acute Respiratory Syndrome Coronavirus 2, more commonly referred to as SARS-CoV-2 or COVID-19, originated in Wuhan, China, in late 2019 (Zhou et al., 2020). Within months, the once-in-a-generation pandemic spread across the planet. Drastic mitigation efforts ensued, which included universal mask wearing, social distancing, business closings, and working from home (Bourne, 2021). The response to the pandemic had a dramatic impact on education. Schools in the United States closed in 48 states in March 2020 (Marshall, 2022a). Although some schools had already closed locally, Nebraska and Maine were the last two states to formally close schools on April 1 and April 2, 2020, respectively, and schools across the country remained closed for the remainder of the 2019–2020 school year.*

The Unprecedented Shift to Remote Learning

Merriam-Webster's 2020 Word of the Year was *pandemic*. It just as easily could have been *unprecedented*. When schools closed for in-person learning, teachers were forced to teach in ways in which most were never trained (Marshall, Shannon, & Love, 2020), and students were asked to learn in ways to which they were unaccustomed (Carpenter & Dunn, 2020). In some cases, teachers were given mere hours to gather everything they would need for the next 2 weeks, which many initially believed

*Montana and Wyoming were exceptions to this. Statewide school closures ended on May 6, 2020, in Montana ("Bullock's Stay-at-Home Order Lifted," 2020) and May 15, 2020, in Wyoming ("Wyoming Schools to Remain Closed," 2020); however, local school districts could still elect to remain closed, and many districts did for the duration of the school year.

would be the duration of the crisis (Love & Marshall, 2022). At some schools, faculty and staff worked overtime to put together paper-based instructional packets for students to take home—packets that school leaders later conceded were not pedagogically valuable (Marshall & Neugebauer, 2022). Survey research from March and April 2020 suggests that teachers who taught in schools that relied on instructional packets experienced the lowest professional self-efficacy during this time (Marshall, Shannon, Love, & Norris, in press). Elsewhere, learning pivoted from face-to-face to online in a matter of days (Kaden, 2020; Love & Marshall, 2022). Scholars have been careful to describe this as "emergency remote teaching" instead of "online teaching"; the distinction is important (Hodges, Moore, Lockee, Trust, & Bond, 2020). Like traditional face-to-face teaching, online teaching is a planned exercise in which the lessons, activities, and assessments are aligned and designed with online teaching as the intended mode of delivery. That definition does not describe what occurred in the spring of 2020 (Affouneh, Salha, & Khlaif, 2020; Hodges et al., 2020; Milman, 2020). When schools closed to in-person instruction, teachers were forced to take lessons, activities, and assessments designed for schooling as usual and deliver them remotely—often without the training, materials, or time to do so effectively (Marshall, Shannon, & Love, 2022). Many of the school leaders we interviewed suggested that teachers should take their curriculum, cut it in half, and then cut that in half again (Marshall & Neugebauer, 2022; Vanourek, 2020). So students who remained engaged in their studies were exposed to a fraction of the content they would have been under normal circumstances.

Schools that delivered instruction virtually prior to the pandemic were a noted exception to this. Kingsbury (2021), in survey research, found that parents of students who were enrolled in virtual schools at the time schools were closed for in-person instruction reported substantially better outcomes when compared to those in traditional brick-and-mortar schools who were delivering emergency remote instruction. However, most students learned decidedly less than they should have during the last two months of the 2019–2020 school year.

Reopening Schools for In-Person Learning

Schooling looked quite different across the United States during the 2020–2021 school year. School districts began the year offering one of the following: fully remote, hybrid, or fully in-person learning. For the purposes of this book, *hybrid* instruction will be defined as instruction delivered to the student partially in person and partially remotely. It is important to note that hybrid instruction looked different across contexts. One example of a hybrid learning modality employed during the pandemic was an A/B plan. Under such a plan, the student body would be divided into two roughly even groups. Group A attended in person on Mondays and Tuesdays and Group B on Thursdays and Fridays. Wednesdays were asynchronous for everyone, allowing for additional cleaning in the school and planning time for teachers. Hybrid teaching should not be confused with hyflex teaching (short for hybrid–flexible), which involves teaching students in person and virtually simultaneously (Bower, Dalgarno, Kennedy, Lee, & Kenney, 2015). Decisions about how and when schools would return in the fall of 2020 were often highly debated across communities at school board meetings during the summer of 2020. These debates ranged from the type of instruction schools would provide to safety protocols that schools would enforce. In the end, every school district offered families an option to choose the learning modality for their child, including remote learning options during the 2020–2021 school year (Marshall & Bradley-Dorsey, 2020)—representing the closest thing to a version of universal school choice that had ever been offered in the United States. For the first time in American history, every family had a choice of how their student would attend school.

Some districts around the United States returned to some form of in-person instruction; however, larger school districts were more likely to begin the school year with remote instruction. According to *Education Week* (EdWeek Research Center, 2022), almost three-fourths (74%) of the 100 largest school districts began the school year with remote instruction.* One analysis found that a school district with 100,000 students was almost 10 times less likely to reopen in person in September 2020 than one with 1,000 students (Marshall & Bradley-Dorsey, 2022). Some school districts, such as New York City, based their decisions to keep schools open on the city's case positivity rates (Heyward, 2021). The case positivity rate was the proportion of total COVID-19 tests administered that

*Hawai'i does not have school districts; all public schools report directly to the Hawai'i Department of Education. These analyses exclude public schools in Hawai'i and the District of Columbia ("School Districts' Reopening Plans: A Snapshot," 2020; Marshall & Bradley-Dorsey, 2022).

were positive (Shapiro & Rubenstein, 2020). This was always a flawed statistic because of the denominator. For example, states such as New York and Connecticut tested a lot. By contrast, states such as Oklahoma generally only gave tests to individuals with symptoms during the fall of 2020. During the week of September 14, 2020, Oklahoma had a case positivity rate of 23%.* That was not so much indicative of how widely the virus spread as, rather, who was getting tested, under what circumstances, and how often. If everyone, including those without COVID-19 symptoms, was tested for the virus, then the positivity rate would be much lower than if only those presenting symptoms were administered the test. In New York City, if the case positivity rate eclipsed 3%, schools would be shuttered based on a deal made between then-Mayor Bill de Blasio and the New York City teachers union (Heyward, 2021). This was much more stringent than the 9% case positivity rate threshold put in place by then-Governor Andrew Cuomo (Shapiro, 2020). Schools were closed for in-person instruction on November 19, 2020, when the case positivity rate rose above the 3% threshold for the first time (Heyward, 2021), only to reopen again on November 29 after parents complained and the mayor abandoned the metric for determining when to close schools (Shapiro, 2020).

School closure and reopening policies were not fixed decisions. Many schools toggled back and forth between learning modalities, especially during the fall of 2020 and winter of 2020–2021. By March 1, 2021, more than 90% of school districts were offering some form of in-person learning. School districts that were small (five or fewer schools), rural, and had less access to broadband internet were the most likely to offer in-person learning, whereas larger, more urban districts, as well as those serving a greater proportion of students of color, were more apt to offer only remote learning. Counties with higher rates of mask wearing, as well as those that supported Joe Biden in the 2020 U.S. presidential election, were also more likely to have schools exclusively offering remote instruction. Conversely, districts located in counties with lower mask-wearing rates, as well as those that supported Donald Trump in the 2020 election, were also more likely to remain open. The shifts between modalities

*This figure was calculated from the CDC's COVID-19 Diagnostic Laboratory Testing Time Series archived website (CDC, 2023d). During the week of September 14–20, 2020, a total of 42,803 COVID-19 tests were rendered in the state of Oklahoma, 9,845 of which yielded positive results.

often led to more work for teachers as they were again changing instructional approaches at a moment's notice (Pressley, 2021b; Pressley, Kidd, & Wheatley, 2023). See Table 1.1 for the percent of districts that offered fully remote, hybrid, and fully in-person learning at four time points during the 2020–2021 school year.

The Logistics of Teaching during the Pandemic

As for the teachers, this time period was challenging regardless of their school's reopening modality. Teachers who taught in schools that were fully remote during this period of time had to continue to translate their lesson plans and curricula to an online context (Huck & Zhang, 2021). Although most remote instruction was synchronous at this point, meaning that instruction was online but taking place in real time (Miller, Sellnow, & Strawser, 2021), teachers often delivered lessons to students with their cameras turned off, with little student engagement (Love & Marshall, 2022). In short, teaching remotely in the fall of 2020 was not an easy task.

Teachers delivering instruction in schools—whether fully in person or hybrid—also experienced challenges. As part of a continued effort to curb the spread of COVID-19, schools instituted a range of mitigation strategies. These included social distancing measures, serving lunch in classrooms, and masking mandates (Falk et al., 2021; Love & Marshall, 2022). In some cases, plexiglass was installed at the front of classrooms, and teachers stood behind it when they taught. Evidence suggests that this was not a particularly successful approach to mitigate the spread of the virus, especially given the length of time individuals spend in a classroom together (Eykelbosh, 2021).

A study conducted by Emily Oster and her colleagues (Oster, Jack, Halloran, Schoof, & McLeod, 2021) explored the efficacy of mitigation efforts in three states: Florida (n = 1,453,464), Massachusetts (n = 485,790), and New York (n = 1,223,327). They focused on masking requirements, ventilation improvements, and student population density in schools. Most schools around the United States required masks for students and staff alike (Marshall & Bradley-Dorsey, 2020). Because of this, studying the efficacy of masking in most contexts was difficult given the lack of a control group. Florida represents an exception to this. Oster and her colleagues found that mask requirements (whether for staff, students,

TABLE 1.1. Distribution of School Districts by Learning Modality in 2020–2021

	Fully remote (%)				Hybrid (%)				Fully in-person (%)			
	9/5	11/2	3/1	6/7	9/5	11/2	3/1	6/7	9/5	11/2	3/1	6/7
All districts	25	19	8	1	41	45	52	45	34	36	39	54
High achievement	18	14	4	0	46	49	56	43	36	37	41	57
Low achievement	30	24	13	2	37	40	49	46	32	35	38	52
High broadband	33	26	12	1	42	48	59	51	25	27	30	48
Low broadband	33	12	4	1	44	41	45	37	40	48	51	62
High poverty	27	20	10	2	37	41	49	44	36	39	41	55
Low poverty	23	18	7	1	46	48	56	46	32	34	37	54
High minority	36	28	14	0	38	42	55	50	26	29	31	49
Low minority	9	7	14	2	46	48	49	38	45	45	50	61
Large districts (12+ schools)	48	35	18	2	34	43	58	56	18	22	25	43
Medium districts (6–11 schools)	37	28	13	1	40	47	58	52	22	25	29	47
Small districts (3–5 schools)	15	12	5	1	42	43	48	39	43	45	47	60
Rural	14	11	4	1	42	42	46	37	45	47	51	62
Suburban	38	28	12	2	45	52	66	56	18	20	22	43
Urban	50	39	21	2	33	40	54	55	17	21	25	43
Top third of COVID cases	12	13	10	0	43	40	59	46	45	45	31	54
Middle third of COVID-19 cases	25	16	9	1	37	46	51	43	37	25	40	56
Bottom third of COVID-19 cases	27	29	6	1	43	47	46	45	31	22	48	53
High mask wearing	40	29	10	2	40	49	62	55	20	22	24	43
Low mask wearing	9	8	7	0	42	40	41	33	48	52	57	67
Biden districts	47	36	18	2	41	49	64	60	12	15	18	38
Trump districts	12	9	2	0	42	42	46	36	46	49	52	64

Note. Biden districts/Trump districts reflect municipality vote in 2020 presidential election. Data from Malkus et al. (2022).

or both) had no statistically significant impact on student and staff case rates in Florida schools. Given that Florida is one of the few settings in which a comparison could be made, it is worth noting that these findings may or may not generalize to other settings in the United States. Regardless of their efficacy, teachers had to contend with enforcing masking policies on top of their assigned duties—an especially difficult task with younger learners.

Similarly, they found that ventilation improvements were not associated with case rates. This could be explained by the range of ventilation improvements from one context to another. It is possible that some efforts were more robust than others and possibly did make a difference in the COVID-19 spread; however, this was not found in this particular study. Surprisingly, they found that schools with greater student density were significantly associated with *lower* rates of COVID-19. One might have hypothesized the opposite to be true. One possible explanation for this is that the study only accounted for what happens in schools, and out-of-school activities may have been different for students in low-density (often, more rural) schools than for those in high-density schools. It is also possible that social distancing measures that were put in place were ineffective at reducing the spread.

Teachers who were in schools in person had to do more than simply manage COVID-19 mitigation efforts. As we noted, every family had the option of electing remote instruction for their children. Schools that were open for in-person learning had to find ways to educate remote students as well. In most settings, this manifested in one of three ways. Perhaps the most common solution was having teachers deliver instruction in a hyflex modality, simultaneously teaching students in person and those who were joining virtually. Just as most teachers were not trained for the remote instruction they were forced to deliver in March 2020 (Marshall, Shannon, & Love, 2022; Thompson, Darwich, & Bartlett, 2020), teachers who had to meet the needs of in-person and virtual students at the same time were not trained for this mode of instruction, either. Bartlett's (2022) review of modified learning modalities employed during the pandemic found that teaching hyflex was especially difficult for teachers. Other models included schools with teachers responsible for both in-person students and remote students, albeit not simultaneously (Marshall, Love, Shannon, & Neugebauer, 2023). In these schools, teachers had a roster of virtual students they were responsible for; however, in most of these instances, the remote students were learning asynchronously. Some schools had dedicated teachers to teach virtual students, freeing those serving students in classrooms to solely focus on educating them. Overall, the teachers who taught in person during the 2020–2021 school year, whether it was their choice or not, had to overcome many challenges that frankly they were not prepared for and that often led to a lot more work and stress.

"A Return to Normalcy"

During the 1920 U.S. presidential election campaign, Warren Harding's campaign called for "a return to normalcy" (Gerstle, Rosenberg, & Rosenberg, 1999). World War I had just concluded a couple of years prior, the United States was in the midst of an economic downturn, and the 1918–1920 flu pandemic had wreaked havoc across the United States and the world. A century later, the phrase would be widely used again—this time referencing a recovery from COVID-19. The 2021–2022 school year was billed as a return to normalcy, with most of the more stringent mitigation measures retired. The lone exception was masking. The CDC (2022) issued guidance suggesting that masks be required indoors in schools. Just over 60% of schools began 2021–2022 with mask mandates, which held steady until about mid-February 2022. The emergence of the omicron variant in late 2021 and its subvariants in 2022 led to increased COVID-19 infection rates (Wang et al., 2022). The omicron variant also rendered vaccination less efficacious; many of those who were vaccinated contracted and spread the virus, which was not the case with previous variants. The good news was that, although more contagious and less shielded by vaccines, omicron was also less deadly, leading to fewer serious cases requiring hospitalization. The omicron variant is noteworthy because it marked the first variant of COVID-19 that did *not* overly disrupt schools. With the exception of a handful of isolated examples, such as the COVID-19-related teacher strike in Chicago Public Schools in early 2022 (Peréz & Kapos, 2022), schools did not close, and additional mitigation measures were not employed despite the spike in cases that came with omicron. By early March 2022, fewer than 10% of schools continued to require indoor masking. Teachers, however, reported that the 2021–2022 school year was the most difficult year they experienced during the pandemic, a point that we discuss in further detail in Chapters 4 and 5. As of this writing (May 2023), COVID-19 mitigation efforts have long concluded in every realm of American life, save for masking in doctors' offices in a handful of states and a few professional academic organizations that continued to require vaccination, including boosters, for conference attendees in the spring of 2023. Although the crisis itself may appear to be over and COVID-19 has become endemic, the aftermath of what took place during the intervening years will continue to affect K–12 education for some time to come.

A Pair of Lessons Learned

This book explores two overarching lessons learned from the pandemic: the impact of the policy failure of prolonged school closures on students and the impact that COVID-19-related policy had on teachers since March 2020. This is not a simple narrative, and the two threads are at times in tension with one another. However, we believe it is important to understand both of these for schools to move forward in the most productive manner. There are those who might claim that prolonged school closures were wrongheaded and that teachers were to blame. There are others who might claim that school closures were prudent and that teachers have had a tough go of it since March 2020. We believe two things can be true simultaneously—prolonged school closures were ineffective, and the job of being a teacher has become unsustainably challenging since the start of the pandemic. Chapter 2 discusses the folly of prolonged school closures in greater detail.

In Chapters 3 and 4, we explore the impact of school closures on children academically, socially, and mentally. Given how few children were seriously affected by the virus (e.g., Lee, Hu, Chen, Huang, & Hsueh, 2020), children have disproportionately borne the brunt of policy decisions that kept schools closed for long durations. At the same time, the job of being a teacher, which was difficult prior to the pandemic, became increasingly challenging. Teaching became tremendously more difficult during the pandemic whether teachers were teaching online for extended periods—often using video conferencing software (e.g., Zoom) with their students' cameras turned off—or whether they were in person in schools, teaching the students in front of them and remote students simultaneously while managing virus mitigation measures. Chapters 5 and 6 discuss teacher well-being and teacher labor markets in the aftermath of the crisis. In Chapter 7, we explore the changes that occurred in schools during the crisis and focus on the changes that are likely to remain common practice beyond the pandemic. As David Tyack and Larry Cuban observed in their 1995 book *Tinkering toward Utopia*, schools have historically resisted change. Perhaps this moment is different. In Chapter 8, we focus on what teachers need to be successful moving forward. In each focus group we conducted in the fall of 2022, we asked teachers a simple question: What do you need to succeed in your job? Their answers are revealing and important for school leaders and policymakers to understand to keep talented teachers in the classroom. Finally, in Chapter 9 we focus on where schools go from here, as schools face the consequences of decisions made during the pandemic. We hope this last chapter challenges school leaders, policymakers, and researchers to understand the state of schools and reflect on the best approaches to supporting teachers and students moving forward.

Chapter 2

The Case against Prolonged School Closures

Schools were shuttered worldwide as part of a larger effort to curb the spread of the COVID-19 virus. At the pandemic's peak, more than 1.5 billion students in more than 190 countries were engaged in emergency remote learning, representing 94% of the world's students (UNESCO, 2020). The case for closing schools was rather straightforward but involved some tradeoffs (Maranto, 2020a; Marshall, 2022b; Tan, 2021). Schools were shut down because they are sites where many people gather, and they could facilitate the spread of a respiratory virus like COVID-19. Policymakers privileged safety over learning by closing schools as part of an effort to keep individuals safe. They believed the benefits of curbing community spread would outweigh any drawbacks associated with closing schools. Looking back, it is fair to say that this was a miscalculation of grand proportions.

Both of us are professors and former teachers who study K–12 education. Suffice it to say, public health and epidemiology are outside our areas of expertise. However, given the nature of this public health crisis, we were forced to consult the medical literature to better understand the nature of this crisis and the impact it was having on schools.* When an author writes a book, he or she is often asked: What surprised you the most when you were conducting your research for the project? For us, it was exactly how much was known about the relative safety of reopening schools at the time American schools were shuttered. Evidence from East Asia and Europe, available as early as summer 2020, suggested that

*This prompted Marshall to publish a narrative review on pediatric mental health (Marshall, 2023a). See Chapter 4 for more on student well-being during the pandemic.

schools were not vectors of COVID-19 transmission (e.g., Iwata, Doi, & Miyakoshi, 2020). By the fall of 2020, there was evidence that the same was true in the United States (e.g., Varma et al., 2021). These were not isolated studies published in obscure outlets; they include studies published in the top medical journals (e.g., *Journal of the American Medical Association* [*JAMA*], *The Lancet*) and those the CDC published in their academic journals (e.g., Leidman et al., 2021).

To be clear, we are not blaming educators or principals for not knowing this information. Those who worked in schools—like everyone else—can be forgiven for the widespread fear and panic that was felt by most people during the early months of the pandemic. We recall wiping down our groceries with disinfecting wipes in the early weeks, crossing to the other side of the road on daily walks to keep a safe distance, and limiting social gatherings to those that were outdoors. In hindsight, was this an overreaction? Yes—but, in the moment, little was known about COVID-19, and the public often just heard about positive case counts, hospitalizations, and death counts on the local news (Horák, Lazaroiu, G., & Valášková, 2020). At the time, we simply didn't know what we didn't know. There were reports of some educators updating their wills prior to the start of the 2020–2021 school year out of fear that going to work might cause them to succumb to COVID-19 (Waldrop, 2020). For some teachers with preexisting health conditions, these fears were perhaps understandable based on the information available to the public. It would be unreasonable for anyone to suggest that middle school math teachers or elementary school assistant principals should have been following the medical literature or keeping tabs on CDC journals.

We are not suggesting that the initial school closures were a mistake. Closing schools from March 2020 through the remainder of the 2019–2020 school year was certainly defensible and a prudent measure of caution. However, the following four things were true by the summer of 2020: (1) The COVID-19 pandemic was a public health crisis; (2) keeping children from attending school was a radical attempt at mitigating viral spread; (3) those in positions of power should have had advisors who *were* keeping tabs on the available data; and (4) reopening schools as soon as there was evidence that doing so was safe should have been the top priority for decision makers. Prolonged school closures during the COVID-19 pandemic were perhaps one of the greatest mistakes made in the history of American public education, and the consequences will be felt for many years to come.

The next three chapters provide an overview of the impact that pandemic policy has had on student academics and on student and teacher well-being. This chapter discusses school closure and reopening policies, explores the disparate impact that these decisions had on historically disadvantaged children, and examines a range of reasons that were offered for keeping schools closed in the face of contravening evidence.

School Closures and the Impact on the Marginalized

According to analyses conducted by World Bank economist Harry Patrinos (2023), the average country worldwide closed its schools for 21 weeks. School closures in the United States were shorter for some students—approximately 8 weeks for students in schools that started fall 2020 in person—because of the annual tradition of summer break. However, in other U.S. jurisdictions, school closures lasted more than a year, or more than double the worldwide average. For example, schools in much of California were closed for more than 15 months.

We discuss the impact that COVID-19 policy decisions had on student academics at greater length in the next chapter. However, given the disparities in terms of access to learning in person, it is worth exploring the impact that school closures had on academic achievement gaps. These gaps widened during the prolonged school closures for students of color (Peterson, 2020), for low-income students (Christakis, 2020; Munro et al., 2023; Peterson, 2020; Viner et al., 2021), and for students receiving special education services (Munro et al., 2023). For most students, online learning was no substitute for in-person instruction (Peterson, 2020; Christakis, 2020). White students whose families were above the federal poverty lines had the option of sending their kids to school to learn, more so than did families living in poverty and/or families of color (Oster, Jack, Halloran, Schoof, McLeod, Yang, et al., 2021). Between January and April 2021, access to full-time in-person learning increased markedly for all race/ethnicity groups. In January 2021, fewer than 40% of students were learning in person. However, by April 2021, almost three-quarters of non-Hispanic White students had access to fully in-person learning, whereas non-White students had substantially less opportunity to attend school in person. Access to in-person learning did not necessarily equate to children learning in person, as every family had the ability to opt for a remote option during this time. However, families with the option to allow their children to attend school in person were significantly more likely to do so (Camp & Zamarro, 2022). See Table 2.1 for a comparison of access to in-person learning by race/ethnicity between January 2021 and April 2021.

Reasons Offered for Keeping Schools Closed

A 2007 report sharing the most up-to-date CDC guidance (as of March 2020) outlines measures for dealing with viral pandemics, including non-pharmaceutical interventions such as school closures (CDC, 2007). For a Category 3 pandemic—as COVID-19 would turn out to be, based on the 2007 criteria—the guidance recommends the following: "with respect to the duration of dismissal of children from schools . . . short term (up to 4 weeks) dismissal of students and closure of child-care facilities." Even for a much stronger Category 5 pandemic, the guidance recommends "long-term closures (up to 12 weeks)" (p. 45). Yet, in such places as San Francisco, California (Marshall & Bradley-Dorsey, 2022), and Richmond, Virginia (Love & Marshall, 2022), schools were closed for almost 50 weeks (not counting the 2020 summer break)—more than 12 times the prescribed school closure for a pandemic such as COVID-19 and more than four times the prescribed closure for the most extreme pandemics. Why was this the case? Here, we explore some of the reasons we have come across for this.

TABLE 2.1. Access to Fully In-Person Learning January–April 2021 by Race/Ethnicity

Race/ethnicity	January 2021	April 2021	Δ
Non-Hispanic White	38.0%	74.5%	36.6%
Non-Hispanic Black	32.3%	63.4%	31.1%
Hispanic	35.9%	58.9%	23.0%
Other	26.3%	56.9%	30.6%

Note. Data from Oster, Jack, Halloran, Schoof, McLeod, Yang, et al. (2021). Δ = the difference in access to in-person learning between April 2021 and January 2021.

"Follow the Science"

During the COVID-19 pandemic, and especially during 2020, we were often told to "follow the science." Presumably, this meant that scientific facts and data should guide decisions made during the pandemic about where, when, how, and under what circumstances schools should reopen. Closing schools and disrupting student learning was a radical move, though one that was prudent, given how little was known about the novel coronavirus early on. Analyses conducted by Auger and colleagues (2020) suggest that states that closed their schools earlier experienced fewer deaths and hospitalizations due to the virus. In March 2020, days mattered. For example, a state that closed schools on March 12, such as Michigan or Maryland, fared much better than a state that closed its schools on March 19, such as Missouri or Texas. In hindsight, it seems that states that closed schools early made a wise policy decision. However, it is worth noting that states that had not closed their schools early were also states that had not ordered other facets of society (e.g., most businesses) to close, either, rendering it difficult to isolate the impact of schools remaining open.

Studies conducted since the initial wave of COVID-19 tell a different story. A systematic review of 40 studies examined COVID-19 and school closure and reopening decisions and found that these decisions had little to no impact on community spread of the virus (Walsh et al., 2021). After New York City reopened its schools, Varma and colleagues (2021) studied the impact of the policy decision on community spread. They were interested in learning whether schools were the vectors of transmission critics of the reopening policy feared them to be. They followed COVID-19 cases among school employees and students between October 2020 and December 2020. They found that teachers and students had lower rates of infection than the community at large. Similarly, a report from the CDC COVID-19 Early Response Team examined data from March 1 and December 12, 2020, and found no significant differences in community spread between counties in which schools had reopened and counties in which they had not (Leidman et al., 2021). Though the differences were not statistically significant, counties in which schools remained closed had slightly *higher* rates of infection, which Dasgupta (2022) notes is "not what you'd expect if extended school closures worked" (p. 125).

Other studies have similarly found no relationship between school learning modality (fully remote, hybrid, fully in person) and COVID-19 cases or hospitalizations (Esposito & Principi, 2020; Harris, Ziedan, & Hassig, 2021; Iwata et al., 2020; Michelson & Samuels-Kalow, 2022). This can partly be attributed to an argument we have made elsewhere—that children are not at home in isolation when they are not in school (see Marshall & Bradley-Dorsey, 2022; Maranto & Marshall, 2023; Marshall, 2023). Bourne (2021) has argued convincingly that school closures likely meant that children were more likely to be in daycare or around others. This was especially true for single parents and frontline workers, whose children more likely to be with grandparents and other, more vulnerable individuals when schools were closed.

Several states included provisions in their fall 2020 reopening guidance that explicitly tied learning modality decisions to COVID-19 case numbers (Marshall & Bradley-Dorsey, 2020, 2022). For example, Maine coded individual counties by color based on risk (Maine Department of Education, 2020a, 2020b). Counties were coded as being (1) *red* (high risk), (2) *yellow* (elevated risk), or (3) *green* (low risk); the directive specified the use of remote instruction for red counties, hybrid instruction for yellow counties, and fully in-person instruction for green counties. As of Labor Day 2020, every county in the state was designated as green (Marshall & Bradley-Dorsey, 2020). Several other states similarly tied pandemic mitigation guidance to data.

Although the policy that was developed in many states seemed to be guided by science and data, in practice, many of the decisions were not. Decisions made about reopening seemed to reflect politics over facts (Boyack & DeAngelis, 2023; DeAngelis & Makridis, 2021; Flanders, 2021; Grossman, Reckhow, Strunk, & Turner, 2021; Hartney & Finger, 2021; Henderson, Peterson, & West, 2020). The stated policy in both traditionally Republican-leaning states (e.g., Florida, Arkansas) and Democrat-leaning states (e.g., Illinois, Massachusetts) recommended in-person learning. Areas with strong teacher unions were more likely to reopen schools with remote learning (DeAngelis & Makridis, 2021; Flanders, 2021; Marianno, 2021). Indeed, Marianno (2021) found a relationship between the length of collective bargaining agreements (CBAs) and a reluctance to reopen schools. The length of CBAs was used as a proxy for union strength. It was also found that areas that tended to vote for Republicans were more favorable toward school reopening and those that tended to vote for Democrats were more hesitant. As further evidence of this, the American Enterprise Institute's Return2Learn tracker (Malkus et al., 2022) found that, in the week of the 2020 presidential election, 36% of counties that supported Joe Biden exclusively offered remote instruction, compared with only 9% of counties that supported Donald Trump's reelection efforts, reflecting the influence of local partisan politics. Collins (2023) found that the strongest predictor of one's support for reopening schools was trust in the CDC's information about COVID-19—except they found that the *less* one trusted the CDC, the more likely one was to support in-person learning. This is all concerning. The public should be able to trust institutions like the CDC during public health-related crises. It should be troubling that decisions that dramatically affected the lives of children were based on anything other than data. The case we make here is not a partisan one; education and health-related data should have mattered more than politics at this moment in time.

In October 2020, three epidemiologists from Harvard, Oxford, and Stanford universities met in Great Barrington, Massachusetts, and penned what became known as the Great Barrington Declaration (Kulldorf, Gupta, & Bhattacharya, 2020). In it, Kulldorf and colleagues noted their concern about the lockdowns and closures that had been a primary feature of COVID-19 mitigation policy. They expressed alarm at the potential physical health, mental health, and economic impacts that these policies were having on people and called for society to reopen while protecting those most vulnerable to the virus. Although their declaration was more about society at large, they did address schools, unequivocally declaring: "Keeping students out of school is a grave injustice. Keeping these measures in place until a vaccine is available will cause irreparable damage, with the underprivileged disproportionately harmed." The declaration has been signed by more than 16,000 medical and public health scientists and more than 47,000 medical practitioners. At the time it was published, the trio was lambasted by those who supported the more stringent policies in place. A "groupthink" had developed among many that seemed to equate science with strict lockdown policies, not empirical studies or data, as it traditionally had been (Joffe, 2021), and these epidemiologists' recommendations were going against the grain at the time they made them. However, two things are clear now. First, they were correct about schools, and, indeed, the underprivileged have been disproportionately harmed. Second, the data available by the fall of 2020 demonstrated that reopening schools did not put teachers and students at additional risk of COVID-19 (e.g., Varma et al., 2021). Those in charge should have followed the science.

Protect the Children

We now know that COVID-19 did not significantly affect children; the virus was primarily an adults' disease. Compared with adults, children were far more likely to be asymptomatic or to have mild symptoms and far less likely to be hospitalized by the virus (Bhopal, Bagaria, & Bhopal, 2020; de Souza, Nada, Nogueira, Pereira, & Brandão, 2020; European Centre for Disease Prevention and Control, 2020; Haleemunnissa, Didel, Swami, Singh, & Vyas, 2021; Lee et al., 2020; Munro et al., 2023). As of March 8, 2023, 0.13% of all deaths in the United States involving COVID-19 throughout the pandemic were among persons ages 0–17 (National Center for Health Statistics, 2023). Deaths involving COVID-19 accounted for only 1.4% of all deaths involving persons under the age of 18 from March 2020 through March 2023.* For individuals 18 and up, deaths involving COVID-19 accounted for 11.7% of all deaths. Although children were relatively safe from the virus itself, they suffered academically, socially, and emotionally during this time (Duckworth et al., 2021; Felfe et al., 2023; Halloran, Jack, Okun, & Oster, 2021; Marshall, 2022b). Christakis, Van Cleve, and Zimmerman (2020) put it this way in their *JAMA Network Open* article:

> Although the risks of keeping schools open drove decisions made in the early phases of the pandemic, the probable harm to children associated with school closure [was] less explicitly discussed. The public debate has pitted "school closures" against "lives saved," or the education of children against the health of the community. Presenting tradeoffs in this way obscures the very real health consequences of interrupted education. (p. 2)

The tradeoffs Christakis and colleagues note failed to properly account for children's mental health, social well-being, and academic needs.

In an April 2020 commentary published in *The Lancet Public Health*, Van Lancker and Parolin called school closures "a social crisis in the making," noting that they "will have long-lasting consequences for children in low-income families" (p. e244). United Nations Secretary-General António Guterres described school closures as an "educational catastrophe," noting that as many as 24 million students may be at risk

---

*"Deaths involving COVID-19" means that the patient tested positive at the time of death. COVID-19 was identified as the underlying cause of these deaths 91% of the time in 2020, 90% of the time in 2021, and 76% of the time in 2022 (CDC, 2023b).

of dropping out worldwide (UNESCO, 2020). Given the evidence from Europe and Southeast Asia, as well as the early evidence from the fall of 2020 in the United States, school leaders and policymakers should have reopened schools in many areas far in advance of when they did. Schools that stayed closed the longest often disproportionately served children of color and children living in poverty (Armitage & Nellums, 2020; Dooley, Simpson, & Beers, 2020; Van Lancker & Parolin, 2020)—leaving already marginalized populations even more disadvantaged than before the pandemic. As Christakis wrote in *JAMA Pediatrics* in May 2020, "No credible scientist, learning expert, teacher, or parent believes that children aged 5 to 10 years can meaningfully engage in online learning without considerable parental involvement, which many families with low incomes are unable to provide because parents must work outside the home" (p. 928). Additionally, school closures meant that children suffering from cases of abuse and neglect outside of school lost an important source of reported allegations of maltreatment—adults in schools. Studies investigating trends in the reporting of cases of child abuse and neglect in the United States found precipitous drops in these types of allegations after March 2020 (Baron, Goldstein, & Wallace, 2020; Nguyen, 2021). Of course, it is possible that the number of these heinous events did indeed decrease during the early months of the pandemic, but unfortunately it is more likely the case that instances of abuse and neglect simply went unreported. Overall, children were relatively safe from the pandemic. It was pandemic policy that harmed them the most.

Protect the Adults

Some subpopulations of adults were at much greater risk from COVID-19, especially compared with children. According to the CDC (2023c), individuals with chronic kidney or liver disease; chronic lung diseases, including asthma; cancer; diabetes; and those who are overweight or obese face elevated risks due to the virus. Of course, some adults who worked in schools had one or more of these conditions. As such, measures should have been taken to protect vulnerable adults during this time (Maranto, Marshall, & Bradley-Dorsey, 2020; Maranto, 2020b; Viner et al., 2021).

Each state released a reopening plan in the summer of 2020 outlining what schooling would look like that fall. Marshall and his colleague Martha Bradley-Dorsey (2020) reviewed each state's plan and found that, fortunately, several states' plans explicitly included language aimed at protecting the vulnerable. The plans of Alabama, Arkansas, California, Colorado, Nevada, Oklahoma, and Pennsylvania encouraged school districts to provide alternative work duties for adults at greater risk, to include allowing them to work from home for an extended time. Schools delivering instruction in person still had a population of students whose families opted for remote instruction, so putting vulnerable teachers in charge of remote learning was also an option. The plans of two states—Alaska and Connecticut—specifically suggested that. Several other states included provisions in their plans to develop flexible leave, ensuring that faculty and staff would not be penalized for quarantines or leave due to illness, including COVID-19. This was important to ensure that individuals did not feel required to come to work when sick in order to earn their full paychecks. Finally, some states tied the protection of vulnerable workers to community spread. For example, Idaho required school workers to come to work in person when there was no community spread ("Idaho Back to School Framework," 2020). However, additional community spread would trigger remote work for vulnerable faculty and staff. To summarize, it was prudent to be concerned about vulnerable adults—especially in the early months of the pandemic.

The Need for Additional Resources

Another reason provided for not immediately reopening schools was the need for additional resources to do so safely. As we recounted in Chapter 1, in-person schooling with COVID-19 mitigation efforts was not easy to pull off. Much of what was needed cost money—which many cash-strapped school districts did not have in abundance. Fortunately, the March 2020 Coronavirus Aid, Relief, and Economic Security (CARES) Act included more than $30 billion for education, including $13.23 billion for elementary and secondary education (U.S. Department of Education Office of Elementary and Secondary Education, 2023) through Elementary and Secondary School Emergency Relief (ESSER) funds. School districts, charter schools, preschools, and nonpublic schools could apply for this funding to address COVID-19's impact, provide remote instruction, and develop and implement a return to normal school operations. In December 2020, the Coronavirus Response and Relief Supplemental Appropriations Act (CRRSA) was signed into law (U.S. Department of Education Office of Elementary and Secondary Education, 2023), providing an additional $54.3 million to the ESSER funds. In March 2021, the American Rescue Plan (ARP) became law, which allocated an additional $112 billion for ESSER funds (Silberstein & Roza, 2023). To put this in perspective, the entire budget of the U.S. Department of Education (2019) in the fiscal year 2019 was just over $104 billion, and a substantial portion of that goes to higher education. In short, the ESSER relief funds more than doubled the U.S. Department of Education's budget in both 2020 and 2021.

If a lack of resources was a primary reason schools were closed, one would think that school districts with more resources would also be more likely to reopen for in-person learning. However, evidence suggests that school districts did not fail to reopen due to a lack of funding. DeAngelis and Makridis (2022) examined data from over 12,000 school districts from the fall of 2020. After controlling for district enrollment, for the percentage of the county that voted for Trump in 2016, for COVID-19 cases per capita, and for COVID-19 deaths per capita, they found no significant relationship between the amount of funding a district had and whether it had reopened for in-person instruction. If anything, they found weak evidence for the opposite—a 1% increase in funding was associated with a .03 percentage point rise in the likelihood that the district was exclusively employing remote instruction, albeit significant at the .10 level. Funding likely shaped many of the decisions made in the spring of 2020 when the crisis began. However, by the fall of that year, funding no longer adequately explained reopening decisions.

Bureaucratic Incompetence

Finally, at least one additional explanation for prolonged school closures is worth exploring. A May 2023 report from the Fordham Institute notes that some of the hardest hit communities in terms of learning loss were New Haven, Connecticut; St. Louis, Missouri; and Richmond, Virginia—all of which saw average learning loss in math exceeding *1½ years* (McDougald, 2023). Richmond Public Schools (RPS) did not reopen their schools for in-person learning until the fall of 2021, rendering the entire 2020–2021 school year one of remote learning. Marshall and his colleague Savanna Love (Love & Marshall, 2022) collected long-form longitudinal qualitative data from a dozen teachers during that school year. One of the teachers we interviewed was an elementary school teacher in RPS. She explained that she and her colleagues opposed reopening, but not because they did not want to return to the classroom or did not think that it would be better for their students academically. Rather, they viewed the school district administrators as unable to reopen schools competently. The teacher said, "We can't even make it safe and smart and keep control of the building under our administrators in a regular setting, and now you're going to be asking kids to come into a space, stay socially distanced, stay in one room, keeping masks on? To be quite frank, our administrators don't know how to create that. They can't create that in normal [non-pandemic] settings" (Love & Marshall, 2022, p. 45). We share this story not to disparage RPS, but rather to illustrate the need for administrators and district leaders to demonstrate competence and develop trust with their faculty and staff. School leaders lacking trust and rapport during normal times will find it difficult to establish that during times of crisis.

* * *

Every 5 years, the Progress in International Reading Literacy Study (PIRLS) releases a report. In May 2023, the 2021 results were released (National Center for Education Statistics, 2023). Among the 65 participating countries, the United States ranked 53rd in the proportion of its schools closed for longer than 8 weeks (72%). It is clear to us that prolonged school closures were a mistake that affected schools tremendously. This was a mistake that did not need to happen; policymakers should have "followed the science." Although we recognize that the decision to close schools cannot be undone at this point, we hope that policymakers and school leaders will learn some lessons about how to conduct themselves in the future. Decisions should be made based only on facts—in this case, those pertaining to medical science and learning. School leaders should also take heed of the importance of developing trust with faculty and staff members during normal times. When trouble strikes, second-guessing leadership usually leads to poor outcomes. We hope readers of this book will not experience another pandemic of COVID-19's magnitude in their lifetimes. But the decisions were made, and they will have long-term deleterious consequences.

Chapter 3

The Impact on Student Learning

Schools pivoted to emergency instructional plans as the world was locked down due to the COVID-19 pandemic. For many schools, these plans included enough work to keep students busy for a few weeks but lacked the rigor students needed or received prior to the pandemic (e.g., Marshall & Neugebauer, 2022). As a result, many students experienced academic learning loss and a decline in academic progress due to the disruption caused by the pandemic. Several factors may have contributed to learning loss during the pandemic,* including lack of access to technology, reduced instructional time, disruptions to learning, and the emotional toll the pandemic had on students, families, and teachers. The extent of academic learning loss varies depending on a range of factors, including the ages and grade levels of the students, the subject matter, and the specific circumstances of the pandemic in the students' communities. Regardless, policy decisions made during the pandemic have significantly affected the academic progress of many students.

*It is worth noting that the term *learning loss,* though widely used in the aftermath of the pandemic, is not entirely accurate. In most cases, what took place was less about learning loss—that is, students missing material that was previously learned—and more akin to a lack of opportunity to learn the material in the first place, due to the challenging conditions of schooling during the pandemic. When we use the term, we're ascribing to the meaning *du jour*; however, this is a distinction worth making.

Early National Student Outcomes

Most students across the United States had returned to in-person learning by the start of the 2020–2021 school year when some of the first standardized test data provided school leaders with an idea of where students were as schools moved back to normalcy (Lewis & Kuhfeld, 2021). The Northwest Evaluation Association produces a widely used computer-based assessment regimen that measures within-student growth instead of proficiency, referred to as Measures of Academic Progress, or MAP. MAP growth assessment achievement data were analyzed for more than 6 million students in grades 3–8 in the fall of 2021 in reading and math. Lewis and Kuhfeld (2021) explored the overall trends of these data and compared the fall 2021 results with 2019 results, as well as with the data from the spring of 2021. Students entered the 2021–2022 school year 3–7 percentile points lower in reading and 9–11 percentile points lower in math. This decline was present for all groups of students, but most pronounced for historically disadvantaged students, for students who attended high-poverty schools and mostly remote schools, and for students enrolled in elementary grades. Additionally, the typical gains that would be expected were lower for most students, especially in math and for lower achieving students (Goldhaber et al., 2022). The result was a widening of racial and economic achievement gaps. Nevertheless, some positive findings suggested that student reading gains aligned with pre-pandemic levels and that student scores were stable from spring 2021 to fall 2021 (Lewis & Kuhfeld, 2021).

In the fall of 2022, the National Assessment for Educational Progress (NAEP) released fourth- and eighth-grade math and reading scores after more than 2 years of pandemic schooling. Beyond the decrease in scores, students' confidence in their reading and math skills also decreased (NAEP, 2022a, 2022b). The overall trends painted a grim picture, as it was the most significant decrease in scores in math since the initial assessment in 1990. There were slight (statistically significant) decreases in fourth-grade reading and math scores compared with 2017 and 2019 (see Figure 3.1). This was true for all ethnicities except for Asian and Pacific Islander students, who earned results comparable to the previous years in both subjects. This was a common trend across the United States, as 30 states/jurisdictions experienced a decrease in average reading scores, whereas 44 states/jurisdictions had a decrease in math scores compared with 2019 (NAEP, 2022a, 2022b).

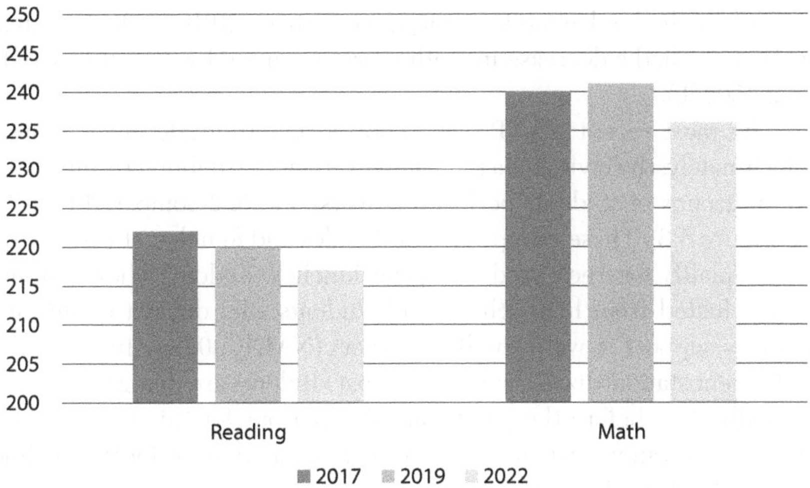

FIGURE 3.1. Fourth-grade National Assessment for Educational Progress (NAEP) scores in reading and math, 2017–2022.

Similar trends continued in the eighth-grade results, with a significant decrease in reading and math scores compared with 2017 and 2019 (see Figure 3.2). Again, all race/ethnicity groups experienced a decrease in average scores except for Asian/Pacific Islander students, who stayed reasonably constant for reading scores. In math, all race/ethnicity groups saw a decrease in 2022 scores. Across the United States, 33 states/

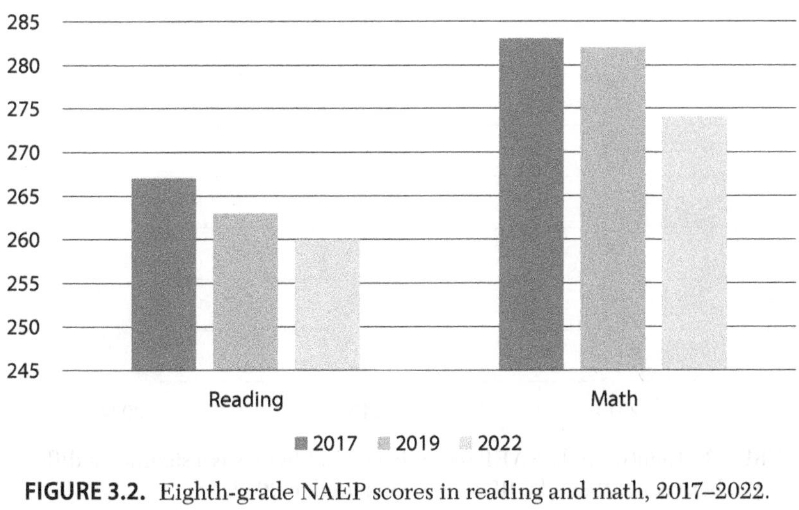

FIGURE 3.2. Eighth-grade NAEP scores in reading and math, 2017–2022.

jurisdictions had a decline in reading scores from 2019, while 48 states/jurisdictions had a decrease in math scores compared with 2019 (NAEP, 2022a, 2022b).

The most recent NAEP data reported eighth-grade civics scores. Unfortunately, the civics data indicated even more troubling results, with several groups of students performing worse in 2022 compared to 2018 (see Figure 3.3). These groups included males and females, students who did not qualify for free or reduced-price lunches, students whose parents had graduated from high school, and students who did not qualify for disability support or were English learners (NAEP, 2022c). In short, the most recent standardized data suggest that students are doing worse academically than before the pandemic. The reasons for this may vary for each student, but we explore some of the possible reasons for the decline in the rest of this chapter.

The Impact of Learning Modality

When schools were forced to close their buildings to in-person learning, school leaders had to decide how to provide instruction and consider the impact that type of instruction would have on student learning. As we discussed in the opening chapter, instruction delivered at the end of the 2019–2020 school year was all remote; decisions made about instructional

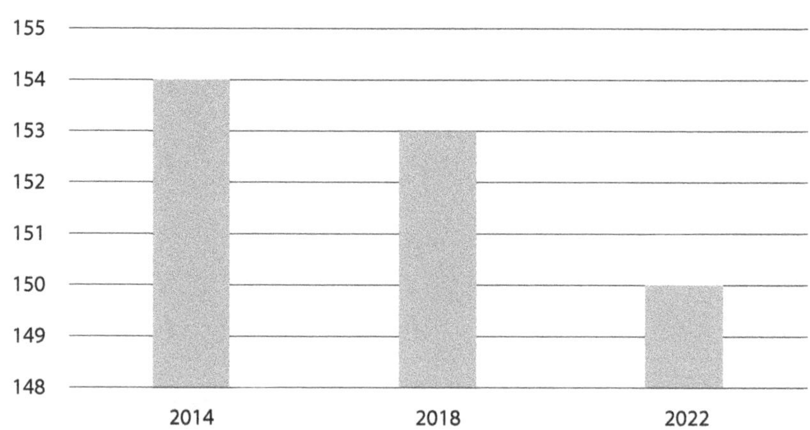

FIGURE 3.3. Eighth-grade NAEP scores in civics. There was a significant difference ($p < .05$) between 2014 and 2018 scores compared to 2022.

modality were more or less limited to one's preference regarding the mix of online synchronous or asynchronous learning or paper-based instructional packets. In many locations, in-person learning resumed in the fall of 2020, and families had the ability to choose whether to enroll their children in person or in a remote learning option. Schools with online and/or hybrid options along with fully in-person instruction allowed families to switch modalities throughout the 2020–2021 school year to provide parents autonomy. Darling-Aduana, Woodyard, Sass, and Barry (2022) found that several factors were associated with parents' choosing virtual instruction, such as low socioeconomic status (SES) and elevated COVID-19 case numbers. By contrast, families with students identified as English language learners, who received special education services, or who came from higher SES backgrounds opted to return to in-person learning more frequently (Darling-Aduana et al., 2022).

With stakeholders making critical decisions about the type of learning students would receive, it is important to understand how learning modalities influenced student achievement. Most students experienced more than just 2 months of virtual learning, and several studies have explored the extent to which this affected academic achievement (e.g., Halloran et al., 2021; Molnár & Hermann, 2023). A study in the United States explored the effects of the different instructional approaches provided during the pandemic (Halloran et al., 2021). Spring 2021 test data were obtained from 12 states (Colorado, Connecticut, Florida, Massachusetts, Minnesota, Nevada, Ohio, Rhode Island, Virginia, West Virginia, Wisconsin, and Wyoming). Overall, there was a decrease in test scores in 2021 compared with the previous year's scores, with a more significant decrease in scores for students who received less in-person instruction (i.e., more hybrid, hyflex, or all virtual instruction). Compared with the studies conducted in Europe (Engzell et al., 2021; Schult, Mahler, Fauth, & Lindner, 2022), Halloran et al. (2021) found a larger decrease in student math scores for those who learned remotely (average of 14%) than for those who received more in-person instruction, who only saw about a 4% decrease in student achievement. Their findings suggested overall declines in test score passing rates of 6.4% in English language arts and 12.5% in math, with significantly larger decreases for Black and Hispanic children and low-income students. In short, in-person learning mattered.

The same group of researchers released a more recent report exploring the pandemic's impact in 21 state tests representing over 5,000 school districts in the United States (Halloran, Hug, Jack, & Oster, 2023). Two years later, Halloran and her colleagues (2023) found evidence of recovery in both English (20%) and math (37%). Thus, this suggests that from spring 2021 to spring 2022, over one-third of students who had a decrease in test scores in 2021 saw improvement in 2022. Although Halloran et al. (2023) found some positive trends with state-standardized testing data, it is still clear that more work is needed to return to pre-pandemic achievement levels.

More positive data are emerging that indicate that students are making progress. For example, a spring 2023 report from North Carolina suggests that students made larger than expected improvements on state standardized test scores in 2022 (North Carolina State Board of Education Department of Public Instruction, 2023). This was specifically true for middle and high school math, third- and fourth-grade reading, and eighth-grade and high school biology. The only subject that did not see improvement was high school English. Notably, students with disabilities and multilingual learners scored closer to their predicted scores than the overall population (i.e., these subgroups made larger than expected gains). However, it is concerning that economically disadvantaged students continue to perform lower than their peers on state assessments. Overall, the test scores from North Carolina suggest that students are slowly recovering from the instructional deficits of the pandemic (North Carolina State Board of Education Department of Public Instruction, 2023).

Learning remotely for an extended time during the COVID-19 pandemic has been associated with learning loss across many studies conducted worldwide (Darling-Aduana et al., 2022; Goldhaber et al., 2022; Kuhfeld, Soland, & Lewis, 2022; Lewis & Kuhfeld, 2021; Pier, Christian, Tymeson, & Meyer, 2021). For example, in a review of 23 studies published from July 2021 to August 2022, one of the major findings was that learning loss was tied to the time students were out of school. Additionally, student attendance during virtual instruction was a significant factor in student achievement during the pandemic (Cohodes et al., 2022). Furthermore, Darling-Aduana and colleagues (2022) found that if students attended all their virtual classes, they received 8.5–10.5 more hours of instruction than their peers who only attended virtual instruction 50% of the time. This may suggest that although learning modality played a role in student learning during the pandemic, other factors influence student achievement. (See Chapter 4 for more on student mental health.)

School leaders needed to consider issues surrounding student access to resources when making decisions about the learning modalities they offered, especially in the early part of the pandemic. For instance, Patrick, Grissom, Woods, and Newsome (2021) found that families with lower SES and rural families had the most difficulty attending virtual instruction because of limited access to high-speed internet. Though some schools provided mobile hotspots for families to access high-speed internet (Carpenter & Dunn, 2020; Tinubu Ali & Herrera, 2020), it often meant that families had to drive to a school parking lot for students to attend classes. The availability of transportation and the feasibility of families, especially ones with multiple children in school, to get to these hotspots daily could have played a role in the attendance of virtual learning. We applaud school leaders for taking actionable steps to support all families. However, lessons must be learned from this crisis if a school ever faces emergency instruction again.

It is critical for school leaders to understand how virtual learning and a lack of opportunity to learn in person impacted students academically. Unfortunately, the results that tie student learning loss to learning modality are not restricted to just one area of the world or one particular study. As schools move back to in-person learning, school leaders and teachers must understand where students are academically as schools transition back to more normalcy. Remediation will be necessary, and it may take years for scores to return to pre-pandemic levels.

Who Was Affected the Most?

Overall, studies conducted during the pandemic suggest that the schools' responses to the pandemic have had a negative impact on student achievement, particularly in the subjects of reading and math. Unfortunately, the data suggest that most student subgroups suffered some learning loss during the pandemic. Now schools are tasked with limiting learning loss and catching students back up to grade-level standards.

On average, students are about a year behind based on early test scores, and students in every grade level suffered some sort of learning loss (Cohodes et al., 2022). Though studies have found severe learning loss occurring across all students, the impact on student achievement varies depending on the context and the type of instruction provided during the pandemic. Several groups of students about whom school leaders should have major concerns are students from lower SES backgrounds and students of different races and ethnicities. Based on some initial studies and data, students from disadvantaged backgrounds have suffered significant learning loss due to the pandemic (e.g., Cohodes et al., 2022; Lewis & Kuhfeld, 2021; Kuhfeld et al., 2022). For example, Kuhfeld et al. (2022) compared grades 3–8 math and reading scores from 2019 to 2021. The authors estimated that the average student in grades 3–8 lost between 5 and 10 months of learning in mathematics and between 3 and 7 months of learning in reading compared with a typical school year. Another critical finding was that the achievement gap grew between low- and high-poverty elementary schools during the 2020–2021 school year. Data suggested that the learning gaps increased by 20% in math and 15% in reading. However, low-poverty schools avoided continued loss once back in person. To put the observed learning loss into perspective, Kuhfeld et al. (2022) found that the decrease in scores from 2019 to 2021 was larger than with other school disruptions by natural disasters, such as Hurricane Katrina in New Orleans and along the coast of the Gulf of Mexico in 2005.

Cohodes and colleagues (2022) found similar findings when exploring the impact of the pandemic on historically marginalized and/or economically disadvantaged students. Low-income students and students of color spent the most time attending school virtually due to school closures and/or COVID-19 outbreaks and had the largest learning losses in a review of studies. It is important to note that students of color who attended schools that returned to in-person learning earlier in the pandemic had no greater learning loss than their peers. However, this was different for the majority. Thus the increase in learning loss has put low-income students and students of color even further behind their peers, with results suggesting that the achievement gap that existed prior to COVID-19 has only increased (Cohodes et al., 2022).

Impact of Grading Policies

When states implemented lockdowns and schools moved to emergency instructional approaches in the spring of 2020, many schools moved to alternative approaches to grading to accommodate the challenges and disruptions caused by the pandemic. In addition, with uncertainty occurring worldwide, many schools provided more flexibility in turning in assignments and assigning course/subject grades for the end of the

2019–2020 school year. The rationale behind altering grading practices was rather straightforward. School leaders did not want students to earn lower grades simply because they did not have adequate access to the resources they needed while learning from home, including a laptop or computing device, reliable broadband internet, and a quiet space where they could engage in learning (Marshall, Shannon, & Love, 2022). We heard a common refrain from school leaders during this time: "Maslow's hierarchy of needs was much more important than Bloom's taxonomy" (Marshall & Neugebauer, 2023, p. 316). In other words, ensuring that students' basic needs were met had to come before academic concerns.

In several school systems, grading procedures were changed so that students could not earn a lower final grade than they had already earned (Sawchuck, 2020; Storey & Slavin, 2020). Equity concerns led policymakers to institute "hold harmless" policies, which meant that a student's performance in the final marking period of the 2019–2020 school year would not count against them. Other school systems moved to a pass–fail system with flexible policies for submitting late work. In most cases, the work submitted was graded for completion rather than accuracy. Another teacher in the first survey we conducted in the spring of 2020 said that only 9 of her 109 students attended her synchronous Zoom lessons, but everyone received an A for the course. This understandably frustrated educators, especially when many were putting extra effort into their teaching during this time. Teachers who were only allowed to deliver asynchronous instruction lacked the ability to interact directly with students, answer questions in real time, or provide meaningful feedback. On the one hand, this made sense due to equity concerns because students did not have equal access to resources at home (Marshall, Shannon, et al., 2023). This was especially true for traditional public school districts, which were much more likely to abandon grading and assessment during the crisis than charter schools were (Opalka & Talkington, 2020). On the other hand, doing away with grades disincentivized effort for those with the resources to still engage in school. In the end, the spring semester of the 2019–2020 school year ended in an anticlimactic manner for most, with proms canceled and graduation ceremonies altered or canceled as well.

A common concern shared by teachers during the initial shutdown was their inability to hold students accountable (Marshall, Shannon, & Love, 2020; Vahle, de Araujo, Han, & Otten, 2023). Teachers we interviewed reported varied student participation during the final marking period of the 2019–2020 school year (Love & Marshall, 2022). A high school Spanish teacher from Colorado said that, of her 60 Spanish I students, she had only a single student who was showing up on Zoom by the end of the school year. The reason for the lack of participation often varied. Students whose families did have access to computers and broadband internet often had to share with parents and siblings. Younger students often did not understand how to log onto video platforms without the support of an older sibling or adult. Some students had parents at home who could help them with schoolwork when they had questions; however, students in single-parent households and students whose parents were frontline workers often did not have the same help at home. This created vastly uneven circumstances—especially for younger learners. However, the lack of meaningful grading also removed an extrinsic motivator for students with the means to participate in school. The Colorado teacher we referenced teaches in one of the wealthiest counties in the United States, yet her students were not learning because they did not have to. Although the instinct to attend to student needs and ensure fairness is understood, the grading policies implemented during this time also removed an extrinsic motivator for *all* students, including those with adequate resources, to participate in school. If one were to interview 100 students during non-pandemic times and ask them if they would rather be at school and do their homework or not go to school and neglect their homework but receive the same grades, many would choose the latter every time.

Several of the teachers who participated in focus groups we conducted in the fall of 2021 and 2022 shared with us that many of their students struggled with reacclimating to grading as usual. Previously standard expectations such as meeting assignment deadlines and having work graded in terms of how correct it was (instead of just for completion) were a challenge for many students. In the wake of these challenges, some teachers have advocated for continued flexibility with student grades.

One idea that has gained some traction is what we'll refer to as "the 50% rule." The 50% rule dictates that no student should earn a grade lower than 50% on any assignment, even if the assignment was never attempted (Coffey, 2023). The case for such a policy would be to prevent students who have a rocky start to a marking period or semester from getting discouraged by making it mathematically difficult for them to catch up. Well-intentioned though it may be, in practice this policy is less than ideal. Coffey (2023) offers the example of a student who earns an

85% in the first marking period, who then subsequently fails to turn in a single assignment for the second marking period. The student's semester grade would end up being a 67.5% (a D+) once 85 and 50 were averaged together, rewarding a student with a passing grade who failed to do any work for half of the semester. As we noted above, some students will do the bare minimum if left to their own devices, and such a grading regime could inadvertently incentivize doing the least possible. Other students who do not believe they will perform much better than a 50% on a given assignment will simply not put forth any effort. Extrinsic motivators such as grades matter—and given the state of student academics following the pandemic, policies that disincentivize effort should be discouraged.

Students Who Had Success

Though most of the literature has suggested that a large amount of learning loss occurred due to the pandemic and the influx of virtual, hybrid, and hyflex learning, several studies have found instances of student success (Cohodes et al., 2022; Hammerstein, König, Dreisörner, & Frey, 2021; Sahin & Matteson, 2022). With most studies suggesting that students are behind, we found it promising that several studies found positive school situations during the pandemic. However, it is important to note that some of these studies' findings may only generalize to some schools or even only some students. For example, Sahin and Matteson (2022) found that student self-efficacy, academic engagement, self-management, and a growth mindset positively influenced math and English language arts scores. Thus students who had high confidence in their ability to take time to engage with the learning materials throughout the pandemic, who self-regulated their learning rather than being told to complete academic activities, and who believed they could succeed academically all showed growth during the pandemic. This is no surprise to us, as these attributes positively affected student achievement before the pandemic (Honicke & Broadbent, 2016; Zimmerman, Bandura, & Martinez-Pons, 1992). Unfortunately, this was not the case for most students during the pandemic. Many students needed access to the required resources (e.g., internet, technology, learning materials) or needed a space they could dedicate to school as families shared office spaces and kitchen tables for school and work.

In a systematic review of studies, Hammerstein et al. (2021) came across three studies that found increased student scores during the pandemic (Meeter, 2021; Spitzer & Musslick, 2021; van der Velde, Sense, Spijkers, Meeter, & van Rijn, 2021). A common theme across all three studies was that students who were already using an online system for completing work, whether it was Google Classroom or another platform, had less of a learning curve when transitioning to online learning in March 2020, as much of their routine was the same regardless of the environment. A similar theme emerged from interviews conducted with charter school leaders in the summer of 2020 (Marshall & Neugebauer, 2023). School leaders who were utilizing online tools such as a learning management system (LMS) prior to the pandemic were in a much better position to pivot to remote learning than those who were not. Additionally, students reported having more success at home due to fewer distractions than in a normal classroom and less time pressure, allowing them to complete activities at their own pace rather than keep up with the class. It is important to note that data from these studies came from the Netherlands (Meeter, 2021; van der Velde et al., 2021) and Germany (Spitzer & Musslick, 2021), which may differ in important ways from the United States. An additional study conducted in Germany also found positive results several months after the lockdown period, after teachers had provided extra group tutoring during the summer (Gore, Fray, Miller, Harris, & Taggart, 2021). Again, the sample demographics from these studies may differ from those in the United States. However, it provides a glimpse of hope that interventions such as extra tutoring may positively affect student achievement gains.

Global Learning Loss

Academic challenges were not unique to American schools during the pandemic. As noted previously, at one point, more than 1.6 billion students from more than 190 countries (more than 90% of the global student population) could not attend school due to pandemic-induced closures (UNESCO, 2020). Early estimates suggest that school closures will cost students trillions in lifetime earnings (Donohue & Miller, 2020; Psacharopoulas, Collis, Patrinos, & Vegas, 2021). In August 2020, UN Secretary-General António Guterres warned that more than 24 million students worldwide were at risk of dropping out of school and "not finding their way back to their studies in 2020 following the COVID-19-induced closures" (UNESCO, 2020).

Scholars from around the globe have examined the academic consequences of school closures. Hevia and colleagues studied learning loss in Mexico, where schools were closed for over a year (Hevia, Vergara-Lope, Velásquez-Durán, & Calderón, 2022). They compared household survey data from 2019 (before the pandemic) to 2021 and interviewed more than 3,000 children ages 10–15. They found that students' ability levels decreased in reading (0.34–0.45 standard deviation [*SD*] decrease) and math (0.62–0.82 *SD* decrease) for every age group and at every SES level. A similar story unfolded in Belize. In reading, national test results show more than a 25% drop from the 2018–2019 school year to 2021–2022 for fifth-grade students and a 14.5% drop for eighth-grade students (Näslund-Hadley, Alonzo, Villanueva, Gideon, & Flowers, 2023). The declines were much more pronounced for mathematics, in which fifth-grade test scores dropped 35% from 2018–2019 to 2021–2022, and eighth-grade test scores fell 41.1% during the same time frame. Student dropout rates increased by 51% in the 2020–2021 school year compared with the previous year.

Molnár and Hermann (2023) explored the short- and long-term effects of virtual learning on math, reading, and science based on test data from 55,000 Hungarian students. In Hungary, kindergarten returned to in-person learning after 10 weeks of remote learning, whereas elementary and secondary students did not return in person until fall of 2020 (approximately 24 weeks out of school due to the pandemic and summer break). During the 2020–2021 school year, schools in Hungary had numerous school closures between September and March due to COVID-19 outbreaks. In addition, Hungary had a second mandatory government school lockdown, which lasted 6 weeks for students in kindergarten through grade 4 and 9 weeks for grades 5–8. Thus, from March 2020 through the end of 2021, kindergartners spent at least 16 weeks at home (with no official virtual learning), students in grades 1–4 experienced at least 19 weeks of remote learning, and students in grades 5–8 spent at least 22 weeks learning virtually. The results suggested that kindergarten and elementary grades (1–4) were negatively affected by the lack of in-person learning compared with older students. Specifically, kindergarten and first-grade students felt the largest impact in math, while second- through fourth-grade students were most affected in reading. Additionally, second- through fourth-grade students from lower SES homes made very little, if any, progress during the virtual learning period.

In a study conducted in the Netherlands, Engzell et al. (2021) collected data from nearly 350,000 students who experienced a relatively short lockdown (8 weeks) compared with schools in many parts of the United States and worldwide. Even with a shortened lockdown duration, Dutch students had the equivalent of one-fifth of a school year in learning loss, which was close to the length of the lockdown. Similar to other studies discussed in this chapter (e.g., Kuhfeld et al., 2022), students from less educated households had an even greater loss (up to 60% larger).

Students in Germany faced a similar amount of time on lockdown (2 months) compared with the Netherlands. Schult and colleagues (2022) explored the impact of the pandemic on student learning through reading and math standardized assessments given to over 80,000 German students in the fall of 2020. Because the tests are given each September, Schult and colleagues could compare the 2020 results with the previous 3 years' scores. Unsurprisingly, scores in the fall of 2020 were lower than those of the previous 3 years; however, students labeled as lower achieving in reading reached their pre-pandemic levels. Unfortunately, this was not the case for lower achieving math students, who continued to catch up to their pre-pandemic achievement levels. Additionally, lower SES was positively associated with larger learning losses in math.

The World Bank and UNESCO Institute for Statistics define *learning poverty* as "being unable to read and understand simple text by age 10" (World Bank, 2022). Simulation studies conducted in 2020 estimated that learning poverty would increase from 53% globally to 63% without substantial interventions to remediate pandemic learning loss (World Bank, 2022). A 2022 report found that learning poverty had increased to 70% globally, with the sharpest increases in Latin America, South Asia, and the Caribbean—regions that closed their schools for the longest durations (UNICEF, 2022). Learning poverty figures were admittedly high for students prior to the pandemic in Mexico (Hevia et al., 2022). However, these figures increased substantially by 2021. In 2019, 42% of low-SES 10-year-olds could not read or understand simple text; 2 years later that figure increased almost 28 points to 67.7%. The trends were also true for students in the top SES quartile. Almost 28% of 10-year-old students met the definition for learning poverty in 2019; 2 years later that figure increased more than 15 points to 43.1%.

World Bank economist Harry Patrinos (2023) studied learning loss across 41 countries (which represent two-thirds of the world's population). He found that the longer schools were closed, the greater the learning loss. Countries closed their schools for 21 weeks on average,* and this was associated with an average learning loss of 0.23 *SD*, or close to a year's worth of learning. Patrinos ran a simple regression model with a single predictor—the number of weeks schools were closed—and found that it significantly predicted learning loss and explained almost 42% of the variance alone. A fair-minded person might wonder whether other factors played a more significant role than school closures. After all, countries differ in important ways from one another. There are a range of types of governments (e.g., democracies, dictatorships), different health concerns (e.g., COVID-19 prevalence, vaccination rates), infrastructure (e.g., internet access), and economic conditions (e.g., gross domestic product [GDP], unionization levels) that all vary across countries. When Patrinos ran a second model that controlled for several factors, including COVID-19 death rates, the prevalence of private schools, internet access, pre-pandemic school quality, COVID-19 vaccination rates, the stringency of lockdowns, unionization, level of democracy, and GDP, the number of weeks closed remained the only significant predictor of learning loss. See Figures 3.4 and 3.5 for data on learning loss and the number of weeks schools were closed, respectively, by country.

Supporting Student Academics Moving Forward

It is clear that most students experienced learning loss during the pandemic (e.g., Asadullah et al., 2023; Patrinos, 2022), and this should be a major concern for school leaders, teachers, parents, and students. Many schools and educational systems have implemented various strategies to address the issues, such as extended learning time, tutoring, summer school programs, and targeted interventions for students falling behind. Additionally, some teachers and school leaders have emphasized the importance of social–emotional learning and mental health support, recognizing that students' well-being is critical to their academic success

*For these analyses, the United States was considered to have closed schools for 8 weeks, because the annual summer break was not counted as school closure time, and approximately half of schools opened for in-person learning in fall 2020.

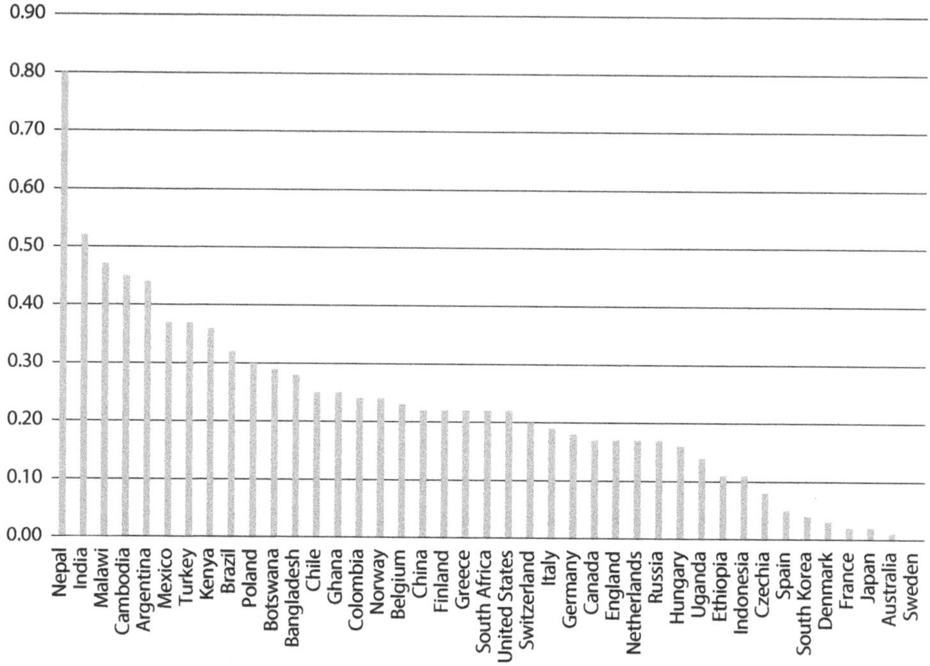

FIGURE 3.4. Average learning loss by country in standard deviations (*SD*). Data from Patrinos (2023).

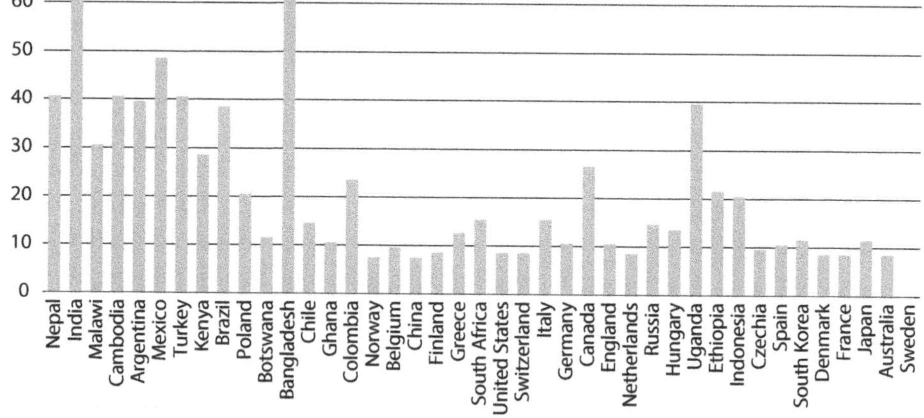

FIGURE 3.5. Weeks schools were closed by country due to COVID-19. Data from Patrinos (2023).

(see Chapters 4 and 7). We have attended national education conferences at which we have heard some researchers speak dismissively about learning loss, but if we care about children's learning and academics, this is a matter that must be taken seriously.

High-Dose Tutoring

Schools should develop and implement targeted interventions to support students who have experienced academic setbacks due to the pandemic. Among the interventions that have demonstrated the greatest success is high-dose tutoring (HDT). Patrinos (2022) defines HDT as "consisting of intensive engagement that occurs one-to-one in very small groups on a sustained, daily basis, during the school day or after school to help students accelerate their learning" (pp. 184–185). Ample evidence exists demonstrating the effectiveness of this intervention. Two separate meta-analyses conducted prior to the pandemic found academic improvements of 0.36 and 0.37 *SD*, respectively (Dietrichson, Bøg, Filges, & Jørgensen, 2017; Nickow, Oreopoulos, & Quan, 2020). Both analyses found HDT more effective than other interventions, including summer programs, after-school programs, and small-group instruction. A study conducted in the Netherlands found that HDT was able to make up 40% of the math achievement gap between low- and high-SES students (de Ree et al., 2023). In India, students suffered among the worst pandemic-era learning deficits in the world (0.70 *SD* for math and 0.34 *SD* for language; Singh, Romero, & Muralidharan, 2022). Six months after schools reopened, students made up approximately two-thirds of the losses, and one study estimates that about a quarter of those gains can be attributed to HDT. Other, similar tutoring efforts have been tried as well. For example, Kraft, List, Livingston, and Sadoff (2022) studied an experimental pilot program that used college students as volunteers to tutor middle school students online one on one. They found positive effects for the initiative; however, the gains were much smaller than studies have found for HDT.

Michael Goldstein and Bowen Paulle (2021) focused on HDT as a possible solution for pandemic learning loss. Both authors have successfully led HDT programs in Boston and Amsterdam, respectively, and both of their programs led to extraordinary academic gains for low-income students. However, they urge caution in scaling up efforts in the wake of the pandemic. Steven Sawchuck (2022) echoes these sentiments, noting several challenges that may exist in implementing HDT, including the costs, the logistics of integrating it into existing practice, and the capacity some schools may not have—especially if they lack the personnel to implement tutoring to fidelity.

The Role of Artificial Intelligence

Sal Khan, founder of the Khan Academy, sees artificial intelligence (AI) as part of the solution. In a spring 2023 TED talk, he stated, "I think we're at the cusp of using AI for probably the biggest positive transformation that education has ever seen. The way we're going to do that is by giving every student on the planet an artificially intelligent, but amazing, personal tutor" (Gendron, 2023). Khanmigo, which launched in the spring of 2023, is an AI chatbot that can assist students with a range of subjects including math, writing, and computer science. Khanmigo helps students find the answers themselves, in contrast to ChatGPT, which is more apt to simply give its users the answer. Rick Hess (2023) shares the optimism about what AI may be able to help achieve in tutoring but urges us to not let its promise displace meaningful human interaction, namely in the form of tech-enabled mentoring. He writes: "tutoring is mostly about conveying content and explaining concepts, while mentoring is beneficial precisely because kids also benefit from access to a broad array of role models and supportive adults. AI tutoring can help with the former, but not the latter" (p. 3). Hess's argument aligns with new findings from a study conducted by Matthew Kraft and his colleagues (Kraft, Bolves, & Hurd, 2023). They studied the impact that informal mentoring from teachers, counselors, and athletic coaches has on students' long-term success and found that these relationships can translate to an almost 10% increase in college attendance. In other words, human relationships matter. Although we agree that AI potentially presents great promise in helping students learn, we agree with these words of caution. Given the current state of pediatric and adolescent mental health (more on this in the next chapter), we don't know that encouraging kids to exist in a world that includes fewer human interactions is a good idea.

* * *

Some of the few groups of students who had success learning during the pandemic found that virtual learning provided flexible learning options that allowed students to learn at their own pace and in their preferred format. Schools might consider providing various learning options, including hybrid and online learning, to support students facing challenges with traditional in-person learning. However, this option may only be ideal for some students and should be used cautiously. Other groups of students who were successful during the pandemic had had technology incorporated into their learning before the COVID-19 shutdown. This use of technology in the classroom allowed an easier transition to online learning during the pandemic. Schools may consider future curricula incorporating technology into daily or weekly lessons that can be completed in multiple settings (i.e., in class or at home). If schools move to incorporate more technology, school leaders must address the inequities regarding technology. Schools should prioritize equity by addressing the digital divide, providing access to technology, and ensuring that students from disadvantaged backgrounds receive targeted support.

Finally, school leaders must understand that students will be behind for a while, and there is no overnight fix to catching students up. It must also be understood that teachers already have a lot on their plates. (See Chapter 5 for more on teacher well-being.) School leaders must recognize that teachers are professionals and know what is best for their students. Addressing student learning loss will not happen simply by requiring teachers to implement new programs, putting pressure on teachers to raise state test scores, or requiring more from teachers on a daily basis. Instead, school leaders must work with teachers to develop appropriate action plans that incorporate teacher perspectives, provide teachers autonomy within the classroom, and support all students in chipping away at the learning loss from the pandemic.

In summary, the COVID-19 pandemic has significantly affected student academic learning, leading to disruptions in the learning process, reduced instructional time, and changes in assessment and grading methods. Addressing these challenges will require a multifaceted approach that involves investment in technology and online resources, providing support for students' mental health needs, and implementing effective learning strategies to address gaps in learning. School leaders must recognize that student recovery will take time and that adjusting expectations and outcomes may be necessary for the short term. Interventions such as high-dose tutoring and AI tutoring hold significant promise to help students recover some of the losses they have incurred. Finally, school leaders must not put unrealistic expectations and pressure on teachers now but instead focus on student growth.

Chapter 4

The Impact on Student Mental and Social Well-Being

Student academics was not the only thing affected by the COVID-19 mitigation measures. Student mental health and well-being also suffered tremendously (e.g., Naff, Williams, Furman-Darby, & Yeung, 2022; Viner et al., 2022). According to a report from the Center on Reinventing Public Education, one in seven young people experienced a "major depressive episode" in 2021 (Gross & Hamilton, 2023, p. 4), and, as of April 2023, 70% of public schools reported an increase in the percentage of students seeking mental health support. What we currently see manifesting in children may only scratch the surface of the nature of the problem. According to the National Association of Pediatric Nurse Practitioners and colleagues (2020), mental health disorders can often present symptoms 2–4 years after a traumatic experience. In this chapter, we share what is currently known about the mental health impacts resulting from COVID-19 mitigation measures, which subpopulations may be more vulnerable, and what some of the protective factors are that lead to improved mental health in youth.

What Is Known about COVID-19 Mental Health Impacts

As discussed in Chapter 2, evidence shows that the actual health risks of COVID-19 to children were minimal (Bhopal et al., 2020; CDC COVID-19 Response Team, 2020; Haleemunnissa et al., 2021). Children were less susceptible to the virus (Lee et al., 2020; Xu et al., 2020), and those who contracted COVID-19 tended to have milder symptoms (European Centre for Disease Prevention and Control, 2020; Lee et al., 2020) and were hospitalized at less than one-fourth the rate of adults (Gandhi & Noble, 2021). However, the measures implemented to mitigate the spread of COVID-19 led to increased mental health risks for youth (Chu & Lake, 2021; Gotlib et al., in press; Hawrilenko, Kroshus, Tandon, & Christakis, 2021; Kishida, Tsuda, Waite, Creswell, & Ishikawa; 2021; Liu et al., 2020; Van Lancker & Parolin, 2020). This was evidenced by an increase of 75% in mental health–related hospitalizations in 2020 over 2019 (Gandhi & Noble, 2021). In addition, pediatric emergency room visits for mental health issues increased 31% from April to October 2020 (Leeb et al., 2020), and 20% of all teen hospitalizations during the first 3 months of 2021 were due to psychiatric emergencies, not COVID-19 (Gandhi & Noble, 2021). To understand the impact of the pandemic compared with previous years, consider a study conducted in Canada that compared data from the same time period (April 1–October 31) across 3 years: 2018, 2019, and 2020 (Stewart, Vasudeva, Van Dyke, & Poss, 2022). Compared with 2018 and 2019, they found that mental health assessments among children significantly decreased, with the greatest decline experienced by children from low-income neighborhoods. In other words, at a time of increased need for mental health services, those with the greatest needs were getting less help than they had been pre-pandemic.

Posttraumatic stress disorder (PTSD), depression, and anxiety have all been documented in individuals who have lived through disaster conditions, and pandemics are no exception (Bartek, Peck, Garzon, & Van Cleve, 2020). When schools closed in March 2020, students lost more than their primary source of academic learning. Schools also serve as central hubs that support student social and emotional needs, serve meals, and provide mental health services. Approximately 3 million students receive mental health services through a school-based program (Golberstein, Wen, & Miller, 2020; Hoffman & Miller, 2020). As discussed in Chapter 1, policies concerning school closures and reopenings involved tradeoffs. However, it is evident now that coronavirus mitigation efforts were overweighted against students' physical, mental, academic, and social needs. When quarantines are necessitated, they should be as short-lived as possible, as longer quarantines are associated with poorer psychological outcomes (Brooks et al., 2020; Tan, 2021). In the United States, prolonged school closures were implemented in several states and cities, and these had severe consequences for student well-being, especially concerning symptoms of loneliness, anxiety, stress, and depression, as well as suicidal ideation and incidence.

Loneliness and Isolation

When schools closed abruptly in March 2020, students' lives, routines, and social networks were disrupted. Students no longer had the opportunity to connect with their peers before or after class, at recess, or in the lunchroom. Rather, the only contact students had with their peers and teachers became exclusively virtual (Marshall, 2022a; Wyse, Stickney, Butz, Beckler, & Close, 2020). The sudden absence of a social network left many students feeling greater levels of loneliness (Ellis, Dumas, & Forbes, 2020). Loades and colleagues (2020) conducted a systematic review of 63 studies exploring the impact of social isolation and loneliness on mental health in previously healthy children and adolescents (i.e., those who were not diagnosed with a mental health disorder prior to the pandemic). They found that the duration of loneliness was correlated with mental health symptoms; longer lockdowns and school closures led to decreasing mental health (Loades et al., 2020). They also found that the duration of loneliness mattered much more than the intensity of the feelings of loneliness. In addition, a longitudinal study in the United States found that loneliness increased during the pandemic (Rogers, Ha, & Ockey, 2021). Similarly, a study of adolescents in Turkey found that school closures increased anxiety and loneliness (Kilinçel, Kilinçel, Muratdaği, Aydin, & Usta, 2021). Isolation and its impact on a person's mental health is not a new phenomenon. For example, a study of 586 participants affected by the H1N1 influenza found that quarantine and isolation can lead to PTSD in both parents and children (Sprang & Silman, 2013). To address the increased loneliness, young people often spent additional time online connecting with peers; however, this was also found to be associated with increased levels of depression.

Anxiety and Stress

Quarantine and social isolation had detrimental effects on mental health, and studies have found that anxiety increased in youth during school closures and lockdowns (Ravens-Sieberer et al., 2022; Rogers et al., 2021;

Salzano et al., 2021; Stewart et al., 2022). One of the more extensive studies on the impact of the pandemic involved survey research in March 2020 conducted in more than 30 countries, representing every continent except Antarctica, and found no geographic differences in the perceived stress that participants reported (Gamonol-Limcaoco et al., 2022). They did, however, find that females and younger participants had the highest stress levels. Overall, the COVID-19 pandemic produced high anticipatory anxiety, causing people to have increased levels of fear.

One possible source of the increased stress and anxiety may have come from the media coverage throughout the pandemic. A person could not turn on a television or scroll through social media without hearing about the latest positive case rates and the spread of the virus. Exposure to an excessive amount of information about the possibility of getting infected may have caused a lot of stress and anxiety for some individuals, although it is difficult to separate this anxiety from general feelings of loneliness and/or the financial impact caused by lockdowns related to the virus (Horesh & Brown, 2020). CNN even had a running ticker on the right side of the screen on its broadcasts that tallied the number of COVID-19 cases and deaths to date. News of the pandemic's wrath was everywhere.

Other factors that influenced anxiety included having a previous psychiatric referral (Kilinçel et al., 2021; Rousseau & Miconi, 2020), having a family member test positive for COVID-19 (Kilinçel et al., 2021), and being frustrated with online learning. For example, a study of 163 adolescents in the San Francisco Bay area involved the administration of a survey that included scales measuring anxiety and depression before and during the pandemic and found that anxiety had increased by half of a standard deviation (Gotlib et al., in press). A longitudinal study was conducted in New York that surveyed adolescents monthly between March and July 2020 and found that anxiety symptoms peaked in late April and early May—corresponding with the peak in infection rates (Hawes, Szenczy, Olino, Nelson, & Klein, 2021). These symptoms subsided in parallel with COVID-19 infection rates, which decreased between May and July 2020 in New York. Additionally, Magson and colleagues (2021) studied adolescent mental health in Australia, one of the most stringently locked down countries in the world during COVID-19. They surveyed 248 adolescents at two time points—prior to the outbreak and 2 months after the implementation of government restrictions and remote learning. Frustrations with online learning led to increased mental health problems. They also found that COVID-19-related distress, or fear of contracting the virus, was highly correlated with anxiety levels. So adolescents were contending with stressors related to how they learned, their isolation, and the virus itself simultaneously. As such, it is altogether unsurprising that their levels of anxiety and depressive symptoms increased across the two survey administrations.

Depression and Suicidality

Children and adolescents also experienced elevated levels of depression and suicidality during the pandemic. Children who experienced extended periods of isolation were three times as likely to develop symptoms of depression (Loades et al., 2020), which could partly explain why children whose parents were frontline workers were also more likely to exhibit signs of depression (Mansfield et al., 2021). Compared with pre-pandemic levels, symptoms of depression in children and adolescents increased during COVID-19 (Bignardi et al., 2020; Cheng et al., 2021; Gotlib et al., in press; Ravens-Sieberer et al., 2022; Rogers et al., 2021; Stewart et al., 2022; Tang, Xiang, Cheung, & Xiang, 2021), with girls (Chen et al., 2020; Mansfield et al., 2021; Oosterhoff, Palmer, Wilson, & Shook, 2020; Pisano et al., 2021) and older students (Chen et al., 2020) reporting statistically greater levels. Those who exhibited depressive symptoms prior to the COVID-19 outbreak were also more likely to exhibit increased symptoms during the pandemic (Pisano et al., 2021). A study of more than 10,000 students between the ages of 8 and 13 in England found that girls had significantly higher levels of depression compared with boys (Mansfield et al., 2021); other studies have echoed this finding (Chen et al., 2020; Oosterhoff et al., 2020; Pisano et al., 2021). One possible explanation for this may be the lack of social interactions students had at the beginning of the pandemic. During the pandemic, students were generally not permitted to interact with peers, and the absence of a social network can be stressful. Social isolation has been found to have greater effects on females than males (Senst, Baimoukhametova, Sterley, & Bains, 2016). One of the major concerns with the increase of loneliness and other mental health issues is that loneliness, anxiety, and stress are often precursors to depression and suicidal ideation and incidence (Rodriguez-Quintana et al., 2021). A meta-analysis and systematic literature review found that loneliness was a significant predictor of suicidal ideation and incidence and that depression was a significant mediator (McClelland, Evans, Nowland, Ferguson, & O'Connor, 2020). Teen suicide increased markedly during the early months of the pandemic (e.g., Hou, Mao, Dong, Cai, & Deng, 2020). This was particularly true for teenage girls, for whom incidents were up 50% (Yard et al., 2021). In one study, researchers surveyed 505 Italian adolescents during the lockdowns and school closures and found that 14.3% reported intentionally harming themselves or attempting suicide, behaviors associated with elevated levels of anxiety and depression (Cena et al., 2022). The COVID-19 lockdown took a major toll on everyone but was especially hard on kids and adolescents who often had few interactions beyond those that were online.

Adolescent Mental Health Trends

The CDC (2023a) conducts a biannual survey, the Youth Risk Behavior Survey. We compared their 2011 findings with the most recent findings from 2021, and the results are alarming. See Table 4.1 for a comparison between the 2011 and 2021 survey results. For each of the five categories listed, mental health outcomes were decidedly worse in 2021 than they were a decade prior. Adolescent girls fared worse than boys in every category, and not just by a little bit. In 2011, 28% of all adolescents reported persistent feelings of sadness or hopelessness in the previous 12 months. A decade later (and during the pandemic), that figure had increased by 50%, or 14 percentage points, to 42%. Adolescent girls fared the worst, with almost 3 in 5 (57%) reporting persistent feelings of sadness or hopelessness. Females were also twice as likely than males to report poor mental health (41% vs. 18%), to seriously consider attempting suicide (30% vs. 14%), to make a suicide plan (24% vs. 12%), or to attempt suicide (13% vs. 7%). As we noted at the start of the chapter, adolescent mental health was trending in the wrong direction before the pandemic. However, the current figures are disconcerting, to say the least.

The Influence of Parents

The mental health of parents can also play a critical role in how children react, as studies have found that parents with anxiety disorder can

TABLE 4.1. Comparing Adolescent Mental Health 2011–2021

The percentage of high school students who:	2011 %	2021 %
Experienced persistent feelings of sadness or hopelessness	28	42
Female	36	57
Male	21	29
Experienced poor mental health[a]	—	29
Female	—	41
Male	—	18
Seriously considered attempting suicide	16	22
Female	19	30
Male	13	14
Made a suicide plan	13	18
Female	15	24
Male	11	12
Attempted suicide	8	10
Female	10	13
Male	6	7

Note. From CDC (2023). In the public domain.
[a]Variable introduced in 2021 survey.

model problem behaviors, resulting in their transferring their anxiety to their children (Aktar, Nikolić, & Bögels, 2017; Woodruff-Borden, Morrow, Bourland, & Cambron, 2022). Additionally, Aktar and colleagues (2017) note that for those with anxiety disorder, "uncertainty is intolerable . . . and that worry helps to cope with uncertainty" (p. 137). In other words, parents with this disorder inadvertently teach their kids to use worrying as a coping mechanism. Similarly, Aktar and colleagues (Aktar, Majdandžić, de Vente, & Bögels 2014) conducted a study that found that toddlers of parents with social anxiety exhibited more fear and avoidance behaviors than their peers. The same was true during the COVID-19 pandemic. Evidence from Italy and Spain suggests that if a child's primary caregiver perceived the COVID-19 pandemic as a threat to their family's well-being, their children were sadder, lonelier, more nervous and uneasy, had more difficulty concentrating, and were more afraid of COVID-19 infection (Orgilés, Morales, Delvecchio, Mazzeschi, & Espada, 2020). This is particularly noteworthy during the COVID-19 pandemic, as many parents may have felt anxieties and stressors because of financial instability, balancing careers and kids' schooling from home, or food shortages.

Parents also became “proxy educators,” especially during the early months of remote instruction. As Davis and her colleagues (Davis, Grooms, Ortega, Rubalcaba, & Vargas, 2020) note, “Since the transition to remote learning, proxy educators have been expected to retain teaching knowledge, teach individualized content, assess the emotional needs of [their children] . . . all in addition to their existing responsibilities [as parents]” (p. 61). They studied the relationship between their children’s academics and parents’ mental health during this time. Parents whose children struggled with remote instruction experienced significantly elevated anxiety and depressive symptoms. When children struggled to learn, parents struggled with their mental health. This becomes particularly concerning when parents blame themselves for their child’s academic struggles. Khoury, Kaur, and Gonzalez (2021) studied maternal relationships and the extent to which mothers internalized problems during the pandemic and found a significant relationship between maternal anxiety and increases in internalizing problems. This suggests that remote learning did not just affect kids but their parents as well. In short, parents faced a number of new stressors during the first few months of the pandemic. These anxieties and stressors continued as families had to decide how they wanted their kid(s) to return to school in the fall of 2020. How parents reacted to the pandemic had the potential to have a decisive impact on how their children experienced the crisis as well.

The news here is not all bad. One of the silver linings of the lockdowns and school closures for some families was that they were able to spend more quality time with one another (Penner, Ortiz, & Sharp, 2021). Research has shown that this served as a protective measure for many students (Marshall, in press). Additionally, Ellis and colleagues (2020) found that young people who spent more time with their families during lockdowns and school closures reported lower levels of depression. A study of youth in the Czech Republic found that 79% of adolescents reported positive interactions with their families during the pandemic and that this was associated with better mental health (Ng, Cosma, Svacina, Boniel-Nissim, & Badura, 2021). Though the pandemic introduced mental health challenges, the lockdowns also provided opportunities for families to spend more time with each other, and in many cases these interactions had a positive influence on their mental health. If spending quality time with one’s family can help mitigate poor mental health outcomes during a crisis, this is likely just as true during non-pandemic times as well.

The Influence of Peers

Lockdown and school closure policies forced students to live and learn in isolation, away from their peers and teachers. A chief result of this was an increase in screen time, stemming from its uses for remote learning and also for social interaction (Haidt, 2023). Madigan, Eirich, Pador, McArthur, and Neville (2022) conducted a meta-analysis to understand changes in child and adolescent screen time during the COVID-19 pandemic. After reviewing 136 articles, they found that screen time increased more than 50%, excluding time spent on remote learning. Prior to COVID-19, there had been increasing concerns about adolescent mental health, especially regarding the impact that increased screen time and social media play in this (McCrae, Gettings, & Purssell, 2017; Twenge, 2017). In addition, a meta-analysis of 38 studies found a negative relationship between social media use and student well-being (Marciano, Ostroumova, Schulz, & Camerini, 2022). Research conducted in the Gaza Strip found a significant relationship between social media use and fear and panic, especially related to COVID-19 (Radwan, Radwan, & Radwan, 2020). Female students were affected more than males. In summary, increased screen time and social media use during the pandemic led to declining levels of mental health in students. However, were screens always bad for youth? The answer to that question is . . . it depends.

Ellis and colleagues (2020) found that although social media use led to increased levels of depression and loneliness, connecting with friends virtually led to reduced levels of depression. Furthermore, Magis-Weinberg and colleagues (Magis-Weinberg, Gys, Berger, Domoff, & Dahl, 2021) conducted a longitudinal study of youth in Peru and found that the nature of social interactions that took place virtually and through social media dictated whether the use of these digital tools was positive or negative. Positive social interactions, even on social media, led to reduced feelings of loneliness and isolation. By contrast, negative social interactions led to the inverse. Previous research has found that adolescents who have strong ties to one another outside of the digital world tend to have more positive interactions online, which are associated with improved well-being (Burke & Kraut, 2016). However, the same was not found to be true of online interactions between individuals who did not have as strong a relationship. Finally, David Naff and his colleagues (2022) conducted a systematic review of the literature on student mental health during the pandemic. They found that moderate use of social media could serve as a positive coping mechanism for students who otherwise could not interact with friends; however, it was not a substitute for in-person interactions. During the pandemic, students' interactions with peers through screens were ubiquitous. As such, understanding the nuances of the impact of those interactions is important.

* * *

The COVID-19 pandemic and its associated mitigation efforts have led to concerning mental health trends in children and adolescents. To be fair, these trends were moving in the wrong direction prior to 2020 (Lukianoff & Haidt, 2018); however, they have been exacerbated by the pandemic. A spring 2023 EdChoice/Morning Consult poll found that roughly half of American teens were happy and felt positive about their futures (EdChoice, 2023a). They were positive about academics and their family relationships, but least satisfied with their mental health and the support they received to address it. The 2021 Adolescent Behaviors and Experiences Survey found that students who felt close to others at school had substantially better mental health than those who did not (Jones et al., 2022). They were happier, reported lower levels of persistent sadness, and thought about and attempted suicide far less often. In short, relationships and connections with others matter. Addressing mental health issues is outside our expertise, so we entrust that to others. However, at least part of the solution may be as simple as finding ways to ensure that every student who walks into a school has at least one adult who knows him or her, one who is invested in his or her success. Schools cannot be expected to address this problem alone. At the same time, schools cannot ignore these trends, either. School leaders must make student mental health a priority moving forward by providing schools and teachers with the necessary resources.

Chapter 5

The Impact on Teacher Well-Being

From the pandemic's start, teachers were frontline workers with multiple roles, including providing instruction to students in various formats (i.e., virtual, hybrid, in person) and implementing safety protocols as schools shifted back to offering in-person instruction. This was done while teachers balanced their personal and work lives, learned new instructional approaches, and tried to keep themselves and family members safe from a virus the world knew very little about. When schools were remote, teachers who were also parents had to juggle helping their children learn remotely while figuring out how to teach online (Clark et al., 2021; Marshall, Shannon, & Love, 2022). Throughout this period, school leaders made many critical decisions on when and how students and teachers would return to the classroom. However, across most of the United States, these decisions were often made with little input from teachers as states and school boards implemented top-down decisions that teachers were expected to follow (Pressley et al., 2023; Storey & Slavin, 2020). We believe it is important for K–12 education stakeholders to understand how the additional expectations teachers experienced during the pandemic affected their stress, anxiety, morale, and burnout.

Teacher burnout was an issue prior to the pandemic. Causes of burnout in teachers vary, but previous research has found heavy workloads, low pay, lack of resources, and lack of autonomy to be associated with teacher burnout (Ferguson, Frost, & Hall, 2012; McCarthy, Lambert, Lineback, Fitchett, & Baddouh, 2016; Pearson & Moomaw, 2005). The pandemic only exacerbated these issues (Chan, Sharkey, Lawrie, Arch,

& Nylund-Gibson, 2021; Herman, Sebastian, Reinke, & Huang, 2021; Pressley, 2021a; Pressley, Marshall, & Moore, in press). As noted previously, teachers were not trained to teach and support students through a global pandemic. Before the spring of 2020, most school districts did not offer teachers professional development (PD) on how to deliver instruction online (Marshall, Shannon, & Love, 2022). Needless to say, the tough job of teaching became even more difficult during the pandemic, with teachers continuing to work through the impact of the pandemic 3 years later.

During the pandemic, teachers' mental health and well-being declined due to increased workloads, uncertainty, a lack of social support, a lack of connectedness with colleagues and students, and coping strategies, and reduced autonomy within the classroom (Fleming, Calvert, & Turner, 2023; Kim, Oxley, & Asbury, 2022; Schiller, Wilcox, Leo, Khan, & Ávila, 2023; Walter & Fox, 2021). This led teachers to seek more mental health support to help deal with the additional burdens. In a spring 2022 national survey, 29% of schools reported an increased number of teachers seeking mental health support since the pandemic's beginning (Institute of Education Sciences, 2022). These findings are similar to what we found in our May 2022 survey, with 33.1% of teachers reporting that they had received mental health counseling since the start of the pandemic (Pressley, Marshall, Love, & Neugebauer, 2022). See Table 5.1 for a comparison of our survey findings from 2022 and 2023.

TABLE 5.1. Teachers Seeking Mental Health Counseling: Comparing 2022 and 2023 Data

Since the beginning of the school year, have you seen a counselor for mental health reasons?	Spring 2022 (N = 830)		Spring 2023 (N = 927)	
	N	%	*N*	%
Yes, I have seen a counselor for mental health reasons.	275	33.13	236	25.46
No, I have not seen anyone for mental health reasons.	545	65.66	512	55.23
I looked into it but did not see anyone for mental health reasons.[a]	—	—	172	18.55
Prefer not to answer.	10	1.20	10	0.76

[a]Variable introduced in spring 2023 survey (credit to Denise Bozek and Rachael Estes of Auburn University for prompting us to ask participants this question).

Teacher well-being is important, as it may affect a teacher's energy level, productivity, overall effectiveness with students, and desire to remain in the profession (Bottiani, Duran, Pas, & Bradshaw, 2019; Savaş, Bozgeyik, & Eser, 2014; Skaalvik & Skaalvik, 2015). Ultimately, a teacher's well-being may influence his or her effectiveness within the classroom. This is critical because a highly effective teacher will prioritize student learning through specific remediation, support student self-regulation, and establish a classroom environment that is managed and motivates student learning (Pressley, Croyle, & Edgar, 2020; Stronge, 2018). These essential characteristics often increase student achievement (Pressley, Mohan, Raphael, & Fingeret, 2007; Roehrig et al., 2012). By prioritizing teacher well-being, school leaders can support teacher development, and, in turn, teachers can better establish effective learning environments for their students. This chapter sheds light on the research conducted during the pandemic focused on teacher well-being, specifically teacher stress, burnout, morale, and mental health. Because the pandemic placed different stressors on teachers at different times, we first examine the literature on teacher well-being in 2020–2021 and then do the same for the 2021–2022 and 2022–2023 school years. At the end of the chapter, we summarize the lessons learned throughout for supporting teacher well-being.

Teacher Well-Being during 2020–2021

The spring of 2020 brought the world to a halt, and teachers were forced to transition to virtual instruction at a moment's notice, going from the standard, everyday, in-person classroom experience to teaching their students from their kitchen tables. With such a sudden shift in teaching, it is unsurprising that teachers experienced high levels of stress. An early study conducted during the pandemic found that 81% of teachers reported high levels of stress often or all of the time during the pandemic (Mathews, Streit, & Smith, 2020), while Chan et al. (2021) found that nearly half of their elementary teacher sample reported high stress levels. The increase in stress was often due to multiple factors, including the new instructional requirements, the support or lack of support teachers received for the instructional changes, teachers' attempts to balance work and life, and the increase in teacher workloads (e.g., Chan et al., 2021; Sokal, Trudel, & Babb, 2020b; Walter & Fox, 2021). Although teachers had busy workloads previously, the increase in workloads during the pandemic often was due to the extra time needed to plan and prepare for virtual instruction, leading to extended teaching hours to connect with students who could not get online at the scheduled virtual instruction times, and having to take time to learn new LMS (Love & Marshall, 2022; Marshall, Shannon, & Love, 2020; Walter & Fox, 2021). Throughout the spring of 2020, teachers shared several ideas that would have made the transition easier, including receiving more support in implementing virtual instruction and emotional support (Chan et al., 2021; Hassan, Mirza, & Hussain, 2020). In addition, Chan et al. (2021) found that teachers who had collaborated with other teachers, who had regular communication with administrators, and who were flexible suffered less stress at the beginning of the pandemic. In some cases, teachers said that they did not have enough resources to perform their jobs adequately (Marshall, Shannon, & Love, 2022). However, in other instances, teachers said that they were given too much to adequately digest at once. As Baker and colleagues (2021) note, "Flooding teachers with resources during the initial transition to online teaching, which was intended to be helpful, was perceived by teachers as burdensome" (p. 492). An, Kaplan-Rakowski, and colleagues (2021) surveyed teachers from 25 states and found that, whereas about half of their sample found online teaching in the early months of the pandemic to be "challenging but rewarding" (p. 2597), another 21% indicated that they were struggling with online teaching. About 60% indicated that online teaching was stressful, and fewer than 1 in 5 preferred it to the classroom.

One study compared teacher well-being in the spring of 2019 with the spring of 2020 in Australia right before the shutdown occurred (Fray, Jaremus, Gore, Miller, & Harris, 2022). Through survey and interview data, Fray and her colleagues got an insight into how teachers felt during the initial transition period of the pandemic. A common theme among teachers was decreased morale and the struggle to balance work and family. Teachers attributed the lack of balance to the increase in workloads required of teachers to support students' remote learning (Fray et al., 2022). This feeling of being overworked continued through 2020, even after Australian schools returned to in-person instruction. Teachers shared the pressure to catch students up on missed content during remote instruction (Fray et al., 2022). Not all research on teachers suggested negative outcomes, though. One interesting finding came from a study conducted in Germany, which suggested that although teachers had fewer resources available to them when schools shifted online, teacher fatigue decreased (Hilger, Scheibe, Frenzel, & Keller, 2021). In addition, the authors suggested that the shift to online teaching led to fewer day-to-day stressors being put on teachers compared with in-person teaching. Though most teachers did find some relief in the demands placed on them, two groups of teachers experienced more demands, specifically, less experienced teachers and teachers who also cared for others in their homes (Hilger et al., 2021).

In view of all the changes that took place during the spring of 2020, Wright and colleagues (Wright, Weinberg, Sample McMeeking, Lin Hunter, & Balgopal, 2022) asked teachers about their experiences and perceptions of district and school decisions at the beginning of the pandemic, as well as when schools returned in the fall of 2020. Teachers noted that most of the changes made at the initial outbreak focused on student well-being, including ensuring that families had reliable internet access, learning materials, and food security. Only 25% of teachers believed their districts provided clear communication with teachers at the beginning of the pandemic (Wright et al., 2022). Another study conducted during the spring of 2020 explored teacher job satisfaction in April 2020 among a group of teachers in Germany (Stang-Rabrig, Brüggemann, Lorenz, & McElvany, 2022). Overall, teachers surveyed were satisfied with their jobs; however, female teachers reported higher stress levels than male teachers. Factors influencing stress included technical difficulties, computer problems, and an increased workload. These demands also had a positive association with teacher exhaustion. Additionally, teachers with lower self-efficacy had higher levels of exhaustion. On a positive note, the support teachers received from other teachers and school administrators and a teacher's ability to innovate on the fly positively affected their job satisfaction (Stang-Rabrig et al., 2022).

During the summer of 2020, counties, states, and school leaders debated how and when students and teachers should return to the classroom. For most, this was done on a case-by-case basis, which led to schools and districts establishing different instructional plans: Some schools bounced between formats depending on COVID-19 case counts, whereas other school leaders pushed for a return to all in person and some opted for more hybrid, hyflex, or virtual approaches to limit the number of students within a classroom environment (Marshall & Bradley-Dorsey, 2022). However, no matter the plan, teachers took on the responsibility of providing instruction with the understanding of having to follow local and state mitigation measures. Wright et al. (2022) found that fewer teachers (25% in spring 2020 compared with 13% in fall 2020) reported that school leaders made decisions to support teacher well-being. The focus on teacher well-being also shifted from communication to professional development.

As county, district, and school leaders debated how to return to teaching, Matthew Hirshberg and his colleagues (Hirshberg, Davidson, & Goldberg, 2023) explored teacher and school staff members' mental health. These researchers found that teachers reported clinically meaningful anxiety and depressive symptoms, with those reporting lower income levels (less than $40,000) more likely to report higher stress and depression levels. Unfortunately, most participants who fell within this category were classroom teachers (likely teachers new to the career) or teacher assistants. These teachers and staff members also had the highest risk of not returning to their jobs (Hirshberg et al., 2023).

Other data collected early in the 2020–2021 school year found that teachers had high levels of burnout and anxiety (Marshall, Smith, Love, Neugebauer, & Shannon, in press; McMakin, Ballin, & Fullerton, 2023; Pressley, 2021a, 2021b; Pressley, Ha, & Learn, 2021; Pressley & Ha, 2021; Trinidad, 2021). Specifically, Pressley found that teachers had higher levels of burnout in the fall of 2020, about a month into the school year. At this point in the pandemic and return to school, teachers reported having anxiety communicating with administrators and parents, and fear of contracting the COVID-19 virus as significant predictors of burnout (Pressley, 2021a). In a study of elementary teachers alone, Pressley et al. (2021) found that virtual teachers had the most significant increase in stress during the first month of the 2020 school year compared with teachers engaging with other instructional formats. In addition, teacher anxiety was influenced by communication within the school (which included both administrators and parents) and teacher stress. Lastly, Pressley and Ha (2021) explored a more advanced model of teacher psychological well-being and found that teacher instructional and engagement efficacy and administrative support affected teacher stress.

Following up on one of the first studies conducted in the fall of 2020 (Pressley, 2021a), Pressley conducted a mixed-method study to learn more about teacher stress and anxiety sources (Pressley, 2021b). Teachers responded that they felt overwhelmed by the amount of work, especially those who taught in hybrid or hyflex models. In addition, many teachers commented that they felt unsupported by school administrators who set unrealistic expectations for student learning. For example, teachers voiced frustration about needing more time to complete all the expectations, including developing multiple versions of lesson plans (in person and remote) and learning the new LMS. Teachers often voiced frustration with parents during this time. Many teachers felt unsupported with remote learning and believed parents had unrealistic expectations of them during this period. This included cases in which parents did not force kids to log on and participate in the online lessons or to complete the required assignments. Teachers also felt blamed for technology issues that were out of their hands and for students' not completing the necessary work. Furthermore, some teachers faced major criticism from parents on social media and at school board meetings about the policies put in place, almost all of which were outside teachers' locus of control. With all that teachers faced during the first return-to-school phase of the pandemic (fall 2020), it is unsurprising that teacher well-being significantly decreased.

As the first full school year progressed, other studies found similar results, with teachers having high rates of stress, anxiety, and burnout throughout the year (e.g., Kotowski, Davis, & Barratt, 2022; Kush, Badillo-Goicoechea, Musci, & Stuart, 2022; Westphal, Kalinowski, Hoferichter, & Vock, 2022). Some of the reasons for the decrease in teacher well-being during the pandemic included teachers having to learn new approaches to teaching virtually (Marshall, Shannon, & Love, 2020; Sokal et al., 2020a), teachers being forced to balance their work and home lives (Love & Marshall, 2022), engage with unsupportive parents (Sokal et al., 2020b), and make due with limited available resources (Rabaglietti, Lattke, Tesauri, Settanni, & De Lorenzo, 2021).

One surprising report found that teachers reported higher stress levels than health care workers during the pandemic due to the demands made of them (Kush et al., 2022). The high stress levels were especially true for teachers who taught remotely, as they reported higher rates of depression and isolation than teachers who taught in person during the pandemic. In addition, female teachers reported significantly higher anxiety rates than their male counterparts (Kush et al., 2022). Similarly, Kotowski et al. (2022) surveyed more than 700 teachers in the Cincinnati area and found that 72% reported feeling very or extremely stressed. In addition, over half (57%) felt burnt out and often struggled to balance their work and home lives at least some of the time (57%). Lastly, Hutchison et al. (2022) found that teachers and school staff across Western Canada reported higher-than-average anxiety levels during the 2021–2022 school year. The reported teacher anxiety levels were also higher during than before the pandemic. Some factors associated with higher anxiety included increased contact time with students, gender, and age—with female and younger teachers having the highest anxiety levels.

In year 2 of a longitudinal study, Jeffrey Keese and his colleagues (Keese, McIntush, & Waxman, 2022) interviewed 14 teachers to learn about the experiences of the pandemic. By the spring of 2021, teachers were glad to have their students back in person, even with the safety protocols in place. However, not all students were back in person by this time, and managing multiple learning modalities led to increased workloads and teacher stress. Because of this, teachers expressed "feelings of being always on" and being exhausted. One positive note teachers shared was that they felt they had more autonomy in what and how they were teaching, especially compared with the spring of 2020. Though teachers had more positive feelings about the direction the profession was going than they had earlier in the pandemic, they were still frustrated with their voices and needs often not being considered by district leaders when making decisions (Keese et al., 2022).

As researchers published more studies on the impact of the pandemic on teachers, similar results emerged worldwide. Teachers worldwide took on new stressors and anxieties that had a major impact on their teaching careers (e.g., Jakubowski & Sitko-Dominik, 2021; Sokal, Trudel, & Babb, 2021; Walter & Fox, 2021). For example, Ma, Chutiyami, Zhang, and Nicoll (2022) conducted a systematic review and meta-analysis of 54 studies across 22 countries. The results found that teachers had high levels of stress, anxiety, and depression due to online teaching, increased workloads, and reduced job satisfaction. In another scoping review that explored 67 studies worldwide, Agyapong, Obuobi-Donkor, Burback, and Wei (2022) calculated the median scores for teacher stress, burnout, anxiety, and depression. The researchers found that 67% of teachers felt high stress, 60.9% felt burnt out, 39.6% had high anxiety, and 14% suffered from depression in studies they classified as "high quality." These psychological aspects were associated with gender, marriage status, teaching experience, class size, job satisfaction, and subject taught (Agyapong et al., 2022). In a study that included teachers worldwide, Billaudeau, Obuobi-Donkor, Burback, and Wei (2022) found that feeling safe at work and having higher levels of autonomy within the classroom were positively associated with well-being for teachers in France, Canada, Belgium, Morocco, and Mexico.

Teacher Burnout

As discussed in more detail in the next chapter, very few teachers left teaching in the spring of 2020; however, teacher burnout increased the longer the pandemic lingered, from 25% of teachers indicating that burnout was a major concern in the spring of 2021 to 57% by the fall of 2021. Those teaching in virtual, hyflex, and hybrid formats had especially high rates of burnout compared with those only teaching in person (Kaufman & Diliberti, 2021). For teachers tasked with teaching virtually in some form, an increase in teacher stress and burnout became a major concern: Teachers were having to teach themselves new skills while simultaneously preparing for and providing instruction to students (Sokal et al., 2020a, 2020b, 2021). With the increase of workloads and the need for more support, it was common for teachers to teach beyond the typical workday during the pandemic, often putting in more than a typical 40-hour work week (Kaden, 2020; Love & Marshall, 2022). We understand that 40-plus-hour work weeks have been common for teachers for some time, with or without a crisis. However, teachers' workloads during the pandemic increased (Marshall, Shannon, et al., 2023). Increasing the work that already-overworked individuals have to do would likely take a toll on anyone.

School and district leadership greatly influenced teachers' levels of burnout during the COVID-19 pandemic (Sokal et al., 2021). Specifically, teachers who planned to leave teaching had negative comments about their building administrators and blamed them for issues leading to their burnout. In addition, teachers shared feelings of being "devalued and disregarded" (Sokal et al., 2021, p. 7). Pressley and his colleagues found similar findings when surveying teacher perspectives at the end of the 2020–2021 school year (Pressley et al., 2023). Specifically, they explored differences in teachers' perspectives based on how they perceived the return-to-learning plans put together by school leaders during the 2020–2021 school year. Teachers who did not believe their district put together a successful back-to-school plan had significantly higher levels of burnout than those who did believe their district put together an effective plan (Pressley et al., 2023). Some of the reasons for this included extra work required of teachers, the lack of administrative support, and difficulty implementing the required COVID-19 safety protocols. Specifically, teachers commented that their extra work was due to the multiple changes in the schedule throughout the year, with teachers often experiencing changes in instructional formats and in class rosters as parents moved their children from one instructional format to another, or due to quarantine requirements. Teachers who taught hybrid or hyflex instruction were most frustrated due to the requirements to teach in multiple formats or provide instruction to both in-person and online students simultaneously. In addition, many teachers did not feel supported by school leadership because they were never consulted about the plans to return to the classroom during the school year. School leaders did not fully understand the day-to-day workings of the "COVID classroom," and the "figure it out" attitudes of some districts led to inequities across schools. Finally, teachers struggled to implement and enforce COVID-19 safety protocols. In some instances, socially distancing students was not physically possible, and teachers said that they did their best with the limited supplies available. Besides the safety issues, teachers often did not feel that the technology provided by school leaders was adequate for the virtual, hybrid, or hyflex instructional requirements, which led to inequities in instructional quality (Pressley et al., 2023).

Teacher well-being during the first full year of the pandemic was an issue, and district leaders were beginning to take notice. Through interviews with district leaders, Carver-Thomas, Leung, and Burns (2021) found that California district leaders understood that teacher burnout and the workload being asked of them was a major problem, so much so that many school leaders feared it might lead to a large increase in teacher attrition. An increase in early retirements and resignations led to greater teacher shortages in the Golden State—a state already facing a teacher shortage problem. This was especially an issue for rural schools with limited access to new teachers from teacher preparation programs.

Teacher Well-Being during 2021–2022

Most of the literature on teacher well-being has focused on the first year and a half of the pandemic; however, the psychological impact of the pandemic on teachers did not disappear at the end of the 2020–2021 school year. As teachers returned to the classroom for the second full year of the pandemic, many schools returned to more normal instructional approaches with some residual COVID-19 safety protocols in place, depending on where they were. At this point in the pandemic, schools across the United States ranged in protocols, with some schools returning to pre-pandemic policies, while others still required masks but eased social distancing and cleaning requirements. This was also a point in the pandemic when vaccines were widely available for adults and children. Any teacher who wished to get vaccinated had the opportunity to do so by the first day of the 2021–2022 school year. As the school year progressed, states and schools began to ease up on COVID-19 safety protocols throughout the spring of 2022. Though teachers were beginning to see what was considered more normal classrooms with the loosening of COVID-19 safety protocols, they continued to face challenges within their schools and classrooms that affected their psychological well-being. Some of these challenges included covering classes for teachers who were out sick, as many districts did not allow or did not have the necessary substitute teachers available (Keese & McIntush, 2023). In addition, teachers felt the pressure to provide remedial instruction to prepare students for state standardized tests (which returned after being paused during the spring of 2020), to limit the learning loss, and to continue the use of LMS and other technologies that schools implemented during the pandemic. Furthermore, teachers have also reported feeling overworked, with no time to get job requirements (e.g., grading, lesson planning, and other required preparation) done because they lost planning periods in order to cover classes (Keese & McIntush, 2023). Although many teachers strengthened their relationships with students' families at the start of the pandemic (Love & Marshall, 2022; Marshall & Neugebauer, 2022, 2023), some teachers began to report feeling increased friction with some of their students' parents during the second pandemic year.

As the 2021–2022 school year neared the end, we wanted to understand better how teachers felt. Specifically, we wanted to allow teachers to share their perspectives on the teaching profession, especially with an increase in national media stories about teacher shortages across the United States (e.g., Noonoo, 2022). In a national survey of teachers in the spring of 2022, we explored teacher burnout, morale, mental health, teacher autonomy, attrition, and job satisfaction. When asked, teachers reported high levels of job satisfaction and lower levels of burnout when they felt trusted and respected by school leaders to make decisions about their teaching (Marshall, Neugebauer, Pressley, & Brown-Aliffi, 2023). The feelings were true for teachers regardless of their races or genders, the locations of their schools, or whether their schools qualified as Title I schools (Marshall, Neugebauer, et al., 2023).

We also asked teachers about their morale and mental health.

These were important concepts to understand as, prior to the pandemic, researchers had linked teacher morale to important educational factors such as student achievement (Andrew, Parks, Nelson, & Phi Delta Kappa Commission on Teacher/Faculty Morale, 1985; Houchard, 2005), teacher productivity, and relationships with students (Lumsden, 1998). Some of the factors that affect teacher morale include teacher motivation, effort, and job satisfaction (Huysman, 2008). In addition, Coughlan (1970) also discussed administrative operations, working relationships, school effectiveness, and career fulfillment as factors influencing teacher morale. In the spring of 2022, we found that teachers reported low morale and mental health, with over half the sample indicating low morale (Pressley, Marshall, Love, & Neugebauer, 2022). The analysis found that teaching experience, teacher ethnicity (teachers identifying as White had slightly lower morale than did non-White teachers), job satisfaction, administrative support, teacher autonomy, student mental health, and teacher burnout were significant predictors of teacher morale. In addition, job satisfaction, administrative support, student mental health, and teacher burnout were significant predictors of teacher mental health (Pressley, Marshall, Love, & Neugebauer, 2022). The current results suggest that want to be trusted to make the appropriate decisions for their students rather than being micromanaged by school leaders, who often have been removed from the classroom for several years.

Teacher Well-Being during 2022–2023

In focus groups we completed in the fall of 2022, teacher well-being emerged as a major theme. Specifically, some of the reasons for the lack of teacher well-being included lower administrative support and higher expectations, increased workloads, and less respect given to teachers by society. The role of administrators and the lower support provided to teachers by administrators was a common theme that emerged during the focus groups. As an elementary teacher from Texas commented, "It [teaching] drained me because it was hard. I have an infant at home, and it was a struggle for me this past school year." Later in the focus group, the same teacher discussed more of her and her students' mental challenges. Before sharing the following with us, she walked into a separate room. She explained that her husband is also a teacher and that she did not want to dishearten him.

> "The work is becoming harder. You have to try to teach standards while giving psychology lessons. And teach standards while hoping and praying and having faith or wishing that these kids don't end up dead. I have lost three students this past year. The work is becoming harder. The work is emotional and emotionally taxing. When I leave work I feel like I have nothing to give. . . . The work is hard."

The effects of job stress on teachers' time outside of school hours was also mentioned by an elementary teacher from Virginia: "The pressure of all that fell on the teachers, and there was a lot of pressure from the administration. There were a lot of extra things that we had to do. I was also the lead, and we had a lot of extra meetings that took away from time with my family. It was a lot of stress and a lot of pressure for me." A high school teacher from Wisconsin shared similar feelings of pressure due to unrealistic expectations from administrators: "They [administrators] are expecting me to take kids that have reading levels that are five years below grade level and somehow, in a semester, make it to grade level. That is some crazy teacher magic that I have not discovered. It feels like they are setting me up for failure."

Though several teachers did not feel supported, other teachers did have positive things to say about their administrations. An elementary teacher from Las Vegas, Nevada, said, "I have a very supportive administration and our morale overall at work is good. My principals and my administration are really good at trying to take care of us." (She spoke less positively about the school district's leadership and communication.) Similar thoughts were expressed by a high school teacher from California (you can read more about this teacher's experiences in Chapter 8, in the section "Case Study—Amanda"):

> "They would just pour any resource to help teachers feel more comfortable. If you needed another screen, they would buy you another screen. We all have brand-new computers. Any technology, anything that they could do in their power to support you, you got. I think all our staff knows how fortunate we are to have that much support and to have our voice matter. . . . We had a huge outpouring of people interested in coming and joining us. So I think that the word gets around that you're in this environment. It becomes a highly desirable environment to be in."

For a teacher from Virginia, the transparent communication style of her administrators allowed her to feel more supported:

> "We had so many things that felt out of our control over the last couple of years. Even if our administration said we don't have this information, here is what we do have. The more that they were able to do that fed into feeling supported. We weren't just being thrown off into the wilderness to do things on our own. We were all in it together more. Expressing that definitely did help."

Having supportive administrators can have a major influence on teacher well-being, as teachers can feel heard and respected. To sum it all up, when asked about her supportive administration, a middle school teacher from New Jersey said, "It made all the difference."

Teachers also discussed their workloads during the pandemic. A middle school teacher from Texas said, "Teacher burnout for me last year [2021–2022] was extremely real. We were starting our day at 7:30 in the morning and we were not leaving campus 'til about 4:30 P.M." She continued by commenting how she hoped to make changes in the upcoming school year to limit her burnout. "This year I've actually set some boundaries because of last year. I'm leaving at 4 P.M. I show up at 7:30 and whatever gets done, gets done then. Because I feel used up and unappreciated from the last two and a half years of hell that teachers were put in front of." The feeling of not having enough time in the day would often lead teachers to take work home with them to get everything necessary done. Unfortunately, this has become an expectation in the teaching profession, as an elementary teacher from Illinois commented: "There was always the expectation that you are going to take work home. You are going to do it on the weekend. It is just assumed and expected." This particular teacher told us that she left the classroom at the end of the 2021–2022 school year because of the time requirements expected of teachers.

One final theme that emerged from the focus groups was the lack of respect teachers receive from the public, specifically from stakeholders such as parents and politicians. As a high school teacher from Texas said:

> "It'd be nice if society thought we did something other than babysitting. I don't know where that came from. The lack of respect has been huge. It's in the last ten, fifteen years that it was—you know it used to be, 'Oh, you're a teacher! Oh, thank you for what you do. And

> I so admire people who give themselves to our children. Thank you!' And now it's like, 'Oh, you're just stupid! Why would you do such a terrible job? Well, I disagree. And you're just whitewashing things, or you have an agenda.' Whoa! Where'd that come from? It's been a big switch."

The lack of respect felt by some teachers has led them to consider leaving the profession. A middle school teacher from California remarked that she had begun looking at jobs after the 2021–2022 school year because of how teachers are treated. "I don't see myself in this job for the long run. It's just that everybody's so angry. The kids are angry, the parents are angry, the administration's angry, and you pick up the newspaper, they are angry. Everybody is angry about everything. The amount of money teachers get paid is the punching bag for all of these angry people. It's just not worth it."

Having faced new challenges and overcome many unforeseen obstacles throughout the pandemic, it is not surprising that teachers had an increase in stress, anxiety, and burnout. Though schools and society are moving back to more normalcy in day-to-day lives, school leaders still must understand how the pandemic affected teachers and work to support them in hopes of keeping teachers in the classroom in years to come. As data continue to emerge from the pandemic, it is clear that teachers are still feeling overworked, unsupported, and disrespected for the jobs they are asked to do. Through these focus groups, it was clear that the teachers who participated loved their students and enjoyed having an impact on their students. However, it was also clear that the passion for teaching may not be enough to keep them in the classroom in the future.

By the spring of 2023, teachers and students were 3 years removed from the great disruption that occurred in the spring of 2020. However, there were still residual effects, especially in teacher well-being. A survey of teachers jointly conducted by the National Alliance for Public Charter Schools and The Harris Poll in May 2023 found that 78% of teachers felt that they worked in a "thankless job", 67% reported feeling burned out, and 72% felt overworked (Veney, 2023). Teachers in charter schools were more than twice as likely to report feeling appreciated, valued, and supported compared to teachers in traditional public schools; however, it is worth noting that even in charter schools, more than half of the teachers surveyed did not feel this way.

In our final national survey of teachers (Marshall, Pressley, & Shannon, 2023), we gathered perspectives from more than 800 teachers across 47 states. Our preliminary findings showed that teacher morale and mental health had increased from our 2022 data collection (see Table 5.2). We believe this is a good thing but also are quick to note that the average scores still fall in the medium to low range for morale and mental health. Further, we found that teacher burnout levels stay comparable with just a slight improvement, leading us to believe teacher burnout is still a concern at the end of the 2022–2023 school year. In addition, teachers' average stress measured 4.64 (SD = 1.33) on a 6-point scale. We did not collect the stress levels of teachers in previous data collections, but the 2023 preliminary analysis suggests teachers feel a high level of stress. See Table 5.2 for a comparison of teachers between our 2022 and 2023 survey administrations.

Supporting Teacher Well-Being

Even before the pandemic, teacher well-being and burnout were matters of concern. However, the pandemic exacerbated these issues, and school leaders need to be aware of this. Before we get into specific recommendations, we must urge caution to school leaders. It is important that school

TABLE 5.2. Comparing Teacher Well-Being and Job Satisfaction—Spring 2022 to Spring 2023

	Spring 2022 *M* (*SD*)	Spring 2023 *M* (*SD*)	Comparison
Teacher morale	3.74 (2.31)	4.75 (2.31)	Medium/large improvement***
Teacher mental health	3.90 (2.16)	5.01 (2.34)	Large improvement***
Teacher burnout	15.28 (3.27)	14.71 (3.57)	Small improvement***
Job satisfaction	14.33 (4.26)	14. 63 (4.45)	Same
Stress[a]	—	4.64 (1.33)	—

Note. Comparisons made by calculating independent-samples t-tests between the 2 years. Teacher morale, teacher mental health, and stress were all measured with a single item. Teacher burnout was measured using a 3-item scale (Pressley, Marshall, & Moore, in press). Job satisfaction was measured using a teacher job satisfaction scale (Skaalvik & Skaalvik, 2011).

[a]Variable introduced in spring 2023 survey.

***$p < .001$.

leaders understand teachers' needs but also understand that they cannot place additional burdens on teachers. Supporting teacher well-being will take a balance of support and listening to teachers.

School environment is a major factor that affects teacher well-being and burnout, a factor that school leaders can influence. Milam, Butler, and Vanderhaar (2022) found that school climate significantly predicted teacher well-being in 2020 and 2022. School leaders must consider the well-being of their faculty when making critical decisions. They can start by communicating with teachers about what the teachers need to be successful. Similarly, Jasper Maas and colleagues (2022) found that a successful school environment has school leaders that provide social support and is well structured with necessary teacher resources (Maas et al., 2022). (We explore this topic more in Chapter 8.) Administrators can also support teachers' well-being by providing more mental health resources, such as telehealth resources or access to professional counselors. In our spring 2023 survey (Marshall, Pressley, et al., 2023), we learned that just under 12% of teachers had access to a therapist at school. Another 12% of teachers commented that there were formal mindfulness activities (e.g., yoga) planned to help with their well-being. School leaders may also explore opportunities throughout the school year to provide teachers with mental health days or days to catch up on daily tasks such as grading and lesson plans rather than requiring PD. Fewer than 10% of teachers reported that they were formally allowed to take mental health days; however, teachers have used their sick days for these purposes for years.

Administrative support was found to be an important aspect of school climate in multiple studies conducted prior to the pandemic (e.g., Bottiani et al., 2019; Ryan et al., 2017). Teachers with school administrators who (1) supported classroom management to address student misbehavior (Bottiani et al., 2019), (2) established positive relationships with teachers (Margolis & Nagel, 2006), and (3) downplayed the pressure for students to perform on state standardized tests increased levels of well-being in their faculty (Ryan et al., 2017). In addition, school leaders who included teacher voices in decision-making processes and provided resources needed throughout the pandemic had fewer burnt-out teachers. Along these same lines, school leaders must also provide flexibility with instruction and set realistic expectations for teachers. This includes accepting that many students fell behind but also trusting teachers to make sound decisions to support student learning (Chan et al., 2021;

Walter & Fox, 2021), as well as supporting teachers who have difficulties with students or students' parents. Teachers must know that the school administrators have their backs.

Furthermore, school leaders must trust and respect teachers as professionals and give them autonomy in their classrooms. Providing teachers more autonomy will allow them to employ the most appropriate instructional approaches for their students, establish classroom management routines, and select appropriate PD for the areas they want to improve. School leaders can reflect on some of the mandated decisions pushed down on teachers to determine whether there are areas in which teachers can have more autonomy rather than having a blanket policy for all teachers. This should be done at the school level, as teachers in specific grade levels or subjects or with varying levels of experience may need different things throughout the year, and central office personnel are likely to know less about what these needs are than school building leadership. There is one approach to creating teacher well-being that we are less supportive of, and that is the use of some nonmonetary incentives. Providing incentives is often meant to promote well-being and recognize the hard work teachers have put into the job. Providing incentives such as "dress down days" or food is nice; however, these do not support teacher well-being.

Another approach to supporting teacher well-being is through interventions that promote aspects such as mindfulness, yoga, and stress-reducing activities (see Agyapong, Brett-MacLean, Burback, Agyapong, & Wei, 2023, for a scoping review). For example, Summer Braun and her colleagues (Braun, Roeser, & Mashburn, 2020) found positive results from implementing a mindfulness-based program with kindergarten through third-grade teachers. Over half of the teachers reported personal and professional benefits of the program, with positive effects on teacher well-being, occupational health, and teaching practices. Though Braun and colleagues (2020) found positive results, it is important to note that the study only included 21 teachers and that the PD included almost 28 hours of training. As noted by the study's authors, future research and implementation should consider shorter intervention programs to limit the extra time required for participation (Braun et al., 2020). We believe interventions such as this show promise but agree with Braun and her colleagues that a shorter intervention program is critical if implemented with teachers. Successful interventions with teachers may be a good first step in supporting teacher well-being; however, interventions cannot add more to teachers' to-do lists. This would make them just another requirement they must complete and likely become a form of stress rather than support.

It is also important to understand and research schools and areas that are having success when it comes to teacher well-being. Mississippi is one of two states with 2022 state test scores that were better than their 2019 figures (South Carolina was the other). As such, we explored our spring 2023 teacher survey data to understand whether Mississippi teachers fared any differently than teachers from other states in terms of job satisfaction, self-efficacy, morale, mental health, or their likelihood of remaining in their jobs for another 3 years (or more). We shared our findings in an op-ed in the *Northeast Mississippi Daily Journal* (Marshall & Pressley, 2023). What we learned was interesting. The teachers we surveyed from Mississippi reported higher levels for all five of the variables given in the preceding sentence. They were also disproportionately less likely to have access to therapists at school, mental health days, or formal mindfulness programming. As we stated earlier, there is likely some benefit in all three of these resources, as well as others. It is possible that Mississippi teachers would fare even better if they had access to these resources. However, our findings from Mississippi also demonstrate that simply placing additional resources in schools does not guarantee that teacher well-being improves.

Finally, school leaders should take steps to provide appropriate resources to teachers and find ways to appropriately compensate teachers for the jobs they are completing (Mackenzie, 2007). Throughout the pandemic, teachers have increased the number of hours spent prepping and providing instruction (Kaden, 2020; Pressley, 2021b) with little to no additional compensation. School leaders and policymakers need to find ways to compensate teachers appropriately for the work they have put and will continue to put into supporting student learning. This will be especially true as teachers debate whether they will stay in the classroom post-pandemic. (See Chapter 6 for more discussion on the teacher workforce.) It is important to note that money is not going to fix the teachers' well-being problem. As Pendola (2022b) found, a majority of teachers did not prioritize monetary rewards but, rather, wanted to be treated and respected as professionals. In addition, teachers want to see school leaders put in an effort to protect their time and understand the realities of the teaching profession (Pendola, 2022b).

Supporting Teacher Workloads

Teacher workloads have continued to grow and grow over the past several years. School leaders need to reflect on teacher workloads and the requirements and expectations of teachers. It will be important to explore ways to provide more balance to teacher schedules and limit the amount of extra work required of them. This may include the following:

- Reviewing procedures for covering extra classes
- Protecting planning periods from other meetings or duties
- Blocking out and protecting collaboration and grade-level or subject planning time
- Limiting required meetings and professional development on teacher workdays
- Exploring alternative ways to recruit more substitute teachers

Adding to teacher workloads are the many trainings, PD workshops, and extra meetings that teachers must attend throughout the school year. These requirements take up teacher time before and after school, as well as during planning time. We understand some trainings are necessary for teachers, and good PD can help teachers become even better teachers. However, it is important for school leaders to limit the mandatory requirements and provide teachers with some autonomy in completing them. One way that school leaders can offer PD while making sure it is a good use of teacher time is to provide teachers autonomy in selecting the PD they attend.

One example of supporting teacher workloads and autonomy came from a district in Virginia that required teachers to participate in at least 8 hours of PD a year. Rather than requiring teachers to attend multiple, district-selected PD sessions throughout the year, the district allows grade-level or subject teams to determine what area they would like to focus on during their PD time and how they want to accomplish the required PD. Thus, teachers have the autonomy to choose the area they want or need extra support in and to decide whether PD would be one long day or broken up across multiple days. For example, one particular middle school subject team decided to have teachers attend PD for one full teacher workday during the year to allow the teachers to have the remaining teacher workdays to implement aspects learned at the PD and catch up on other work such as grading, lesson planning, and connecting with parents or guardians. This approach gave teachers the required PD for the year but only took up one day rather than using up 1–2 hours over multiple teacher workdays during the year. An approach like this gives teachers some flexibility throughout the year during teacher workdays and gives grade and subject teams autonomy in selecting PD that is useful to their specific needs. This was not the case in the case study that we present in Chapter 6, which mandated specific PD for teachers throughout the year.

* * *

Throughout the pandemic, teachers have worked as frontline workers who changed their instructional approaches immediately, learned new technology requirements, and implemented required safety protocols to provide the best instruction possible to their students. As schools have returned to normalcy, teachers have again been tasked with a lot, including recovering pandemic-era learning loss and teaching students how to be students again. Through all of this, teachers have become worn down. School leaders need to take a moment to pause and assess teacher well-being and mental health to provide appropriate support to teachers.

Chapter 6

The Impact on Teacher Labor Markets

For five decades starting in the 1970s, the teaching profession saw a rise in the number of individuals seeking to enter the profession (Kraft & Lyon, 2022). However, since 2010, there has been a steady fall in demand to enter the field. The increase in teachers leaving the profession has only become more prominent since the COVID-19 pandemic, when teachers had to transition to new pedagogical approaches at a moment's notice and implement safety protocols that no one prior to 2020 would have ever imagined. Though the COVID-19 pandemic has undoubtedly been a factor in the increasing number of teachers leaving the field, it is not the sole reason. Even before the COVID-19 pandemic, almost 50% of teachers were leaving the classroom within the first 5 years of their teaching careers (Ingersoll, Merrill, & May, 2014; Papay, Bacher-Hicks, Page, & Marinell, 2017; Ryan et al., 2017), and about 8% of teachers were leaving annually (National Center for Education Statistics, 2016). As such, school leaders need to understand why teachers leave and incorporate ways to support teacher retention.

Why Teachers Leave

Of those teachers that left teaching, the major reasons for their exits were the stress they felt on a day-to-day basis and increased teacher workloads (Carver-Thomas et al., 2021; Diliberti, Schwartz, & Grant, 2021). Other factors that have led to the decline in number of teachers include pay, working conditions, accountability regimens, a lack of autonomy, and safety issues within the school building (Kraft & Lyon, 2022). These concerns have led to the lowest level of teacher job satisfaction in over half a century. With numerous reports by national media outlets of teacher shortages across the country, it is critical to understand how the pandemic affected the teacher workforce and how current teacher attrition rates compare with pre-pandemic times (e.g., Fortin & Fawcett, 2022; Vivinetto, 2022). With such a dim outlook on the profession, it is important for school leaders to understand the current state of teachers and teacher attrition as they begin to formulate plans to recruit and retain teachers for their schools.

In a national survey conducted by the EdWeek Research Center at Merrimack College in the spring of 2022, teachers reported all-time low job satisfaction scores (EdWeek Research Center, 2022; Kurtz, 2022; Will, 2022) and overall dissatisfaction with the teaching profession (Kaufman & Diliberti, 2021). One interesting finding from this survey was that even though teachers had low job satisfaction, they still wanted to teach and loved influencing kids. This aligns with Pendola and colleagues' (Pendola, Marshall, Pressley, & Trammell, 2023) findings from a survey of Alabama teachers. They found that despite the sources of dissatisfaction, teachers were still dedicated to teaching and caring for their students. Other aspects of the job that pushed teachers to consider leaving the classroom included an increased workload and the need to support kids academically, socially, and emotionally. In addition, teachers did not report feeling respected for the time and work they are asked to put into the profession (Will, 2022). Furthermore, teachers reported longer work days during and after the pandemic, with teachers reporting working on average 54 hours a week (Kurtz, 2022), which aligned with Kaufman and Diliberti's (2021) review of national surveys, finding that over half the teachers surveyed across the United States reported working more than 48 hours per week during the fall of 2020. Of the teachers who intended to stay in teaching, 44% reported they planned to leave in the next 2 years (Kurtz, 2022).

With a decrease in overall teacher job satisfaction across the United States, it is important to understand its effect on teacher attrition and grasp its impact on schools. Schools and districts often see several negative effects when teachers leave their careers. For one, finding new teachers is often expensive and takes extra resources that schools could use toward other ends (Barnes, Crowe, & Schaefer, 2007; Milanowski & Odden, 2007). In addition, it often has a negative effect on student learning, as novice teachers are often not as effective as more experienced teachers (e.g., Ronfeldt, Loeb, & Wyckoff, 2013). More specifically, when schools see large teacher turnover, it has a negative effect on student achievement, with economically disadvantaged students hurt the most (Sorensen & Ladd, 2020). However, it is first important to understand the attrition process and how attrition trends shifted during the COVID-19 pandemic.

Leaving Is a Process, Not an Event

Teachers become increasingly likely to leave the classroom when there is a mismatch between what attracts them to the job and what the job is actually like (Gallant & Riley, 2014; Pendola, 2022a). Consider someone who gets into teaching because he or she is passionate about teaching children to read. But then he or she is handed a scripted curriculum and is expected to implement it with fidelity. In addition, the teacher has to take attendance in three different ways—in a form submitted to the office, in a binder for the teacher's records, and online. And then the teacher has to complete multiple weekly progress sheets for every student. Each task we just described asks the teacher to expend his or her time completing tasks that are not directly related to the passion for teaching kids to read, and the scripted curriculum limits the amount of creativity and autonomy to teach. As such, the gulf widens between this teacher's expectations for what the job of being a teacher would be with what it is like on a daily basis. Andrew Pendola's (2022a) research has found that teachers who are stuck with these conflicting expectations become dissatisfied with their jobs, and that dissatisfaction leads teachers to increasingly take steps toward exiting the profession.

This is not altogether different from students who fail to complete high school. Dropping out is a process, one that is the culmination of several events leading up to that point (Feldman, Smith, & Waxman, 2017; Fine, 1991; Marshall, 2022c; Rumberger, 2011). High school students who drop out rarely wake up one morning and decide to do so. The same is true for teachers who leave the profession (Gallant & Riley, 2014; Willett & Singer, 1991). Gallant and Riley (2014) describe the decision to leave as "the end of a protracted process" (p. 574) and note that a *pre-exit stage* often precedes quitting: "The pre-exit phase of leaving [involves] considerable sense of disillusionment [where teachers feel] let down by leadership and/or veteran colleagues and [lose] any expectation of things improving" (Gallant & Riley, 2014, p. 575). Thus the idea of leaving teaching does not occur overnight and is not the result of one event but, rather, a series of occurrences that lead to one believing the job will not improve. One could argue that this occurred more regularly during the pandemic, as teachers were asked to do more and received less support (Pressley, 2021a; Sokal et al., 2021; Walter & Fox, 2021).

Teacher Attrition Trends during COVID-19

During the early stages of the pandemic, teacher attrition slowed down compared with previous years (Bastian & Fuller, 2022; Goldhaber & Theobald, 2022; Rosenberg & Anderson, 2021). Teachers did not want to risk the job security of teaching for a potential new career outside of education due to economic uncertainty. Nationally, however, several reports conducted in the spring of 2021 indicated no increase in teachers leaving. These national reports did find an increase in teacher burnout and low levels of teacher job satisfaction (Rosenberg & Anderson, 2021; Zamarro, Camp, Fuchsman, & McGee, 2022). For example, Zamarro and her colleagues (2022) found health concerns and the requirement that teachers provide alternative instructional approaches (i.e., remote or hybrid) as possible reasons that may lead to an increase in teachers considering leaving; however, these reasons were not leading teachers to take the final step of leaving the field. Among teachers who did leave the profession between March 2020 and June 2021, almost half cited working conditions due to the pandemic as the reason (Diliberti et al., 2021).

As teachers wrapped up the first full year of teaching during the COVID-19 pandemic, a national RAND report on teachers found that nearly 25% of teachers were considering leaving their jobs at the end of the 2020–2021 school year (Steiner & Woo, 2021). Prior to the pandemic, about 16% of teachers reported leaving their jobs on an annual basis, about half of which transferred to a different school and half of which left the profession altogether. The main reasons for such a high rate of teachers considering leaving teaching were stress, burnout, and depression. Other reasons focused on the teaching conditions during the pandemic and the technology issues teachers faced during remote instruction (Steiner & Woo, 2021).

Unfortunately, this trend of teachers only considering leaving, but ultimately staying in the profession did not continue, as some states saw increased teacher attrition by the end of the 2021–2022 school year (e.g., Bastian & Fuller, 2022; Camp, Zamarro, & McGee, 2022). A second national survey, conducted by the National Education Association (NEA; Jotkoff, 2022) during the spring of 2022, found that increased pandemic-related stress contributed to 55% of NEA educators developing exit plans, which was a sizable increase from what was reported in August 2021 (31%; Jotkoff, 2022). In addition, because of teacher attrition and teacher shortages in schools, almost 75% of teachers reported having to cover extra classes or duties, which led to more work for the teachers. Furthermore, both reports (Jotkoff, 2022; Steiner & Woo, 2021) found that teachers of color were more likely to leave than other teachers.

In the national teacher surveys we administered in May 2022 and May 2023, we asked teachers whether they considered leaving their current positions and whether they had looked at job postings and/or applied for other jobs the previous year (see Table 6.1). We found that three-fourths of teachers thought about leaving teaching during the 2021–2022 school year, with over half exploring nonteaching jobs (Marshall, Pressley, Neugebauer, & Shannon, 2022). Though teachers' looking at alternative jobs does not always equate to their leaving, we found that almost a quarter of those teachers did apply for jobs outside of teaching during the 2021–2022 school year. By the end of the 2022–2023 school year,

TABLE 6.1. Actions Teachers Completed Regarding Their Careers from Spring 2022 to Spring 2023

	May 2022 survey (N = 830)		April–May 2023 survey (N = 913)	
	N	%	N	%
Considered leaving job during year	634	76.4	690	75.6
Looked at postings for other teaching jobs	420	50.6	517	56.6
Applied for other teaching jobs	170	20.4	186	20.4
Looked at postings for other ed. jobs[a]	—	—	394	43.2
Applied for other ed. jobs[a]	—	—	186	20.4
Looked at postings for noneducation jobs	478	57.6	492	53.9
Applied for noneducation jobs	159	19.2	154	16.9

Note. Other ed. jobs = nonteaching jobs in K–12 education. Teachers could select all applicable options.

[a]Variable introduced in spring 2023 survey.

we found similar numbers, with three-fourths of teachers still considering leaving teaching. One bright note was that, although there was an increase in teachers looking at other teaching jobs, there was a decrease in teachers applying for noneducation jobs. Thus, most teachers considering leaving their current jobs were looking to stay in the field of education rather than leaving it entirely.

A national study of six large, urban districts across the United States found increases in teacher attrition for early-career teachers who taught in high-poverty schools (Rosenberg & Anderson, 2021), which have historically had high turnover rates. Additionally, Rosenberg and Anderson (2021) found that in the spring of 2020, aspects such as the increased workloads and teaching during the pandemic made teachers more likely to leave. Further, Jake Bryant and his colleagues (Bryant, Ram, Scott, & Williams, 2023) surveyed more than 1,800 teachers between February and May 2022. They found that nearly one-third of teachers indicated that they planned to leave education, and they estimated that this would equate to nearly 900,000 teachers across the United States leaving K–12 education. Though only some teachers who plan to leave education actually do so, these numbers and the previous national studies suggest a major issue within the teaching profession. The groups with the highest attrition rate included younger teachers, teachers teaching in low-income districts, teachers teaching in school districts that disproportionately educate non-White students, and teachers teaching either at the prekindergarten or high school levels (Bryant et al., 2023). Factors influencing teacher attrition included compensation (e.g., pay and benefits), expectations, well-being, leadership, and the lack of flexibility within the school environment. Overall, national reports suggest that teacher attrition leveled off at the start of the pandemic—but began to increase following the initial year.

State-Level Attrition Reports

States responded differently during the pandemic. This was especially true regarding the access that families had to in-person learning. Here, we focus on reports from five states—Arkansas, California, Massachusetts, North Carolina, and Washington. Of the five, Arkansas offered in-person learning to far more students than the others (Oster, Jack,

Halloran, Schoof, McLeod, Yang, et al., 2021). Arkansas was one of only three states in which students of color had more access to learning in person than White students, and the only state among the five we explore.* See Table 6.2 for the proportion of students in each state that had access to in-person learning during the 2020–2021 school year. Similar to the national reports, several state-level reports have found that teacher attrition slowed during the first year of the pandemic in 2020 but increased during the spring of 2021, with some states reporting a higher number of teachers leaving teaching than before the pandemic (Bastian & Fuller, 2022; Camp et al., 2022). Overall, teacher attrition in North Carolina rose about 3% from the first to the second year of the COVID-19 pandemic, which Bastian and Fuller (2022) equated to approximately 2,800 teachers leaving. In Arkansas, Camp et al. (2022) found similar turnover rates after the first year of the COVID-19 pandemic, which equated to rates comparable to before the pandemic. However, by the end of the second full year of the pandemic (2021–2022), Arkansas also saw an additional increase of about 2% of teachers leaving the classroom.

There was an overall increase in teachers leaving some states, but

TABLE 6.2. Proportion of Students Who Had Access to In-Person Learning—September 2020–April 2021

State	% students with access to fully in-person learning	Δ between White/non-White students with access
Arkansas	81.5	21.3
California	4.0	−5.8
Massachusetts	6.8	−4.6
North Carolina	25.5	−4.6
Washington	2.8	−1.1

Note. The delta (Δ) between White and non-White students represents the mean difference between the percentage of students for each demographic group in terms of access to fully remote instruction. A positive number indicates that more non-White students had access to in-person learning than White students. A negative number indicates that more White students had access to in-person learning than non-White students. From Oster, Jack, Halloran, Schoof, McLeod, Yang, et al. (2021). In the public domain.

*There was no difference in access to in-person learning by race/ethnicity in four states (Delaware, Hawaii, Montana, Wyoming) and the District of Columbia (Oster, Jack, Halloran, Schoof, McLeod, Yang, et al., 2021).

some subgroups saw a larger increase in teacher attrition than others. For example, researchers found an increase in North Carolina during the second year of the pandemic specifically for three groups, including those who were new to the profession, teachers of color, and teachers who previously had earned high teaching evaluations (i.e., highly effective teachers; Bastian & Fuller, 2022, 2023). Although Arkansas, Massachusetts, and North Carolina each experienced an increase in minority teacher attrition, it was a small increase in North Carolina (about 5%) compared with other subgroups of teachers, such as newer teachers, which had almost a 31% increase in attrition rate (Bacher-Hicks, Chi, & Orellana, 2022; Bastian & Fuller, 2023; Camp et al., 2022). Finally, in Arkansas, teachers whose learning modalities changed during the 2020–2021 school year (e.g., from virtual to hybrid to in person or vice versa) were more likely to leave teaching (Camp et al., 2022).

In one of the first reports on teacher attrition for the 2022–2023 school year, Andrew Camp and colleagues continued following the trends observed in Arkansas (Camp, Zamarro, & McGee, 2023). One of the major findings from their report was that teacher attrition continued to grow, with 5% of teachers leaving teaching at the beginning of the 2022–2023 school year. Camp et al. (2023) described this as "a relatively large increase in turnover," equivalent to north of 1,200 teachers leaving the teaching field—more than prior to the COVID-19 pandemic. Through a more detailed analysis, the researchers found that the increase in attrition was due to 2% of teachers not just leaving teaching but moving to noninstructional roles (e.g., school and district administrators, instructional coaches). One interesting finding from this report was that 80% of teachers who left teaching in the fall of 2021 did not find new jobs immediately. Camp et al. (2023) suggest that this may indicate that teachers are not leaving education for higher paying jobs "but rather by other factors, potentially including job dissatisfaction and working conditions" (p. 8).

A report sharing findings from qualitative research conducted in California found a shortage of teachers across the state, meaning that school leaders either had unfilled vacancies or hired uncertified teachers (Carver-Thomas et al., 2021). The hardest hit areas included math and science as well as special education and bilingual education classrooms. Besides hiring uncertified teachers, school leaders reported increasing class sizes and eliminating courses with small enrollments at the secondary level, which sometimes resulted in teachers teaching courses for which they were not certified (Carver-Thomas et al., 2021). California schools also faced a substitute teacher shortage, which was a problem during the pandemic when teachers were required to quarantine. One of the reasons for the shortage was that retired teachers, who previously often stepped into substitute teaching roles, had health concerns or were not comfortable with the new technology used in the classrooms. Because of the substitute shortages, teachers often have had to cover classes or take on larger classes, leading teachers to feel overworked (Marshall, Pressley, Neugebauer, & Shannon, 2022; Pressley, 2021b). Finally, California schools saw an increase in teacher retirement and resignation compared with previous years. One of the main reasons for the increase in retirement and resignation was the need to learn the new technology associated with distance learning. Given that only 4% of California's students had access to in-person instruction between September 2020 and April 2021, instruction was almost exclusively delivered online (Oster, Jack, Halloran, Schoof, McLeod, Yang, et al., 2021). However, this put California school leaders in a tough position because many feared that reopening schools during the pandemic might lead to even more early retirements or resignations (Carver-Thomas et al., 2021).

Dan Goldhaber and Roddy Theobald (2022) explored teacher attrition trends in the state of Washington during the pandemic. During the 2020–2021 school year, only 2.8% of students in the state had access to in-person instruction, making Washington one of three states with less access than California. Washington schools did not have an increase in attrition during the spring and fall of 2020; however, they faced a slight increase in teachers leaving for nonteaching jobs during the spring and summer of 2021. In addition, they found an increase in teachers changing schools after the 2021 school year. This increase in teacher turnover led to hundreds of teacher openings heading into the 2021–2022 school year. However, Goldhaber and Theobald (2022) noted that the percentage of teachers leaving Washington schools was consistent with pre-pandemic teacher attrition. Goldhaber and Theobald did not believe there was a mass exodus of teachers, but that school leaders should take reports of teacher burnout seriously, as teacher attrition may hit specific schools and areas harder than others. Findings from our 2023 national survey of teachers suggest a strong negative relationship between burnout and one's likelihood of remaining in the classroom over the following 3 years. As such, we believe Goldhaber and Theobald's concerns are legitimate.

Schools Hit Hardest

In North Carolina, schools that serve low-income students and a high percentage of students of color saw an increase in teacher attrition. Though schools with these characteristics faced high attrition rates prior to the pandemic, this trend has continued or become even more of an issue throughout the pandemic (Bacher-Hicks et al., 2022). Similarly, data from Arkansas suggest that schools serving lower SES students were hardest hit. Schools with large percentages of students on free or reduced-price lunch programs had the highest teacher attrition rates (Camp et al., 2022). Carver-Thomas et al. (2021) found similar results in California with elevated levels of teacher attrition in schools serving low-income families. In addition, schools located in small, rural districts in California also struggled to recruit and retain teachers compared with larger districts in urban and suburban areas of the state. These trends align with previous literature suggesting that schools in rural and high-poverty contexts are often difficult to staff (Maranto & Shuls, 2013; Pendola & Fuller, 2018; Sharpe, Marshall, & Shetty, 2022).

Teacher Pipeline Problems

The teacher shortage problem is not only an issue due to teachers leaving but is also fueled by the shortage of teachers completing teacher preparation programs and entering the profession. Reports have found that teaching vacancies receive fewer applications than before the pandemic (Kaufman & Diliberti, 2021). In addition, Carter-Thomas et al. (2021) found that California schools had a limited number of certified teachers due to fewer teachers completing education programs. Similar trends have occurred in Virginia, where the number of completers in traditional educational preparation programs has decreased by 50% from 2011 to 2021 (Hanel & McGraw, 2023). Reasons for the decrease in future teachers completing education programs included increased testing requirements for students and limited financial resources for teacher education programs (Carter-Thomas et al., 2021). Another reason for this may be the average teacher salary; researchers at the University of Virginia found that between 2002 and 2022 teacher salaries in Virginia increased by 48.8%; however, after adjusting for inflation, salaries have decreased by 9.1%, with all of the decrease occurring since the 2008 economic downturn (Hanel & McGraw, 2023). Additionally, 62% of parents do not want their children to become teachers because of the low pay, the stress, and the lack of respect associated with being a teacher (Phi Delta Kappan, 2022). Thus teaching may be becoming a less attractive career for someone to consider.

Some Positive Notes

Though the national and state reports found an increase in teachers leaving the classroom, there are some positive aspects to report. For example, North Carolina hired more teachers at the beginning of the 2021–2022 school year than in the previous 5 years. The increase in hired teachers may be due to North Carolina's focus on supporting new teachers with extra support and resources, with some of the noted resources including coaching, professional development, time for planning and grade-level collaboration, and a pay increase (Bastian & Fuller, 2022). Massachusetts saw an increase in the diversity of newly hired teachers and found that most Black and Latino teachers stayed in their teaching positions, which has led to increasing diversity across the teaching profession (Bacher-Hicks et al., 2021). In Arkansas, Camp et al. (2021) found no increase in new teachers leaving the field compared with previous years, which differed from North Carolina, but suggested that new Arkansas teachers stayed longer than 1 year.

It is important to note that, overall, early research has not found a mass exodus of teachers. As Camp et al. (2022) point out, the attrition rate in Arkansas did increase, but not at a rate that would put every school in a position of having unfilled positions. In addition, Zamarro et al. (2022) found that more teachers are *considering* leaving than *actually* leaving the profession. Our May 2022 national teacher survey yielded similar findings—many teachers stated they were considering leaving the classroom, but far fewer had immediate plans to do so (Marshall, Pressley, Neugebauer, & Shannon, 2022). For now, this is a good sign; however, if schools see teachers who are considering leaving beginning to follow through in significant numbers, this may lead to a larger teacher shortage, even if the increase is just 1–2% (Goldhaber & Theobald, 2022). That could exacerbate teacher attrition trends in disadvantaged schools, including schools serving high concentrations of students living in poverty or rural families (Camp et al., 2021; Carver-Thomas et al., 2021).

Supporting Teacher Retention

As we noted at the beginning of the chapter, some schools and districts faced teacher shortages before the pandemic (e.g., Edwards, Kraft, Christian, & Candelaria, 2022; Gais, Backstrom, Frank, & Wagner, 2019; Sorensen, Frank, Gais, & Sun, 2018). Some factors influencing teacher shortages before 2020 included school working conditions and teacher salaries. School leaders also saw schools with fewer early-career teachers applying for positions and high teacher turnover rates, leading to difficulty filling teaching positions (Edwards et al., 2022). Edwards and their colleagues suggest that the factors influencing teacher vacancies before the pandemic continued throughout and after the pandemic. Recent research has found that schools with strong leadership that demonstrate transparent communication with teachers, have fair expectations, and take time to recognize their teachers were more likely to keep teacher morale up during the pandemic (Marshall, Neugebauer, et al., 2023; Pressley, Marshall, Love, & Neugebauer, 2022; Sokal et al., 2021; Walter & Fox, 2021). Additionally, school districts that offered professional development in areas of need and provided time for teachers to collaborate with each other had a higher rate of success in keeping teachers during the pandemic (Kraft, Simon, & Lyon, 2021).

To limit teacher attrition, school leaders and policymakers will need to take action. Some actionable steps include raising teacher pay, especially for early-career teachers, to provide incentives to stay in the profession (Carver-Thomas et al., 2021; Edwards et al., 2022; Hendricks, 2014; Viano, Pham, Henry, Kho, & Zimmer, 2020). However, school leaders would also need to raise the pay of all teachers to recognize the work veteran teachers have put into teaching and their willingness to stay in the classroom. Too often we have heard from veteran teachers who have had to resign and reapply to their jobs to get on a new and higher pay scale. Though more money may not resolve all of the issues teachers face, it may provide security for teachers who took on multiple jobs to support their families and help them feel compensated for their work. We applaud policymakers who have taken actionable steps to increase teacher salaries in their states and would encourage them to continue further with financial support to all teachers.

Increasing teacher compensation alone is not a solution; we discuss this in greater detail in Chapter 8. School leaders must reflect on teachers' working conditions (Edwards et al., 2022; Ladd, 2011; Lovison &

Mo, 2022; Viano et al., 2020). For example, in the same NEA survey, Jotkoff (2022) found that 94% of teachers supported additional mental health support, and 90% supported less paperwork to address teacher burnout. Similarly, Lovison and Mo (2022) found that teachers would rather have additional personnel in schools, including school counselors, nurses, and special education teachers, than a 10% raise. Other actionable steps might include creating sustainable workloads for teachers and staff, providing enough substitute teachers throughout the school year to limit teacher coverage of extra classes or eliminate having larger classes when another teacher is out, and providing professional development in areas of teacher and student needs (Carver-Thomas et al., 2021; Kaufman & Diliberti, 2021). (See Chapter 5 for more on supporting teacher well-being.)

School District Partnerships and Teacher Residencies

Some schools and districts partnered with local teacher preparation programs to combat the teacher pipeline issue. Developing partnerships with local teacher preparation programs allows schools to recruit the newest teachers before preservice teachers complete their required coursework (Carver-Thomas et al., 2021). In addition, school systems have partnered with colleges and universities to develop teacher residency programs to address teacher shortages (Carver-Thomas et al., 2021). Whereas traditional teacher preparation programs tend to privilege coursework over practicum experience (Fraser & Lefty, 2018; Zeichner, 2018) and many alternative certification programs tend to privilege practice over courses (Gastic, 2014; Sharpe et al., 2022), teacher residency programs offer a strong combination of the two models. In a typical teacher residency model, preservice teachers get a full year of teaching experience under a teacher mentor and often receive financial support for their work (McKnight, Hope, Marrs, & Pitre-Martin, 2022; Sims, Lord, Megos, & Mitchell, 2023). At the same time, program participants complete university and college coursework, earn a teaching license, and often a graduate degree. The pairing of practice and coursework allows residents to put new knowledge into practice while under the guidance of a veteran teacher (Marshall, Varier, Hope, & Abrams, 2020). Graduates commit to working in a high-needs school after graduation, and schools get a guaranteed teacher for the next several years (Carver-Thomas et al., 2021).

Preservice teachers who complete student teaching in a typical teacher preparation program enter a classroom and teach for 12–16 weeks, usually in the spring, months after classroom norms have already been established by a more veteran teacher. By spending an entire year in the classroom, teacher residents get to see how classroom norms are developed and experience the entire arc of a school year prior to having a classroom of their own. The extended practicum experience has been found to allow preservice teachers additional opportunities to learn from mistakes, develop their teacher presence, and establish a healthy work–life balance (Marshall, Scott, & Wan, 2021). Researchers have found that teacher residency programs have a high success rate in retaining teachers and positively affecting student achievement (Guha, Hyler, & Darling-Hammond, 2016; Papay, West, Fullerton, & Kane, 2012; Yun & DeMoss, 2020). Advocates for teacher residencies often tout the high retention rates found among graduates; perhaps just as important, research has demonstrated that veteran teachers who mentor teacher residents are positively affected, too (Hope, Abrams, & Marshall, 2022). Teachers who participate as mentors report feeling rejuvenated about teaching and have indicated that it has also kept them in the classroom.

CASE STUDY: CASEY

In one of the focus groups we conducted in the fall of 2022, we spoke with an elementary school teacher who shared candidly with us why she stayed in teaching, particularly why she remained in the classroom during a very difficult first couple of years during the pandemic.

Casey (a pseudonym) began her teaching career as a second-grade teacher during the heart of the pandemic in the 2020–2021 school year. She teaches in a suburban school in the Tampa, Florida, area and describes her school as one that serves mainly upper-middle-class families. She also considers her school a large elementary school that serves over 1,000 students, with eight to nine teachers on every grade-level team and more than 20 students in every class. When we spoke with Casey about her experiences during the pandemic, she was in the fall semester of her 3rd year of teaching. Though she had taught at the same school for her short career, she had worked for three principals.

During her first year (2020–2021), her district offered families a choice to send their children to school in person or to opt into a virtual classroom. However, families had the option at any point during the year to send their children back to in-person learning when they felt comfortable. This led to many transitions throughout the year as families moved their kids back and forth between online and in-person classrooms. Casey was fortunate in that she was not required to teach hyflex or provide asynchronous instruction and only had to teach the students in her in-person classroom. Casey said that she was very grateful for that and felt that teaching in more than one format would have "done [her] in after about two days." To start the year, masks were mandatory, and if anyone in the class had a positive case, the whole class was sent home for a 2-week quarantine period. During quarantine, instruction moved online. Casey felt very fortunate that her class never had to go into quarantine. Though she never taught online during the 2020–2021 school year, she did have grade-level teammates who did have to go into quarantine, with some even at a moment's notice. One of her colleagues was sent home 5–10 minutes before students were supposed to enter their classroom for the day. Though none of Casey's students tested positive for COVID-19 that year, she still had students out sick consistently throughout the year. Having students out sick was the one aspect that led to more work for her, as she was required to send home 2 weeks' worth of lesson plans with a student if he or she was out sick (without a positive COVID-19 test). This forced her to design lesson plans that students could follow and complete independently or with their parents daily. Because of the required 10 days of quarantine for anyone showing symptoms (with or without a positive COVID-19 test result), Casey provided virtual lessons almost every day of the year. As she described, "it was like doing two jobs at once on some days because you had to get stuff ready for your class and put things together for the kids at home and you never had a ton of notice when that was going to happen."

For the 2021–2022 school year, masks became optional, social distancing was no longer an expectation, and there was no longer an online option for families. Her students who had been part of the online classrooms the previous year entered a physical classroom for the first time since March of their kindergarten year. Though there were no COVID-19 policies in place, Casey still had some parents uncomfortable having their children attend in person. This led to one parent removing their child from her classroom after another student tested positive for COVID-19 in October (however, the parents would later reenroll their child in December after unsuccessfully trying to home school) and a parent contacting her before the first day of school to have their child sit away from other students. She explained, "We were expected to honor parent requests for things like that [COVID-19 requests] because there was still so much uncertainty at that time." Casey remarked that *uncertainty* was the word that best described the start of the 2021–2022 school year.

Although almost half of her 2021–2022 class was enrolled in the all-virtual school in 2020–2021, Casey did not see any meaningful differences between the two groups of students academically. However, she noticed differences in the two groups regarding student behavior and social–emotional needs. She explained that she spent most of her second year of teaching addressing fights and helping students "figure out little problems that developmentally they should have been able to work through." In addition, she saw a lot of behavioral meltdowns from students who stayed online during the 2020–2021 school year. She felt that students who had been online for nearly 2 years "did not know how to cope with peer-to-peer conflict." In addition, students did not know when to be quiet, because, as Casey explained, "there is no mute button. I can't mute them [students] in real life." While students struggle to deal with their social–emotional needs, teachers are expected to teach them how to actually be students—far more than would be typical. However, Casey said that although teaching social–emotional skills is expected, teachers have no required curriculum to follow. "It is a 'figure it out as you go' [scenario], but every class has the freedom to provide academic and social lessons based on classroom needs." Overall, Casey described her teaching experience during the 2021–2022 school year as "intense and highly stressful, but [it] has been great seeing the benefits of educating my students and seeing their growth throughout the year." She discussed several tough student behaviors, including a physically abusive student, that challenged her teaching. Because of this student, Casey had thought about leaving the profession.

Casey immediately praised her current school principal when discussing why she decided to stay in teaching. "Her support is why I stayed. I chose to stay because of her relationship with me, her desire to care for me not just as an employee, but as a person." Casey also shared that her principal's first questions were "Are you okay? How are you feeling? Do you need anything? Can I step into your classroom so you can catch your breath for a minute?" Knowing that she was cared for and respected in her building made a big difference, keeping Casey in the classroom. "I was determined to stay because she [the principal] made me want to. I want to stay in this career because she modeled how to set boundaries."

Casey explained that her principal repeatedly told staff members to "shut off the light switch at the end of the day" to help teachers maintain a healthy life–work balance. "She is such a big advocate for us [teachers] that we respect our personal time, and she honors our personal time as well." In addition, Casey told us that her principal would also stand up for the teachers by taking on tough phone calls with parents. Her principal "stood up for her staff and didn't give in to parent demands. She didn't sugarcoat what was happening, even if it meant a parent had to hear hard words about their kid." Casey said, "I knew I was safe at work at least emotionally because she really did care for me and my students beyond what you would expect from a boss at any other job." Beyond the support, her principal gave all teachers the autonomy and space to do their work. Casey said, "She gave us the freedom to do our jobs as we wanted to, which is what we expected when we accepted jobs [as teachers]." Overall, her principal was someone teachers wanted to work with and for, as Casey commented that about 10 teachers from the principal's former school followed her to this new school.

When asked what teachers need to do their job, Casey said that *time* was the number one aspect. At her school, she must meet with other teachers in her grade level two to three times a week before students arrive. Some meetings help integrate a new curriculum into the grade level, whereas others discuss lesson plans and student data. These meetings require her to come in or stay later to finalize preparations for the day's lessons and activities. Though she does have a common planning time, it often is taken up with taking her students to the location of the gym, music, or art, as her campus is quite big. Casey wished she had more time to plan throughout the day than before or after school hours.

Overall, Casey continues to teach because of the support she receives from her principal and the autonomy she has to teach her students. School leaders can take Casey's case as an opportunity to reflect on how teachers are supported, how much autonomy they provide, and how much time they give teachers to get their daily instructional and administrative tasks done weekly. Reflecting on these needs may make a difference in keeping more teachers in classrooms nationwide.

* * *

National and state reports found a decrease in teacher attrition in the spring of 2020. However, since the spring of 2021, there has been a noted increase in teachers thinking about leaving. State reports have found small increases in teacher attrition, with numbers growing as more recent data become available. Some of the schools hardest hit by teacher attrition include schools serving low-SES families and those located in rural areas. However, some states, such as Massachusetts, have seen an increase in teacher diversity throughout the pandemic. School leaders need to take action to support teachers. Another attrition issue for schools, specifically rural ones, is whether or not they have adequate access to preservice teachers from teacher preparation programs. School leaders should look to develop partnerships and teacher residency programs with local teacher preparation programs to help recruit and retain new teachers. Finally, school leaders must continue to take actionable steps, such as raising teacher pay, providing necessary resources, developing sustainable workloads for teachers and staff, and providing enough substitute teachers.

As we saw with the case study of Casey, support within the school and district is key to teacher retention. Teachers went through a lot during the pandemic. School leaders need to take the time to support their teachers. Casey's principal supported her when she needed it and promoted a work–life balance for her teachers. Previous studies conducted during the pandemic found lack of administrative support to be a key factor in teacher burnout (Pressley, 2021a; Pressley & Ha, 2022). We would encourage all school leaders to reflect on how they support their teachers. Failing to do so could very well result in their best teachers seeking greener pastures.

Chapter 7

What Changes Remain?

> Policy talk about the schools has moved in cycles of gloomy assessments of education and overconfident solutions, producing incoherent guidance in actual reform practice. Hyperbole has often produced public cynicism and skepticism among teachers.
> —DAVID TYACK AND LARRY CUBAN (1995, p. 134)

> The times they are a-changin'.
> —BOB DYLAN (1965)

In their book on public school reform during the 20th century, David Tyack and Larry Cuban (1995) observed that "some innovations seem to die on contact with the institutional reality of the school. It is the rare reform that persists precisely according to plan" (p. 60). As schools move beyond the pandemic and return to normalcy in the classroom, it is a perfect time for school leaders, teachers, students, and parents to reflect on the changes made during COVID-19. Zhao and Watterston (2021) suggest that schools use this time to rethink what was considered the norm for schools by weighing the strengths and weaknesses of synchronous and asynchronous learning during the pandemic.

Many modifications were made in schools that would have been rare before March 2020. Though some of the changes were challenging for teachers, students, and other stakeholders, the pandemic forced teachers to learn how to use new technologies and facilitated increased communication with students (König, Jäger-Biela, & Glutsch, 2020; Love & Marshall, 2022). Prior to 2020, teachers and students had limited experiences with technology, and few districts had spent time and resources preparing teachers to incorporate technology into their instruction (Carpenter & Dunn, 2020, 2022; Marshall, Shannon, & Love, 2020). At the start of the pandemic, many schools got by with paper-based instructional packets; however, schools soon had little choice but to pivot to online platforms as it became clear that students would not be returning to in-person instruction during the spring of 2020 (An et al., 2021; Ferdig, Baumgartner, Hartshorne, Kaplan-Rakowski, & Mouza, 2020; Marshall & Neugebauer, 2022; Marshall, Shannon, & Love, 2022). Aside from the increased use of online resources and technology, schools employed a range of learning modalities and nontraditional schedules. There was also an increased focus on social and emotional learning, which was important given the state of student mental health (see Chapter 4). Finally, parents began seeking educational options other than their assigned traditional public schools far more often than before the pandemic, and the range of options available to them continues to expand.

Increased Technology in Schools

Perhaps the most visible changes in schools have involved technology. For decades there have been calls for increased use of technology in the classroom (Bowman, 1982; Cuban, 1986; Davies & West, 2014; Marshall, 2009; Papert, 1993; Scardamalia & Bereiter, 1994). However, the integration of new technologies in elementary and secondary education was slow moving (e.g., Lu & Overbaugh, 2009). When traditional classroom instruction became impossible due to social distancing measures, everything had to change. Teachers were forced to move their lessons online using various video conferencing platforms (e.g., Zoom, Google Meets) to deliver instruction, as well as to use learning management systems (LMS; e.g., Google Classroom, Canvas) to conduct asynchronous discussions and assign and grade work. Additionally, many schools provided students with laptops or tablets and ensured that all students had internet access. In short, schools have invested time and resources into technology, and because of this, many schools and teachers are now much more prepared if faced with another emergency shutdown (Marshall, Pressley, & Love, 2022).

What Teachers Believed Would Remain

It will not be surprising to see some of the changes to schooling made during COVID-19 extend beyond the crisis. In the earliest months of the COVID-19 pandemic, teachers believed very few changes made during

COVID-19 would continue. Specifically, teachers believed that digital learning days (for both planned instructional days and emergencies) and one-to-one (1:1) devices for students would be the only changes to continue (Marshall, Pressley, & Love, 2022). However, by January 2021, the list of what changes teachers believed would remain continued to grow. Ten months into the pandemic, teachers believed that using LMS and Zoom or other video platforms would continue beyond COVID-19.

Marshall's May 2021 survey asked teachers whether they believed certain technology-based changes would persist in schools beyond the pandemic (Marshall, Smith, et al., in press). Teachers responded on a 6-point Likert scale on which a value of 1 represented a *very unlikely* response and a value of 6 represented a *very likely* response. When we surveyed teachers again in May 2022, we simply asked teachers whether they were employing the same technology-based changes in their schools. See Table 7.1 for a comparison of what teachers projected in May 2021 with what was actually happening in their schools in May 2022.

In May 2021, teachers commented that they believed 1:1 devices would be the most likely of the technology-based COVID-19–era changes to remain. A year later, they were correct, with more than four in five teachers reporting that they continued providing students with computing devices for learning (e.g., Marshall & Neugebauer, 2023; Newberry & Hinchcliff, 2023). Students could use these devices in the classroom and,

TABLE 7.1. Pandemic Changes: Comparing May/June 2021 Teacher Projections with May 2022 Reports

	May–June 2021 (n = 304)	May 2022 (n = 864)
Item	M (SD)	%
1:1 devices for all students	5.04 (1.50)	80.56
Continued LMS use	4.70 (1.56)	54.63
Digital learning days (e.g., bad weather)	3.86 (1.65)	43.52
Full-time online learning option	3.34 (1.97)	57.69
Students attend virtually when absent	2.64 (1.51)	40.51
Having asynchronous learning days	1.78 (1.22)	18.40

Note. May–June 2021 responses represent means and standard deviations regarding the likelihood that participants believed pandemic changes would persist on a 6-point scale. May 2022 responses represent the percentage of participants reporting that these changes persisted through the end of the 2021–2022 school year in their schools.

in some cases, take them home to use for their homework. Continuing to use LMS and incorporating digital learning days were the other two changes teachers believed were more likely than not to persist in schools. More than half (54.63%) of the teachers we surveyed reported that their schools were using an LMS by the conclusion of the 2021–2022 school year. Despite teachers' belief in March 2020 that digital learning days were most likely to stick around, only 43.52% of teachers reported in 2022 that their schools were employing digital learning days.

Changes in Classroom Instruction

Although the COVID-19 pandemic has caused many educational challenges, it has also led to positive changes that are likely to continue in classrooms. Even as traditional classrooms resume, many educators will continue to use digital tools to enhance their teaching practices and engage students. The use of technology can also enable teachers to personalize instruction, adapt to individual learning needs, and provide students with more diverse and engaging learning experiences. For example, teachers started using educational applications, online quizzes, and interactive multimedia to engage students and make learning more accessible. Technology also allowed the creation of virtual classrooms, in which students could collaborate and interact with each other remotely. We believe that teachers and school leaders should embrace the new technology opportunities to engage students in ways they would not otherwise. Today's students are extremely technologically savvy, and providing more opportunities for technology integration into the learning process will certainly allow students to continue growing in this digital era.

Learning Management Systems

Prior to the pandemic, LMS use was ubiquitous on college campuses. However, their use was far less common in K–12 education (Lochner, Conrad, & Graham, 2015). LMS provides multiple benefits such as allowing students to access material digitally on their 1:1 devices, as well as providing a platform for teachers to post lessons and assignments in the LMS.

In our May 2022 teacher survey, we asked about the changes that had taken place in their schools, including what was still being implemented after schools had fully reopened (Pressley et al., in press). One finding that surprised us was that teachers who taught in schools that used an LMS reported higher levels of burnout than teachers who taught in schools that did not use an LMS. This was surprising because having an LMS means not having to cart stacks of papers to grade back and forth from home to school (something both of us had to do as teachers) and being able to access learning materials, whether at school or at home—a feature that would have been nice to have back in March 2020 when teachers had to take as many physical materials as they could home with them when schools closed to in-person instruction.

When we conducted our fall 2022 focus groups, we specifically asked teachers about this, and what teachers shared with us offered some clarification. Those who taught younger students, especially early elementary-grade levels, did not have students complete assigned readings posted in an LMS or submit assignments online. That made sense. But what about those who taught older learners? The teachers with whom we spoke responded that, although they saw the benefits of using an LMS, it became just another thing on their plates. For example, whereas they previously might have had to submit lesson plans to their administrators, now they had to submit them to administrators *and* post them in the LMS so families could access them. In other words, the LMS' affordances did not replace other tasks and make them more efficient; they became an addition to what was already required of teachers. As LMS use becomes the norm and teachers are properly trained on using them, we believe their use will be a net positive for all stakeholders. However, school leaders should be mindful to use the LMS to replace tasks assigned to teachers and not create additional work.

Digital Learning Days

We have seen districts nationwide begin to implement digital learning days, such as New York City (Klein, 2022), the Cherokee County School District in Georgia (2023), and Gwinnett County Public Schools (2023) in Georgia. Additionally, states such as Nebraska and Wisconsin have adopted the option to implement digital learning days on days when teachers and students may have previously been off (Nebraska Department of Education, 2022; Wisconsin Department of Public Instruction, n.d.). For example, schools can now implement digital learning days due to election days or inclement weather (e.g., hurricane or snow days). On these days, teachers post assignments to the LMS and hold office hours for students to ask questions or get help with the online assignment for the day. By using digital learning days, schools could eliminate days at the end of the year or provide longer winter breaks because the digital learning days would eliminate canceled school days throughout the year. However, school leaders must use caution, as these days were often seen as a nice relief for teachers and students throughout the year, and school leaders should be cognizant of overworking teachers and provide days to reset and refresh (Marshall, Love, Shannon, & Neugebauer, 2023; Pressley, 2021b). See Chapter 4 for more on student well-being and Chapter 5 for more on teacher well-being.

Changes in Learning Modalities and Schedules

As described in Chapter 1, schools employed a range of different learning modalities during the pandemic, including fully in-person, hybrid, and remote learning options (e.g., Marshall & Bradley-Dorsey, 2022). Although nontraditional modalities were typically employed as a COVID-19 mitigation effort so that fewer or no students would be in the physical building, the crisis forced schools to try something other than the traditional five-days-per-week 8:00 A.M. to 3:00 P.M. school schedule in a brick-and-mortar building (Newberry & Hinchcliff, 2023). As the saying goes, "necessity is the mother of invention"—an idea derived from Plato's *Republic* (380 B.C./2000). We wondered whether this moment, spawned as a reaction to a crisis, might be the watershed moment when schools began to employ more creative schedules and different modes of instruction. So far, the evidence seems to suggest the contrary is true; schools mostly returned to normal ("Back to School and Back to Normal," 2022).

During the pandemic, many schools delivered instruction asynchronously 1 day per week, often on Wednesdays (Love & Marshall, 2022; Newberry & Hinchcliff, 2023). This allowed teachers to have additional planning time, which was important given the herculean task they were asked to complete (Marshall, Love, Neugebauer, & Smith, 2023). Teachers would often hold office hours during this time so that students who needed additional help could meet with them through video conferencing software such as Zoom. The midweek asynchronous day also allowed for school custodians to do additional cleaning in the school building as part of an effort to curb the spread of COVID-19.

This change in the school schedule was an important feature during the pandemic, but will it endure beyond the crisis? The teachers we surveyed in May 2021 did not think so (see Table 7.1). More than 80% of teachers responded that they believed it was either *unlikely* or *very unlikely* that their school would continue to have asynchronous learning days beyond the crisis. When we surveyed teachers again the following year, fewer than 20% of teachers indicated that they were still doing this. Some would look at those numbers and dismiss this as a revolutionary change. However, if someone were to suggest prior to the pandemic that almost one in five schools would evolve to have an atypical school schedule, no one would have believed them. Since the pandemic, some school districts around the country have begun to shift to 4-day weeks as ways to recruit teachers and support their well-being (Hanson, 2023). The idea of a 4-day week has begun to gain traction over the last decade, and a recent *Phi Delta Kappan* poll found that 53% of the public supported a 4-day schedule, which was a significant increase from 2003, when only 25% of the public supported it (*Phi Delta Kappan*, 2023). Though the change to a 4-day week is one that families, students, and teachers must adjust to, we believe it may have a positive effect on keeping teachers in the classroom. There is still limited research on the effect of 4-day weeks (e.g., Anglum & Park, 2021), so we encourage future research to explore their impact on teacher retention as well as on teacher and student well-being.

CASE STUDY: ALABAMA AEROSPACE AND AVIATION HIGH SCHOOL

The Alabama Aerospace and Aviation High School (hereafter, AAAHS) is a charter school serving grades 9–12 in Bessemer, Alabama.* The school opened its doors in the fall of 2022. As its name suggests, the school is an aerospace- and aviation-themed school that serves all students but seeks to attract those with a particular emphasis on STEM subjects. In terms of technology, the school issues 1:1 devices to students and utilizes an LMS. Each student develops an individualized learning plan and can select different industry-aligned pathways, including those for careers as pilots, air traffic controllers, aircraft maintenance mechanics, and so on. Their permanent location will be near the Bessemer Municipal Airport.

---

*To learn more about AAAHS, visit the school's website at *www.alaahs.org* and see Marshall and Witte, 2023.

For full disclosure, one of us (D. T. M.) was the chair of the Alabama Public Charter School Commission when AAAHS's application to open their school was approved.

Despite opening well after COVID-19 mitigation efforts ceased in Alabama, the school opted to open its doors with every Friday as an asynchronous learning day. Ruben Morris, the school's founder, explained that this allowed them to do three things. First, in an era marked by teacher vacancies and smaller pools of applicants applying for jobs (see Chapter 6), it allowed him to attract a lot of teachers who were drawn to the idea of being able to work from home every Friday. Second, it allowed his students to develop good academic habits for completing work asynchronously—something almost all of the students will likely do at some point if and when they pursue postsecondary education. And finally, students would spend half of the day on Fridays in their pathway—so, for example, those in the aircraft maintenance pathway would get hands-on experience working with airplanes. Delta Airlines donated old engines to the school so that students could gain experience. Instead of spending Friday in the school building, they could work alongside professionals in the aerospace and aviation industry. Thus, this school uses an asynchronous day for students to gain authentic learning experiences and develop good practices with asynchronous learning and as a way to attract a wider pool of teachers to AAAHS.

Social and Emotional Learning

Another change likely to continue is the increased emphasis on social and emotional learning (SEL) in education. SEL refers to the process of acquiring and applying the knowledge, skills, and attitudes necessary to understand and manage emotions, establish and maintain positive relationships, make responsible decisions, and achieve personal and academic goals (Elias, Zins, Weissberg, Frey, & Greenberg, 1997). SEL allows students to practice these skills in a supportive environment and can have a positive impact on students' academic success; it also enhances their mental health and well-being (Elias et al., 1997). As the pandemic has highlighted the importance of student mental health and well-being, many educators will continue prioritizing SEL in their teaching practices (see Chapter 4 for more on student well-being). Schools may also continue to offer counseling services and mindfulness programs to support students' emotional well-being. For example, schools may implement SEL skills, such as self-awareness, self-management, and relationship building. As schools return to normalcy, teachers have and will continue to provide emotional support through mindfulness programs that support student management of stress and anxiety and counseling services to students.

Implementing SEL can positively affect students' mental health and well-being by reducing symptoms of anxiety, depression, and stress (Greenberg, Domitrovich, Weissberg, & Durlak, 2017; LaBelle, 2019). SEL programs provide students with the skills and strategies to identify and regulate their emotions, communicate effectively with others, and develop positive coping mechanisms (Weare & Nind, 2011). Through a meta-analysis of SEL interventions, Weare and Nind (2011) found that they had significant real-world effects when implemented correctly. Specifically, SEL interventions should focus on positive mental health, early intervention with younger students that continues through school, and promoting SEL throughout the whole school environment (Weare & Nind, 2011).

Additionally, SEL can positively affect academic performance by improving students' motivation, attention, and engagement in learning (Payton et al., 2008; Schonfield et al., 2015; Zins, Bloodworth, Weissberg, & Walberg, 2004). When students feel emotionally safe and connected to their teachers and peers, they are more likely to participate in class, ask questions, and take risks in their learning (Durlak, Weissberg, Dymnicki, Taylor, & Schellinger, 2011). Moreover, the self-regulation, goal-setting, and problem-solving skills taught in SEL programs can help students manage their time, prioritize their tasks, and persist in facing challenges, which are key components of academic success (Zins et al., 2004).

SEL can help students learn appropriate behaviors when interacting with others (Payton et al., 2008). As we have heard from teachers in focus groups and surveys, students have returned to school with more behavior problems and developmentally inappropriate behaviors. According to a May 2023 survey of teachers, 74% list student discipline and behavioral issues as the top challenges they face in their jobs (Veney, 2023). This could be due to the different conditions that existed during remote learning. For example, teachers did not always feel the need to correct unruly students when class was on a screen; they could simply mute that student rather than teaching them classroom rules for not talking out of turn. Some older students might not understand that, for example, using their cell phones is inappropriate in most instances during class time, especially when all they did for two years was learn through screens. In addition, SEL can promote positive social behavior and reduce negative behavior, such as bullying and aggression, by promoting student empathy, respect, and cooperation. Students with strong social and emotional skills are better able to understand and appreciate the perspectives of others, resolve conflicts peacefully, and contribute to a positive school culture (Durlak et al., 2011). SEL programs can also improve students' social and emotional competence, such as self-awareness, self-management, social awareness, and relationship skills (Weissberg, Durlak, Domitrovich, & Gullotta, 2015).

Finally, SEL also positively affects teacher well-being, job satisfaction, and self-efficacy (Collie, Shapka, & Perry, 2012; Reyes, Brackett, Rivers, White, & Salovey, 2012). Teachers who possess these competencies are better equipped to handle the emotional demands of their profession and maintain a positive outlook in challenging situations. Consequently, teaching SEL promotes teachers' well-being, reducing burnout rates and enhancing job satisfaction (Kim, Choi, & Lee, 2021). In addition, teachers trained in SEL have increased their academic success by implementing SEL strategies into lessons (Greenberg et al., 2003) and stronger classroom management (Durlak et al., 2011). With the research that supports the benefits of SEL and the student social and emotional well-being we have seen throughout the pandemic (see Chapter 4), we believe SEL should and will be an aspect that is incorporated into classrooms beyond the pandemic.

Virtual Communication

When everything shut down in the early days of the pandemic, most things migrated online—including communication. This included most forms of communication that typically would have taken place in schools, such as parent–teacher conferences, discussions of individualized education plans (IEP), and other meetings between teachers, school leaders, and parents or guardians. At the start of the pandemic, teachers reported anxiety communicating with parents as a leading factor of teacher burnout (Pressley, 2021a). However, by 2021, teachers shared feelings about strengthened communication with parents throughout the pandemic (Marshall, 2022a). As schools adapted throughout the pandemic, it became the norm for meetings with parents and guardians to occur on a video conference platform. For families and teachers, this has made meetings more accessible to all. For example, school leaders no longer have to find time for an administrator, teacher, parents or guardians, and other stakeholders to come together in person for a student's IEP meeting. Everyone can log on from home, their place of work, or other locations rather than having to come to the physical school building. Some schools have also continued using virtual meetings for school staff rather than meeting in person before or after school (Marshall, 2022a). This has allowed teachers to hear important information from school administrators while they prepare their classrooms for the day or pick their kids up from school. Virtual meetings have allowed teachers more flexibility in their use of their time before and after school.

Expanded Educational Opportunity

Most of this chapter has discussed how schools have changed. However, for some, the most substantial change in K–12 education during the pandemic was *where* children were enrolled to learn. Survey research conducted by Dick Carpenter and Joshua Dunn (2020) found that parents mostly viewed the remote instruction that took place in spring 2020 positively. However, as months passed, fewer parents were as excited about remote learning for their children. Enrollment in traditional public schools declined by 3%, which was the largest decline since 1943 (Wall, 2023), and this occurred especially among families who wished their children to learn in person (e.g., Dee, Huffaker, Phillips, & Sagara, 2022). Parents "voted with their feet," and almost 1.5 million students were no longer enrolled in a traditional public school system 3 years after the start of the pandemic. Nationally, independent private school enrollment increased (Scafidi, Tutterow, & Kavanagh, 2021), and enrollment in general increased in more than half of private schools during the 2020–2021 school year (McCluskey, 2021). Private school enrollments increased during the 2020–2021 school year, reversing declines in the early months of the pandemic (McCluskey, 2022). Estimates suggest that charter school enrollment increased between 4.4 and 7% during the 2020–2021 school year (Veney & Jacobs, 2021). See Table 7.2 for enrollment patterns in traditional public schools, charter schools, and private schools between 2017–2018 and 2020–2021.

Some families opted out of traditional schooling altogether, opting to

TABLE 7.2. Student Enrollment by Sector Before and During the Pandemic

	Traditional public schools			Charter schools			Private schools		
Year	*N*	%	Δ%	*N*	%	Δ%	*N*	%	Δ%
2017–2018	44,242,369	77.7	n/a	3,143,269	5.5	n/a	4,898,154	8.7	n/a
2018–2019	44,078,647	77.8	−0.3	3,290,149	5.8	4.7	4,775,529	8.4	−2.5
2019–2020	44,018,621	77.8	−0.1	3,431,230	6.1	4.3	4,652,904	8.2	−2.6
2020–2021	42,804,829	77.1	−2.8	3,581,952	6.5	4.4	4,693,902	8.4	0.9

Note. Data from John Kristof of EdChoice (personal communication, June 8, 2023). The % column represents the sector's market share for that school year. The Δ% represents the within sector change year over year.

home school (Musaddiq, Stange, Bacher-Hicks, & Goodman, 2022) or to create what became known as "pandemic pods"—the schooling of children from a small number of families together (Watson, 2022). Still others explored hybrid home schooling, which can be defined as "a school that for some part of the week educates children in a traditional brick-and-mortar building and for some other part of the week has children educated at home" (McShane, 2021, p. 31). Between 2019–2020 and 2021–2022, New York's traditional public schools dropped 8% in enrollment (Center for New York City Affairs, 2023). The declines were the steepest in New York City, which saw a 13% drop in student enrollment. At the same time, New York City charter school enrollment increased 24%, and home schooling increased 184%.

Beyond the pandemic, these trends are likely to continue. In 2019, 53.9 million students were enrolled in public and private schools, with approximately 85% enrolled in traditional public school systems (National Center for Education Statistics, 2022a), 6% enrolled in public charter schools (National Center for Education Statistics, n.d.), and 9% enrolled in private schools (National Center for Education Statistics, 2022b). In the wake of the pandemic, education savings accounts (ESAs; also known as "universal school choice") bills have been enacted in several states. Similar to health savings accounts, ESAs allow parents to use a portion of the money that would have funded their children's education in a traditional public school system to cover education-related costs, including private school tuition, music lessons, tutoring, online learning programs, special education–related services, and other related services and materials. As of this writing, universal school choice legislation has been passed in Arizona, Arkansas, Florida, Indiana, Iowa, Nebraska, North Carolina,

Oklahoma, Utah, and West Virginia since August 2022 (EdChoice, 2023b). In addition, Mississippi passed three voucher programs that are geared toward students receiving special education services. School choice has always existed for families with the means to afford private school tuition or to purchase a home attached to good schools (Marshall, 2017). As Mike McShane (2023) argued in *Forbes*, increased educational opportunities "will maximize the likelihood that schools will reflect the needs, wants, and values of the families entrusting their children to them." Trends that began during the COVID-19 pandemic may change the educational landscape as we know it. Scholars should seek to understand how these initiatives affect students and teachers alike.

Online Learning Options

The pandemic has shown that remote learning can be an effective alternative to traditional classroom instruction. Of teachers who participated in our May 2022 survey, 58% reported that full-time online options were available in their states, and close to 10% were unsure. Qualitative research conducted with charter school leaders in 2020 found that as many as one-third of school leaders were considering adding an online option, including some who were philosophically opposed to online learning prior to the crisis (Marshall & Neugebauer, 2022, 2023). However, follow-up surveys in the summer of 2021—after schools had reopened everywhere—revealed that only a handful were still considering the option. Although fully remote learning may not be suitable for all students, it can be a valuable option for those who cannot attend school in person, such as those who live in remote areas or have health conditions that prevent them from attending school. Remote learning can also provide more flexibility in scheduling and allow students to learn at their own pace and to complete school work around work schedules, extracurricular activities, and family obligations (Borup & Kennedy, 2017). Studies also suggest that students who have been bullied in traditional schools find solace in online learning, as it allows them to focus on their studies without the social distractions (Borup & Kennedy, 2017; Heinrich, Darling-Aduana, Good, & Cheng, 2019).

Remote learning can also offer students a more personalized learning experience and provide more autonomy (Moe & Chubb, 2009). With remote learning, teachers can use digital tools to create customized lessons and assignments based on students' needs and interests. Teachers can also provide individualized feedback on assignments and assessments, which can help students identify areas in which they need to improve. In addition, it can help students develop time management and self-regulation skills, as they must take responsibility for their learning and manage their time effectively. Though remote learning that was employed during the pandemic was not effective for most students and, thus, is not a viable option for long-term instruction for most students (Duckworth et al., 2021; Halloran et al., 2021), it was effective for specific populations of students (e.g., Aloizou, Chasiotou, Retalis, Daviotis, & Koulouvaris, 2021; Cash, Brinkmann, & Price, 2022; Shaw & Shaw, 2021). For example, Shaw and Shaw (2021) found that attending classes online reduced anxiety for students in special education, and Aloizou and colleagues (2021) found that students diagnosed with autism thrived when they learned through a combination of video conferencing technology and an online educational gaming platform. Dennis Beck and his colleagues (Beck, Maranto, & Lo, 2014) have previously conducted work exploring parental satisfaction in an online charter school and found greater satisfaction among parents with children receiving special education services than others.

Although studies have found that integrating technology well and engaging students with the learning process can lead to increased academic achievement (e.g., Hull & Duch, 2019; Kim et al., 2019), several studies have found that students who attend virtual schools underperform compared with those attending brick-and-mortar schools (e.g., Hamlin, Adams, & Adigun, 2023; Zimmer et al., 2009). There are likely selection biases at play in terms of who elects to enroll in online learning in the first place, but the evidence suggests that online learning is not for every student. However, given that it does seem to work for some students, the option is likely here to stay. In the state of Alabama, all students must take at least one online course to graduate (Digital Learning Collaborative, n.d.). Students in traditional schools have increasingly taken specific courses online (Lin, Kwon, & Zhang, 2019), especially those in smaller school districts or in rural areas (Marietta & Marietta, 2020). Consider the example of a student enrolled in a small school district that does not have either enough students or a teacher to offer Advance Placement French in a traditional classroom setting. Online course choice can allow that student to still be able to take the class, regardless of the school's offerings. A recent study found that more than half of parents whose children attend schools that do not have access to online course choice wish their children did have that option (Kingsbury & Marshall, 2023). In the wake of the pandemic, online learning—including both full-time options and individual course choice—will likely continue to grow.

* * *

The COVID-19 pandemic has caused significant educational disruptions but has also led to some positive changes. The increased use of technology and the acceptance of remote learning as a viable alternative to traditional instruction are likely to continue in today's classrooms. In addition, schools must continue to support student mental health through SEL as a way to promote positive behaviors, as well as to help students self-regulate and catch up developmentally from behaviors that were not taught or supported throughout the pandemic. Further, schools can continue using virtual meeting platforms to connect school leaders, teachers, and parents or guardians. Virtual meeting platforms allow teachers and school leaders to have more flexibility in where they are when attending a meeting, but, more importantly, they provide parents and guardians an opportunity to have easier access to their student's teachers without having to leave work or home and meet in person. Building on these changes and finding new ways to improve education and support student learning and development is essential as we move forward. Expanded educational options and opportunities stemming from the pandemic will create a landscape of more diverse learning options among which families can choose. A common saying during the pandemic among educators was that we learned that "one size fits all" doesn't really fit all. Students have different learning needs, and having more options from which to choose, including virtual options, increases the odds that they will find an option that best fits their individual needs.

Chapter 8

What Do Teachers Need to Be Successful?

Since the spring of 2020, teachers have been through a lot. First called heroes for stepping up to the challenge of pivoting to emergency remote instruction, teachers also received criticism because the packets sent home and remote learning were not challenging enough. Later in the same year, teachers were denounced for having reservations about returning to the classroom in the fall of 2020. Although we have made the case throughout this book that the COVID-19 school closures were a policy mistake with deleterious consequences, it is important to remember that in the summer of 2020, a lot of individuals—including teachers—were still justifiably concerned about the virus given what was known at the time. In addition, throughout the pandemic, teachers reported working increased hours to connect with students and learn new technology for remote, hybrid, and hyflex instruction (Carver-Thomas et al., 2021; Kaden, 2020; Love & Marshall, 2022; Marshall, Love, Shannon, & Neugebauer, 2023) while trying to balance their own health and family interests. As society returned to normalcy, teachers have taken on even more work, addressing the learning loss that occurred during the pandemic, and providing social–emotional support to students who forgot or never learned how to be students in school. This has all taken a toll on teachers.

Teacher Self-Efficacy

Like members of any other profession, teachers want to feel that they can go to work every day and succeed. But during the pandemic, teacher self-efficacy suffered. A person's self-efficacy is his or her perception of his or her ability to complete a task (Bandura, 1997). One's perception of self-efficacy comes from previous success in a specific domain, observing others through vicarious experiences, verbal persuasion, and a person's physiological state (Bandura, 1997). For teachers, self-efficacy focuses on "the teacher's belief in his or her capability to organize and execute a course of action required to accomplish a specific teaching task in a particular context" (Tschannen-Moran, Hoy, & Hoy, 1998, p. 233).

As teachers adjusted to additional instructional demands during the pandemic, researchers found that teacher self-efficacy decreased, especially at the beginning of the pandemic (Marshall, Shannon, et al., in press; Pellerone, 2021; Pressley & Ha, 2022; Walter & Fox, 2021). Survey research conducted by Marshall and his colleagues, David Shannon and Savanna Love, in March–April 2020, showed that self-efficacy levels were low overall, as expected (Marshall, Shannon, et al., in press). What was surprising was that they were low for all teachers, regardless of grade level or subject taught, of whether they taught in urban, rural, or suburban schools, or of contextual factors, including the proportion of their students who had access to broadband internet at home. In addition, Kraft et al. (2021) found that in the spring of 2020, teachers experienced a large decrease in their sense of success as their instruction became remote. Thus teachers did not feel as confident in providing high-quality instruction using the newly required approaches. This was found to be particularly true with regard to the use of LMS. As we noted in the previous chapter, LMS were not commonly used in most K–12 systems prior to the pandemic. However, many school systems immediately invested in LMS to help teachers and students navigate remote learning. Cardullo, Wang, Burton, and Dong (2021) found that how useful teachers perceived the LMS to be significantly predicted their self-efficacy for classroom management, instruction delivery, and student engagement in the spring of 2020. Self-efficacy is important; Lücker and colleagues (2022) found a link between teacher self-efficacy and thoughts about leaving the profession during the pandemic. Teachers with lower levels of self-efficacy were significantly more likely to consider leaving their jobs.

Survey research conducted by Pressley in October 2020 found that elementary teachers in the United States had lower teacher self-efficacy scores than studies conducted before the COVID-19 pandemic, with all teachers who taught remotely having the lowest self-efficacy (Pressley, 2021c). In addition, there were no differences in either instructional or engagement self-efficacy based on years of experience or a teacher's previous success in the classroom. Similar trends were found when looking at all levels: elementary, middle, and high school teachers (Pressley & Ha, 2021). Furthermore, Pressley and Ha (2022) found an association between U.S. K–12 teachers' instructional self-efficacy and their amount of stress, as well as a negative association between administrative support and teachers' engagement efficacy. Teacher self-efficacy was a mediating variable between school administrative support and teacher stress early in the pandemic (Pressley & Ha, 2022).

It was not just teachers in the United States who saw a decrease in self-efficacy during the pandemic. In Italy, Pellerone (2021) found that teacher self-efficacy mediated the relationship between personal accomplishment and teacher burnout. Other findings suggested that the makeup of the class also influenced teacher self-efficacy, with teachers having larger classes and more students with special education needs showing lower self-efficacy early on during the pandemic. Rabaglietti et al. (2021) surveyed teachers across Europe during the initial COVID-19 lockdown. As teachers tried to adjust their instruction to a remote format, they saw a decrease in self-efficacy when facing difficulties with distance learning. Similarly, studies conducted in China (Ma et al., 2021) and Canada (Sokal et al., 2020a) during the COVID-19 pandemic found that lower teacher self-efficacy for remote instruction was associated with a reduced sense of accomplishment and higher levels of burnout.

By the end of the 2020–2021 school year, teacher self-efficacy scores had increased compared with fall 2020, but several factors played critical roles in influencing teacher self-efficacy (Pressley & Rangel, 2023). For instance, emotional exhaustion and personal accomplishment, two aspects of teacher burnout, both influenced teacher overall self-efficacy, as well as self-efficacy for instructional strategies, student engagement, and classroom management. In addition, teachers' previous successes—such as being recognized as Teachers of the Year—prior to the pandemic indicated a positive influence on instructional strategies and classroom management self-efficacy. Finally, school administrative support also positively affected student engagement and classroom management self-efficacy (Pressley & Rangel, 2023).

Megan Tschannen-Moran and Anita Woolfolk Hoy (2001) created an often-used scale to measure teacher self-efficacy. As of this writing, their seminal paper on the topic has been cited more than 10,000 times in the academic literature (Tschannen-Moran et al., 1998). Their scale measures teachers' sense of efficacy in three distinct areas: (1) classroom management, a teacher's ability to manage the classroom environment; (2) student engagement, a teacher's ability to engage students in the content; and (3) instructional strategies, a teacher's ability to provide clear instruction to all students in the class. We measured teacher self-efficacy using their Teacher Sense of Efficacy scale (Tschannen-Moran & Hoy, 2001), on which 1 indicates low efficacy and 9 indicates high efficacy. We looked back at the teacher self-efficacy data we collected throughout the pandemic to explore the changes in teacher self-efficacy across the pandemic (fall 2020, spring 2021, and spring 2023; see Table 8.1). Our figures come from three separate scale administrations and thus do not reflect responses from a consistent group of teachers, which is a limitation. However, we believe these figures are worth considering all the same.

Data collected prior to the pandemic using this scale yielded scores ranging from 6.80 to 8.08 depending on the subscales (Wolters & Daugherty, 2007; Yoo, 2016). The figures we obtained from teachers surveyed in the fall of 2020 were substantially lower and lower across all subscales. The lowest scores, unsurprisingly, came in the beginning stages of the pandemic. Although we only collected data with the Instructional Strategies and Student Engagement subscales, both means were well below pre-pandemic norms. By the conclusion of the 2020–2021 school year, both figures improved, but again not to levels found before the crisis.

Between May 2021 and April–May 2023, overall teacher self-efficacy levels were statistically similar to one another. The good news

TABLE 8.1. Comparing Teacher Self-Efficacy from 2020 to 2023

	October 2020[a]	May 2021[b]	April–May 2023
	M (*SD*)	*M* (*SD*)	*M* (*SD*)
Overall TSES	—	6.34 (1.62)	6.19 (1.18)
Classroom management[c]	—	6.54 (1.79)	6.01 (1.47)
Instructional strategies	5.58 (1.72)	6.53 (1.79)	6.93 (1.24)
Student engagement	5.09 (1.43)	5.96 (1.68)	5.67 (1.40)
N	361	316	917

Note. Teacher self-efficacy was measured using Tschannen-Moran and Hoy's (2001) Teacher Sense of Efficacy (TSES) 9-point scale.

[a]Pressley and Ha (2021); [b]Pressley and Rangel (2023); [c]scale introduced in May 2021 survey.

is that teacher self-efficacy for delivering instruction rose significantly from October 2020 to May 2021 ($p < .001$) and again from May 2021 to April–May 2023 ($p < .001$). However, the same was not true for the other two subscales. Although teacher self-efficacy for student engagement increased from October 2020 to May 2021 ($p < .001$), it dropped again between May 2021 and April–May 2023 ($p < .01$). Teacher self-efficacy for effectively managing a classroom also dropped during the same 2-year stretch, from 6.54 to 6.01 ($p < .001$). These findings are in line with one of the themes we revisit throughout this chapter: Teachers need support with disruptive student behavior. At the same time, these findings also suggest that student engagement has not recovered since the start of the pandemic.

Supporting Teacher Self-Efficacy

Though some aspects of teacher self-efficacy rebounded as the pandemic continued, it is important for school and district administrators to recognize the dip that teachers experienced during the heart of the pandemic. School leaders can use the pandemic as a learning opportunity to understand the impact that learning new instructional approaches might have on teacher self-efficacy.

First, teachers need support with new technologies introduced during the pandemic—especially with LMS. It is also important that school leaders recognize mastery experiences and personal accomplishments. This could take the form of school administrators providing feedback on lesson plans, informal and formative walk-throughs, communicating with teachers about resources they need to support student learning, and supporting teachers through relevant PD opportunities (e.g., Dolighan & Owen, 2021; Fackler & Malmberg, 2016; Kraft et al., 2021; Yoo, 2016). Additionally, school leaders may provide time throughout the school year for teachers to observe and talk with each other to learn collaboratively and to provide opportunities for instructional coaching (Hope, Abrams, & Marshall, 2022; Marshall, Trammell, Shetty, & Woods, 2022; Walsh, Ginger, & Akhavan, 2020). Delivered either by mentors or professional coaches, instructional coaching provides opportunities for less experienced teachers to learn from more experienced teachers through formative observations, modeling lessons, and management techniques, as well as by coteaching lessons (Bandura, 1997; Dembo & Gibson, 1985; Kraft et al., 2021; Siciliano, 2016).

Second, implementing hybrid and remote learning had a major impact on teacher self-efficacy during the pandemic. If schools plan to continue using these instructional approaches or ever need to implement hybrid or remote learning again, school leaders should consider more flexibility with requirements for each type of instructional approach. Providing more autonomy with lessons and requirements may allow teachers to incorporate aspects they are more comfortable with or have previously used in lessons. In addition, school leaders can offer relevant PD to teachers on hybrid and remote learning approaches. Allowing teachers to lead PD provides opportunities for them to learn from one another and can support self-efficacy (Dolighan & Owen, 2021; Kraft et al., 2021; Yoo, 2016). Finally, school leaders need to acknowledge all the work teachers put into practicing their craft. Providing praise and encouragement as teachers are forced to provide new instructional approaches may make a difference in how teachers feel about their instruction and their impact on students (Kraft et al., 2021).

What Do Teachers Need?

This was an important question to us, and one we believe school leaders should be asking themselves as they look to support teachers. To find possible answers, we held focus groups in the fall of 2022 and asked teachers this exact question: What do you need to be successful in the classroom? We found three themes that consistently emerged: (1) a need for respect; (2) support from both school administrators and parents; and (3) autonomy. See Figure 8.1 for a visual depiction of what teachers shared with us.

Respect

There are professions that carry a certain amount of respect, such as serving in the U.S. Armed Forces. Most people realize that we are all better off because some individuals are willing to sacrifice to keep us safe. During the pandemic, frontline workers were afforded similar respect. Most people stayed home and did not leave the house except for necessities, such as groceries. Police officers, firefighters, and hospital and medical staff were frontline workers who did not have the option to do their work from home. Society counted on them—especially doctors and nurses—to

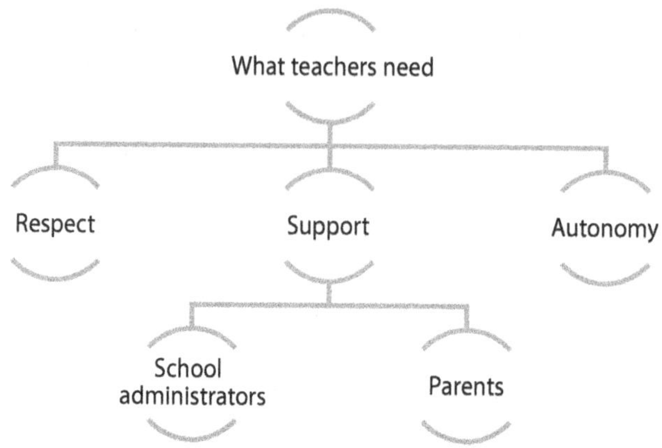

FIGURE 8.1. What teachers need.

continue to work throughout the pandemic, putting themselves at risk and often working longer shifts and more hours in the process (Kinder, 2020). New York City, the largest and most densely populated city in the United States, was one of the hardest hit cities in the country in the early months of the pandemic, both in terms of COVID-19 cases and related deaths (CDC, 2020). As a show of gratitude, every night at 7:00 P.M., residents would open windows or step out on balconies or rooftops to clap, cheer, bang pots and pans, and make noise as a token of appreciation to the frontline workers who were working and risking their lives every day (Jeffery, 2020). In short, frontline workers were considered heroes during the pandemic, and rightfully so.

When schools closed to in-person instruction and every child had to learn from home in March 2020, the job of being a teacher was not the only thing that became more taxing. The job of being a parent of a child who was enrolled in school also became more difficult—and this was particularly true for parents of younger students. During the pandemic, teachers were also among those initially heralded as heroes and as frontline workers (Nerlino, 2023). Many parents across the United States found themselves in awe of the efforts that teachers were putting in to ensure that their children kept learning through the crisis.* However, as the fall of 2020 approached and school districts across the country were

*This was not universally true; some parents found themselves quite disappointed in their school's efforts during this time (e.g., Sonnenschein & Stites, 2021).

deciding whether to reopen their schools for in-person learning, teachers were often disappointed in one of the central reasons touted for doing so—that their students' parents needed child care so they could work. This was articulated in a July 2020 *USA Today* opinion piece:

> The case for reopening schools and daycare centers during the pandemic is strong. Reopening them would provide *much needed child care for parents and other caregivers who need to work* (emphasis added), help feed the 30 million U.S. students who rely on low-cost or free school meals, and prevent further inequitable learning losses. (Wong & Faherty, 2020)

To be fair, the authors of that piece list several other reasons for reopening schools, including ones we have articulated in previous chapters, such as preventing learning loss. They also go on to outline some of the challenges that came with reopening schools, such as the need to quarantine when there were positive COVID-19 cases. Our point is not to pick on the authors of that piece. However, for many teachers who poured their hearts and souls into their classrooms for years, all they heard was that they were glorified child care—and that understandably hurt morale. This point is summarized by a quote from a high school teacher from Texas shared in one of our focus groups:

> "It'd be nice if society thought we did something other than babysitting. The lack of respect has been huge. You know, it used to be: 'Oh, you're a teacher! Thank you for what you do. I so admire people who give themselves to our children. Thank you.' And now it's like . . . 'Why would you do such a terrible job?' "

Teachers spend years perfecting their craft, learning how to create lessons that move students academically. They believe, and as former teachers we agree, that they deserve respect for their efforts beyond their utility as free child care.

Support from School Administrators and Parents

The teachers with whom we spoke also commented that they needed the support of principals and administrators in order to be successful in the classroom. A middle school math teacher from Wisconsin taught in a school that changed administrations during the pandemic. He compared his current administration with the previous one in terms of how they communicated with teachers and staff. "I've been in schools where they . . . send things out at 8:00 P.M. and we get [to school] at 7:00 A.M. and [they] say, 'Why haven't you seen this yet?' I think my current administration is very supportive. They limited a lot of communications at night and understood [our] boundaries. . . . " Similarly, an elementary school teacher from Virginia described what it meant to be supported in her work:

> "I definitely found . . . when I have a lot of administrative support, the school is a much happier place to be and an easier place to work. When I feel known and supported and I feel that my kids are known and cared for at an administrative level, it is a lot easier to do my job. I don't feel like I'm screaming into the void. There are people listening and there are people to help."

The same teacher described how it felt not to have the support of her administrators: "I didn't have that last year and it was horrible. It was really hard to come back this year." Feeling support from administrators was not simply necessary to be a successful teacher; it was a baseline requirement to want to continue in the profession.

The teachers we spoke with also said that it was important to have supportive parents in order to be successful as a teacher, though most of the examples they shared were of situations in which they did not feel supported by their students' parents. Far from the frontline-worker praise they received at the start of the pandemic, 2 years later, teachers described feeling worn down. A first-grade teacher from Massachusetts said, "I think a lot of us felt very beat up by the previous year [2021–2022]. The school board was at us, parents were at us. . . . I think we felt very underappreciated." Other teachers mentioned that the lack of support came from struggles to get responses when they made efforts to communicate with parents. For example, a middle school math teacher from Wisconsin said, "If I reached out to a parent with a concern and they responded to me, they generally responded positively. But most of the time I didn't get much of a response from parents, which was frustrating when the [administrators] say you have to contact parents." Other teachers described feeling as if they were "walking on eggshells" to keep from upsetting parents. A middle school teacher from Arizona gave an example of the tensions between balancing parents' wishes and the realities of school:

> "I think one of the concerns I have is the way that parents see us. I'm always afraid that I'm going to tick a parent off, and I don't feel like I should feel that way. So, yesterday, my teammate was out and we split her class. So, I have 40 kids in my room. One of the kids is not supposed to be in a room of over 25 kids because the parents don't want them around that many people because of COVID. The kid still wears a mask at school, and we've been without masks here in Arizona for a year or something like that, right? So, I'm talking to this kid and say, 'Hey, I heard that your mom doesn't want you in a big group. There's going to be 40 kids in here, so I found someplace else for you to do your work.' Mom is ticked because we singled her out. So, it's like damned if you do, damned if you don't."

This teacher was attempting to accommodate her student's parents' requests, and in doing so was still met with complaints. In the end, teachers need the support of all stakeholders to move students academically. If parents and administrators can respond positively to teacher communication, it is likely that students will have more opportunities to grow and learn throughout the year.

Teacher Autonomy

Finally, teachers pointed out that in order to be successful, they needed to have the autonomy to make instructional decisions that best served the needs of their students. Teaching is both a science and an art, and teachers who have the creative space to design lessons that engage their students are less burned out, are more satisfied with their work, and have better morale and mental health (Marshall, Neugebauer, et al., 2023; Pressley, Marshall, Love, & Neugebauer, 2022). Several of the teachers with whom we spoke brought up situations in which they did not feel they had autonomy, often when they were told to perform tasks that they did not see as relevant to achieving their academic goals in the classroom or being asked to implement a scripted curriculum. A high school teacher from Southern California shared with us that an issue she and her colleagues faced was constantly being asked to implement a new initiative, only to have administrators change their minds after a short period of time. She said, "[Our school leaders] keep introducing these new initiatives and we get completely trained on them, and then they're like, 'never mind.' It gets a little tricky trying to keep up." The time spent attending these trainings and planning to implement these initiatives was time this teacher did not have to grade, plan lessons, or do other tasks more immediately related to her teaching. A secondary teacher from New York was in the same focus group as the California teacher and remarked that he was grateful for the autonomy and flexibility his administrators afforded him and his colleagues—especially when they were doing hybrid teaching during the 2020–2021 school year. He said:

> "I can't imagine trying to work in an environment where I would have admins breathing down my neck every day . . . questioning my every pedagogical decision at the same time as I'm trying to teach half my kids one day, half the next, then all of them at once on Zoom a third day. You know, I'm thankful every day that I had the ability to basically do what I needed to do in the moment to get my kids through the year the best I could."

An elementary teacher from Massachusetts echoed those sentiments: "[my principal] was a teacher herself [and] she firmly believed in staff having more autonomy and trusting that we are professionals." A middle school social studies teacher from Alabama similarly commented, "We were really told what we needed to do, and then it was hands off and get a hold of me if you need something. If we ever needed something, we got a hold of them and that happened. I don't ever think I felt pushed back against [sic]." Just as any professional wants to be able to exercise his or her individual expertise in his or her work, teachers do as well. Findings from our survey research suggest that teachers who report having more autonomy in the classroom are more satisfied with their jobs, have better morale, and are less burned out (Marshall, Neugebauer, et al., 2023; Pressley et al., in press). Teachers who have more autonomy are also more likely to still be in the classroom 3 years later. In short, professional autonomy matters, and it matters quite a bit.

We followed up our focus groups with an additional, brief survey that we administered to teachers in October 2022. We posted the same open-ended question to teachers: "What do teachers need in order to be successful in the classroom?" We received 99 usable responses. Our findings were in line with the responses of the teachers we spoke to in focus groups. The most common unprompted response teachers gave for what they needed to be successful was a supportive administration

(36.4%). Being supported by students' parents was the third most common response (25.3%). Teachers also commented that smaller class sizes and more staffing would help them succeed (29.2%). This was especially important given the context of the pandemic, when teachers were frequently asked to cover their colleagues' classes during their planning periods. Having additional resources (25.3%), better support handling disruptive student behavior (22.2%), and more time (22.2%) were also listed as top-line issues that mattered to teachers. The latter two tend to go hand in hand. McShane (2022) shared findings from a national survey of teachers. The survey revealed that 58% of teachers reported having instructional time interrupted by student discipline issues in the preceding school day and that, of those who reported having interruptions, 86.5% reported having more than one disruption (McShane, 2022). Additionally, 25% of teachers reported spending 3 or more hours per day handling student disciplinary issues, which, over the span of a 180-day school year, is the equivalent of 18 full school days lost. This represents lost time in the classroom; however, it also is time that teachers could spend completing other tasks as well.

Interestingly, increased pay was the seventh most common response from teachers, and more than two-thirds of those who did list "more pay" as something they needed to be successful listed one or more other items first. In the focus groups we did with teachers in the fall of 2022, "more pay" was almost never even brought up. As former teachers ourselves, we certainly are not suggesting that teachers should not be paid more. The Economic Policy Institute estimated that, in 2021, teachers earned 23.5% less pay than other professionals with similar education (Allegretto, 2022). An analysis from the Fordham Institute notes that this gap is made up in part by teachers having 9–10% better benefits than the comparison group (Murray, 2022); however, the gap remains all the same. Our findings suggest, though, that if none of the other above-described issues were addressed (e.g., administrative support), giving teachers a pay raise alone would not lead to greater long-term teacher satisfaction with their jobs. Just over 6% of our sample discussed respect from society/public trust as something that they needed to be successful. See Table 8.2 for a list of what teachers reported needing to succeed in the classroom.

In a similar study, Andrew Pendola (2022b) conducted focus groups with teachers in Alabama to learn what teachers want and need to stay

TABLE 8.2. What Teachers Say They Need

	N	%
Administrative support	36	36.4
More staffing/smaller class sizes	29	29.2
Parent support	25	25.3
Additional resources	25	25.3
Support with disruptive behavior	22	22.2
More time (tasks other than planning)	22	22.2
Better pay	21	21.2
More planning time	20	20.2
Greater professional autonomy	12	12.1
Fewer extra duties	9	9.1
Public trust	6	6.1
Less paperwork	4	4.0
Less political interference	4	4.0
Less professional development	4	4.0
Additional mental health resources	4	4.0
Patience	4	4.0
Students who are willing to learn	4	4.0

in teaching. The results showed that teachers wanted school leaders to respect their time and their professional opinions. Specifically, teachers shared their ideas about ways that school leaders could provide purposeful autonomy and organizational care. Some of the teacher suggestions included blocking and respecting teacher time, as mentioned in Chapter 5, but also included the following:

- Building noninstructional responsibilities (e.g., IEP meetings, team planning, lunch or bus duty) into specific times and routines and include staff and administrators in duties
- Demonstrating that additional responsibilities (e.g., assessments, new curricular objectives) will be offset with the removal of other responsibilities

- Allocating a small discretionary materials fund ($100–300) for each teacher that does not require paperwork to use
- Ensuring that paperwork (e.g., purchase orders, permission forms, discipline referrals) is checked, cleared, and filed by office staff rather than by the teacher
- Implementing software that simplifies recording student attendance
- Simplifying discipline procedures and supports to limit disruptions and maintain focus on the class (e.g., supervised reflection room, centralized referral forms)
- Clearly defining and regularly outlining teachers' job duties, and explicitly acknowledging and providing support for conflicting role directives (e.g., managing 30 or more students while giving instruction to every student, ensuring high achievement while teaching to every student's needs) (pp. 17–18)

Here, we fully agree with Pendola's recommendations and find them to be realistic and doable. We would encourage school leaders to reflect on their district and building policies and to establish procedures that will support teachers rather than make their jobs more difficult.

In addition, Pendola (2022b) suggested leadership and organizational changes that would support teachers:

- Leadership and staff should demonstrate that the decision-making priority is ensuring quality instruction, not making administrative tasks easier for the district or front office.
- Leadership should demonstrate attempts to protect teachers from out-of-touch or misaligned policy and explicitly recognize such misalignment.
- Leadership should ensure that directives (e.g., new literacy strategy) are thought through in terms of implementation, rather than placing the onus for decisions on the classroom teacher.
- Leadership should ensure that all administration and staff share responsibility and offer support for assessment days and protocols. (p. 18)

Once again, we fully support these suggestions and believe that these small changes will not interrupt the organization or daily operations of a school district or school. We believe that making these changes will have a positive impact on teachers and students.

How Not to Support Teachers

Throughout this book, we have made the case that it is clear that the pandemic has had a major impact on teachers. Though we have focused and will continue to focus on how school leaders can support teachers, we would be remiss not to provide evidence of what *not* supporting teachers looks like. One example of this was a social media post shared by multiple teachers from an urban school district in the Mid-Atlantic region of the United States that tragically faced a school shooting. Although these events have become far too common in recent years, this one was particularly troubling. Here, a first-grade teacher who did not receive the necessary support that she and other teachers asked for when dealing with student behavior was the victim. The teacher had previously reported to administrators that one of her students brought bullets to school, to no avail. A week later, the 6-year-old student took a gun out of his bag and shot the teacher in the middle of class. This was after school administrators had received a warning of the gun being at school three times on the day of the incident and after the student had assaulted two staff members the same day (Eckstine, 2023; Natanson & Jouvenal, 2023). In the wake of this tragic event, the now-former school superintendent's first response to teachers and staff members was to send a list of "Tips for Teachers Who Have Concerns about Student Behavior"—a message that was quickly shared and panned on social media by many of the school district's teachers.

The superintendent's "tips" encouraged teachers to face their fears and "take time out to breathe"; practice mindfulness by seeking out helpful books and podcasts; and make sure students understand clear boundaries and don't cross them—all in the immediate aftermath of one of their colleagues being shot by a 6-year-old!

To put it mildly, the district's employees did not receive this well. Telling teachers to face their fears, "utilize a buddy teacher," and seek out podcasts about positive thinking was insulting. In short, this was an altogether inadequate first effort to support teachers immediately following an emergency situation. Unsurprisingly, many teachers voiced their discontent across social media platforms and at the next school board meeting, which included more than 3 hours of open-forum comments to the board and superintendent. From our perspective, this response indicates that the district leader, in this case, the district superintendent, was incredibly out of touch with the teachers in the district. The findings from our research are clear—teachers need support from their administrators, and when they don't have that, they become less satisfied with their jobs, feel less efficacious in their work, experience reduced morale and increased burnout, and ultimately consider pursuing other career opportunities.

CASE STUDY: AMANDA

Amanda (a pseudonym) was one of the teachers who participated in the focus groups we conducted in August and September 2022. She is a 10th-grade biology teacher at a charter school in Sacramento, California. The focus group included her, a teacher from Las Vegas, Nevada, and another teacher from a small town in Kansas. In each focus group we conducted, our first question was open-ended: "Tell me about last school year." In this focus group, the other two teachers shared their experiences first. What they said was similar to what we heard from a number of teachers with whom we spoke. They complained about a lack of communication from school and district leadership and policies changing at a moment's notice with little input from teachers. They shared common frustrations with resources, insufficient time to do their work, and disengaged students. When it was Amanda's turn, she began by expressing how sorry she was to learn what teaching was like for the other two in her focus group. Her experience had been vastly different. It would be easy to write this book and catalog the litany of things that have gone wrong during and since the pandemic. However, we believe it is also important to learn from people and places that are finding success in the classroom. So we conducted an additional interview with Amanda to learn more about her school environment and experience teaching during the pandemic.

What Amanda told us was very much in line with what our survey showed that teachers need—administrative and parental support, resources, time, and professional autonomy. She consistently described the educators in her building as "teachers as designers." This was a phrase she used several times throughout our conversation with her. We asked what she meant by that, and she said the following:

> "I have a lot of freedom because that's what my school is all about. We have this thing called *teachers as designers*. It's one of our fundamental pillars. There's a lot of trust, and autonomy given to us to bring our best selves, our best thinking, our best ideas, and we have a lot of freedom to be able to move within that space. I call it 'playing

> in a sandbox.' So, I'm given a sandbox, and of course, there's barriers to my sandbox. I still have standards. I still have my content that I'm responsible for covering. But I get to get there how I want."

One example of this was a partnership the school had with a municipal wildlife preserve. Amanda was able to secure some funding for buses and took her students to the preserve several times each semester. An employee at the preserve informed Amanda that they had installed game cameras that needed monitoring; however, they did not have the personnel to be able to adequately do that. So, one of the tasks her students completed when they were at the park was to review the camera footage. She said, "I get to take my students out to this preserve, and we get to go hike around. We're doing species counts of all of the plants. We're looking at the game trail cameras and getting kids out hiking, and it's ridiculously fun." Students get to apply what they have learned in the classroom, and, as Amanda put it, "everything they are learning in class [becomes] very, very real." She also describes this as a successful service-learning project in which the data that the students are collecting matter and are actively used by park personnel.

Amanda describes the parents at her school as being very supportive. Because her school is a charter school, no student is assigned to attend the school; parents enroll their kids there because they believe the school meets the needs of their children. During the 2021–2022 school year, when many teachers had to give up their planning periods to cover colleagues' classes when they were out, teachers at Amanda's school had a different experience. She told us that parents stepped up, completed the requirements for substitute teaching, and filled in to cover classes. Impressed by this, we asked whether that was because the school had been intentional with parental buy-in prior to the pandemic. She said that the opposite was actually true. After the school district canceled plans to build a new school in their neighborhood, parents banded together to found the school for their community and for their children. A strong connection with families has been at the center of the school since its inception, and, when the pandemic hit, those connections were already well established.

We asked Amanda about the professional time that is afforded the teachers in her school, and she said that they have an early release day every Wednesday. Every other week, this time is used for professional development. For the rest of the weeks, teachers are given the additional time to collaborate with one another, plan lessons, and handle other tasks related to their jobs. Daily, teachers are given 90-minute planning periods. She credits this professional time and the autonomy that she is given to teach, which allows her to use open-source resources, with her ability to do almost all of her professional work at school. Amanda explains that the professional development and planning time ensures that she and her colleagues are "all working toward a similar goal." She shared, "It's brilliant because it means I can leave at the end of the day. It's great. I'm a 17-year teacher, but I don't take anything home. I don't grade at home. I don't do anything at home. I have two little kids. When I leave, I leave. I'm done. And I have the time to [make that happen]."

Amanda believes that their ethos of teachers as designers, the professional time built into her schedule, and the support she receives from administrators and parents alike make her school an attractive place to work. And this matters in the context of shifting teacher labor markets (see Chapter 6). She describes her colleagues as "an impressive bunch of people," giving the example of the high school physics teacher who previously worked with NASA and had been into space. "She's our physics teacher . . . you're guaranteed to be in her class!" "I think we're all there because we can play in our sandboxes." She and her colleagues feel supported and have the freedom to be creative in the classroom. We said that her school sounded just about perfect, with a bit of skepticism. Amanda rebutted:

> "We're supported and the kids are supported. Things are not perfect. They are not. We are growing and there are growing pains. But it feels like a safe place to make mistakes . . . to try something and not be perfect at it—which I feel like maybe isn't true for my colleagues that teach in [traditional] public schools."

Amanda's school has highly motivated parents and is a school of choice to which parents apply for their children to attend. We understand that is not the case everywhere. However, we maintain that there are important lessons to be learned from Amanda and her school.

* * *

Throughout the pandemic, research has demonstrated that teacher self-efficacy declined, and this decline has been a major factor leading to burnout. School leaders should prioritize supporting teachers as schools return to normal and must understand that there are right and wrong ways to support teachers. School leaders who are out of touch with their teachers' needs may end up hurting teachers more than helping. The teachers we have spoken with want to be respected as professionals and have their time protected. In addition, teachers need to feel supported by administrators and parents regarding their classroom decisions. Teachers want and need to be trusted as professionals to make the best decisions for their students rather than being micromanaged from the top down. Echoing Pendola's (2022b) findings, many of the things that school leaders can do to support their teachers are simple, don't cost additional money, and are effective ways to keep teachers satisfied with their jobs and in the classrooms. When we conducted our focus groups and asked teachers the simple question that this chapter focuses on ("What do you need to be successful?"), one of the most common initial responses we received from our participants was, "Thank you for asking that. No one ever asks us that question." To the extent that is true, that is a shame.

Chapter 9

Where Do We Go from Here?

Lessons Learned from the Pandemic

When we set out to write this book, we were interested in learning what happened in K–12 education in the aftermath of the COVID-19 pandemic. The crisis represented the greatest disruption to American schooling in its history, and we felt it worthwhile to try to learn from this moment. The COVID-19 pandemic has been difficult for students and teachers alike, and we have attempted to highlight a pair of, at times, intersecting and dueling claims regarding the lessons that should be gleaned from the past few years.

First, looking back on the pandemic, long-term school closures were a mistake, possibly the biggest educational policy mistake of the past century. Students suffered substantial learning loss, have substantially worse mental health on average than ever before, and have suffered socially as a result of being forced to live and learn apart from others during the crisis. These facts are especially glaring when taken together with the fact that children did not suffer greatly from the COVID-19 virus itself (e.g., Lee et al., 2020). Although we acknowledge the tremendous challenges of making policy (and practical) decisions during a time of widespread fear and rapidly evolving information, we maintain that school reopening decisions should have been driven by data and little else. Three countries never closed elementary schools (Iceland, Sweden, and Taiwan*; Viner et al., 2021), and Sweden was among the only countries in the world that did not suffer academic learning loss during the pandemic (Patrinos, 2023).

*Taiwan did not close its schools when the initial outbreak took place in early 2020 (National Academies of Sciences, Engineering, and Medicine, 2020). However, they eventually did close schools due to COVID-19 in the spring of 2022 (Everington, 2022).

In many jurisdictions in the United States, schools remained closed long after evidence suggested that they were not vectors of transmission (i.e., the central reason for closing schools in the first place). This policy mistake will have consequences for children long after the mitigation efforts have subsided.

Second, the job of being a teacher was overwhelming for many during the pandemic. All teachers were forced to engage in emergency remote teaching for the final weeks of the 2019–2020 school year. As we outlined in Chapter 1, teachers who were teaching remotely had to figure out how to alter their entire curricula and deliver instruction online that they were used to teaching in a classroom. Teachers who were teaching in person also faced a range of challenges, from enforcing mitigation policies such as masking to dealing with students who were quarantined. In addition, teachers worked longer hours and had to go to extra lengths to do their jobs well since the start of the pandemic. All in all, the job of being a teacher has been unsustainably difficult since March 2020—and that, too, is an important takeaway. As school leaders and policymakers grapple with how to best move forward post-pandemic, they must be mindful of what teachers need—namely, time, support, and autonomy.

The teachers with whom we spoke in our focus groups and, to a lesser extent, the teachers we surveyed told us that they felt disrespected—especially during the pandemic era. In fairness to them, they were asked to go above and beyond during this time, and even small slights probably felt greater during the pandemic. As former teachers, we can empathize with that. However, a 2021 YouGov poll shows that teaching is among the top eight most respected professions in the United States and the seventh most respected profession worldwide (Smith & Ballard, 2021). So teachers claim disrespect, yet the public still indicates that they respect teachers' work—and not by a small margin. According to the YouGov poll, three-fourths of the U.S. population sees teaching as a respectful profession. How can both of these findings be true? It is possible that the public generically respects the teaching profession but acts in ways that teachers find dismissive.

So what might be the causes of the disrespect that teachers face? We speculate that the public has often conflated a few things. First, there is reason to believe that some in the public have conflated the actions of national teacher unions with teachers' views as a whole. As we discussed in Chapter 2, a clear relationship exists between union power and influence and prolonged school closures (Boyack & DeAngelis, 2023;

DeAngelis & Makridis, 2021; Flanders, 2021; Grossman et al., 2021; Hartney & Finger, 2020; Marianno, 2021). Evidence from public school enrollment patterns suggests that public schools only offering remote instruction in 2020–2021 experienced significant disenrollment (Dee et al., 2022), suggesting that many parents desired in-person learning. Parents whose views on school reopening were at odds with those of the national teacher unions may have conflated the special interest groups' position to represent all teachers—a position for which there is no evidence to our knowledge. Evidence suggests that teachers' views often align with the stances taken by their local unions but not necessarily with national union stances (Moe, 2011). Teachers tend to disagree most with national unions on political matters, and evidence suggests that teachers in general are more moderate politically than left- or right-leaning activists (Greene & Paul, 2021; Moe, 2011). In short, parents may have blamed teachers for policy stances that their child's teachers may not have even held.

The same is true for "woke" ideologies. There are certainly examples of teachers espousing extreme views, especially around issues of racial identity and sexuality, that some parents object to being taught in public schools (e.g., Greene & Paul, 2021). For example, a sixth-grade teacher in Orlando, Florida, was put on administrative leave after parents complained that he posted TikTok videos online. The videos depicted him forcing his White students to act as slaves to their Black classmates during Black History Month—fanning, feeding, and bowing before them (Algar, 2023). Regardless of the pedagogical point this teacher was attempting to make, most would agree that forcing middle school students of any race, for any reason, to act as slaves is unequivocally wrong. The school district's superintendent agreed and stated that he was "appalled by the behavior and judgment of the teacher," as well as by the "inappropriate" videos that were posted.

We make this point not to wade into debates over what is appropriate in classrooms. We'll leave that for others to address. Rather, we seek to make a larger point about teachers and what they have experienced during the pandemic. A January 2023 report from the Center for Reinventing Public Education found that almost one in three school district administrators reported that their teachers received verbal or written threats from the public over controversial topics since the start of the 2021–2022 school year (Jochim, Diliberti, Schwartz, Destler, & Hill, 2023). Casey, the teacher we feature in the case study at the conclusion of Chapter 6, discussed this when we interviewed her. She pointed out that though most parents were supportive, some families "undermined" her role as a teacher. She shared her frustration about this with us. "I am a professional and yes, you can trust me to teach your child, and no I am not indoctrinating them. I am not in this job to harm your child—physically, emotionally, or academically, I am in this job because I love [kids and teaching]." Are "woke" incidents such as the one described in the preceding paragraph outliers, or are they indicative of broader trends in public education? The evidence suggests that teachers are generally not ideologues, and it would be a mistake to overly generalize stories of teachers behaving poorly to represent the judgment and behavior of most teachers (Greene & Paul, 2021; Pondiscio, 2023). Though extreme cases do exist, our research suggests that most teachers truly just want what is best for their students.

Another reason teachers may feel disrespected is that they are often the messengers and the first contact for parents. As such, teachers often take the brunt of parent frustrations when the matter is often out of the teacher's hands altogether. Mask-wearing mandates and other safety protocols were examples of this during the pandemic. Teachers had to enforce school district-level decisions about masks, regardless of their personal views. Yet they were likely the first to hear complaints from parents who disagreed either way, whether it was a parent who wanted masks in a setting where they were not required or a parent who opposed them in a setting where they were. Parents concerned with policy decisions would be better served to take them up with school or district administration, rather than venting their frustrations to teachers who likely lack the ability to address them.

In Chapter 4 we discussed student well-being, noting that many children and adolescents experienced diminished mental health during the COVID-19 pandemic (e.g., Marshall, 2022b; Naff et al., 2022). There is evidence that older adults fared better in terms of their mental health, but many younger adults struggled during the crisis (e.g., Park, Choi, & Kim, 2022). Adults—including many teachers and parents alike—faced cognitive concerns about food insecurity, loss of income, and going out in public during the health crisis, including those who did not have a mental health condition prior to the pandemic (Holingue et al., 2020). There were also increases in adult anxiety and depression (Fitzpatrick, Harris, & Drawve, 2020; Holingue et al., 2020; Kessler et al., 2022; Park et al., 2022), both of which were more pronounced for adults ages 18–44, during the pandemic (Czeisler et al., 2021). Czeisler and colleagues (2021) were interested in learning whether differences existed in mental health outcomes between parents of children under the age of 18 and those who were not parents. They found no difference in anxiety or depressive symptoms between adults who were parents; however, parents who were also caregivers of older adults had significantly increased odds of anxiety or depression compared with those who were just parents. Many adults also were consumed with fear of COVID-19, beyond what was reasonably warranted by data, and this, too, led to mental health consequences (Fitzpatrick et al., 2020). In short, many Americans were not the best versions of themselves during the pandemic. People did not always make the best decisions, assumed the worst in each other, and catastrophized situations (Haidt, 2022). A charitable take would assume that at least some of the poor decisions made and interactions that took place between people, including teachers and parents, were the result of some individuals simply not being their best selves.

* * *

Charles Payne (2008), Professor Emeritus at the University of Chicago, once wrote that "most discussion of educational policy and practice is dangerously disconnected from the daily realities of urban schools, especially the bottom-tier schools" (p. 5). This is especially prescient at this moment. Although Payne's remarks were made in reference to his work with Chicago Public Schools, the point holds true for schools beyond our urban centers. There indeed exists a disconnection between the debates between and among policymakers, academics, and pundits and what actually happens in our schools. Schools are navigating the post-pandemic era, which requires addressing the academic, mental health, and social consequences of COVID-19 policies. Policymakers and school leaders will need to make sure that they are listening to teachers and supporting them as they take on this important work. Researchers like us who study schools would be wise to spend more time in schools and focus on what matters if we hope to also make a difference.

Appendix

Overview of Methodology

Throughout this book, we have drawn on research that we have conducted over the course of the last few years, as well as the research of others. We have cited all of the work that has been done for the benefit of those who wish to learn more about how that work was conducted. We have also drawn on findings from three research efforts that, as of this writing, have not been published elsewhere: (1) focus groups conducted in August through September 2022; (2) a brief survey conducted in October 2022; and (3) a survey conducted in April and May 2023. Here we briefly describe those efforts. All three studies were approved by our IRBs, and all participants completed an informed consent form prior to participating.

Fall 2022 Focus Groups

We surveyed teachers in May 2022 (n = 830) as part of our research efforts. See Marshall, Neugebauer, Pressley, and Brown-Aliffi (2023) for an overview of the methodology. We asked teachers to leave an email address if they were interested in participating in follow-up focus groups, and more than 200 teachers did—representing about a quarter of our survey sample. We reached out to these teachers in early August 2022 and asked them whether they were still willing to participate. Ultimately, we ended up conducting focus groups with 40 teachers representing 24 states. A plurality of participants were White (87.5%), female (85.0%), and from the West Coast (20.0%). Focus group participants had been teaching for an average of 18.5 years, which makes them more experienced overall than the teachers who completed our initial survey (M = 13.26 years). See Table A.1 for descriptive statistics for the sample.

TABLE A.1. Descriptive Statistics for 2022 Focus Group Participants

	N	%	*M*	*SD*
Teaching experience			18.50	10.44
Race/ethnicity				
Black or African American	1	2.5		
Hispanic	2	5.0		
Pacific Islander or Native Hawaiian	1	2.5		
White	35	87.5		
More than one race	1	2.5		
Gender				
Female	34	85.0		
Male	6	15.0		
Region of United States				
Northeast	5	12.5		
Mid-Atlantic	7	17.5		
Southeast	6	15.0		
Midwest	7	17.5		
Rocky Mountains	1	2.5		
Southwest	6	15.0		
West Coast/Hawai'i	8	20.0		

All focus groups were conducted via Zoom, and they included teachers from multiple states and time zones—which was sometimes challenging to schedule. The focus groups lasted approximately 1 hour in length and were recorded and transcribed to ensure accuracy. We began each focus group the same way, asking participants generically about their experiences as teachers during the 2021–2022 school year. We did not wish to lead them in a particular direction; rather, we were interested in where they would take the conversation. We asked follow-up questions about student academics, social and emotional well-being, and technology use, if needed. In our May 2022 survey, we found that administrative support and teacher autonomy positively predicted teacher morale, burnout, and job satisfaction (Marshall, Neugebauer, Pressley, & Brown-Aliffi, 2023). Teachers with more support and autonomy also had better morale, were more satisfied with their jobs, and suffered less burnout. We shared these findings with participants and asked them to expand on them. We concluded the focus groups by asking teachers what they needed in order to be successful in the classroom. Their responses to this question form the basis for much of Chapter 8.

Data were analyzed using ATLAS.ti version 9. Codes were created a priori based on the focus group protocol. Additional codes were created based on the transcripts. Emerging themes were identified and reported.

October 2022 Survey

After conducting the focus groups, we decided that we would focus an entire chapter of this book on the question posed in Chapter 8—what do teachers need to be successful? As such, we decided to conduct a brief survey to learn the extent to which these findings mirrored what we heard from teachers during the focus groups. We posted a link to our survey on Facebook and on teacher- and education-related subreddit pages on Reddit. Ninety-nine teachers completed the survey. Similar to our previous survey, a majority of teachers were female (74.7%) and White (85.9%). Almost 1 in 6 participants was a special education teacher (17.3%). A plurality of teachers taught in traditional public schools (85.7%) that were located in suburban settings (43.4%) in the Southwest region of the United States (23.6%). See Table A.2 for descriptive statistics for the sample.

The survey was designed with brevity in mind. We asked the above-listed demographic questions, as well as three open-ended responses. Specifically, we asked teachers the following:

1. What do you need in order to be successful in the classroom?
2. What do your students need in order to be successful?
3. How are your students in terms of their social and emotional well-being?

Descriptive statistics were calculated using SPSS version 28. Qualitative data generated from the open-ended items were analyzed using ATLAS.ti version 23. Initial codes were created based on the focus group findings. Additional codes were created based on the transcripts. Emerging themes were identified and reported. Artificial intelligence was not used during analyses.*

Spring 2023 Survey

We conducted our final survey of teachers in the spring of 2023 to understand their experiences as teachers during the 2022–2023 school year. We invited teachers to participate in the research between April 20, 2023, and May 7, 2023. Participants had to be currently employed as teachers in the United States in order to be eligible to participate in the research. We shared a link to the survey to our personal networks in addition to posting it on social media sites (i.e., Facebook, Twitter, and Reddit). Those who participated were invited to share

*ATLAS.ti version 23 had released a beta version of AI Coding prior to these analyses.

TABLE A.2. Descriptive Statistics for the October 2022 Survey Sample

Variable	*N*	%
Gender (*n* = 99)		
Female	74	83.4
Male	23	15.2
Other	1	1.0
Race/ethnicity (*n* = 99)		
African American/Black	4	4.0
Hispanic	4	4.0
Middle Eastern/North African[a]	1	1.0
White/Caucasian	85	85.9
More than one race	5	2.2
Special education teacher (*n* = 98)	17	17.3
School type (*n* = 98)		
Traditional public school	84	85.7
Charter school	9	9.2
Private school	5	5.1
Geographic location (*n* = 99)		
Rural	14	14.1
Small town	10	10.1
Suburban	43	43.4
Urban	32	32.3
Region of the United States (*n* = 93)		
Northeast	11	11.8
Mid-Atlantic	15	16.1
Southeast	13	14.0
Midwest	14	15.1
Rocky Mountains	3	3.2
Southwest	22	23.7
West Coast/Hawai'i	15	16.1

[a]Self-described.

the link with other teachers they knew if they were so inclined. A total of 967 teachers completed a survey, the majority of whom were female (83.4%) and White (87.4%). About 1 in 6 teachers (15.7%) was a special education teacher, and almost two-thirds (65.6%) taught in a Title I school. A plurality of the study's participants taught in suburban schools (36.8%). See Table A.3 for descriptive statistics for the sample.

TABLE A.3. Descriptive Statistics for the May 2023 Survey Sample

Variable	*N*	%	*M*	*SD*
Age			40.47	10.38
Years of teaching experience			13.46	8.82
Gender				
Female	816	83.4		
Male	139	15.2		
Other	12	1.3		
Race/ethnicity				
African American/Black	39	4.3		
Asian American	10	1.1		
Hispanic	29	3.2		
Native American/Alaskan	2	0.2		
White/Caucasian	797	87.4		
More than one race	20	2.2		
Prefer not to answer	14	1.5		
Title I	593	65.7		
Special education teacher	143	15.7		
School type				
Traditional public school	803	88.0		
Magnet school	19	2.1		
Charter school	40	4.4		
Private school	47	5.2		
Microschool/learning pod	3	0.3		
Geographic location				
Rural	252	27.7		
Small town	141	15.5		
Suburban	335	36.8		
Urban	182	20.0		

References

Affouneh, S., Salha, S., & Khlaif, Z. N. (2020). Designing quality e-learning environments for emergency remote teaching in coronavirus crisis. *Interdisciplinary Journal of Virtual Learning in Medical Sciences, 11*(2), 135–137.

Agyapong, B., Brett-MacLean, P., Burback, L., Agyapong, V. I. O., & Wei, Y. (2023). Interventions to reduce stress and burnout among teachers: A scoping review. *International Journal of Environmental Research and Public Health, 20*(9), 5625.

Agyapong, B., Obuobi-Donkor, G., Burback, L., & Wei, Y. (2022). Stress, burnout, anxiety and depression among teachers: A scoping review. *International Journal of Environmental Research and Public Health, 19*(17), 10706.

Aktar, E., Majdandžić, M., de Vente, W., & Bögels, S. M. (2014). Parental social anxiety disorder prospectively predicts toddlers' fear/avoidance in a social referencing paradigm. *Journal of Child Psychology and Psychiatry and Allied Disciplines, 55*(1), 77–87.

Aktar, E., Nikolić, M., & Bögels, S. M. (2017). Environmental transmission of generalized anxiety disorder from parents to children: Worries, experiential avoidance, and intolerance of uncertainty. *Dialogues in Clinical Neuroscience, 19*(2), 137–147.

Algar, S. (2023, February 22). Florida teacher suspended for using kids as "political props," having White kids bow to Black classmates in TikTok videos. *https://nypost.com/2023/02/22/florida-teacher-suspended-for-using-kids-as-political-props-in-tiktok-videos.*

Allegretto, S. (2022, August 16). The teacher pay penalty has hit a new high. Economic Policy Institute. *www.epi.org/publication/teacher-pay-penalty-2022.*

Aloizou, V., Chasiotou, T., Retalis, S., Daviotis, T., & Koulouvaris, P. (2021). Remote learning for children with special education needs in the era of COVID-19: Beyond teleconferencing sessions. *Educational Media International, 58*(2), 181–201.

An, Y., Kaplan-Rakowski, R., Yang, J., Conan, J., Kinard, W., & Daughrity, L. (2021). Examining K–12 teachers' feelings, experiences, and perspectives regarding online teaching during the early stage of the COVID-19 pandemic. *Educational Technology Research and Development, 69*(5), 2589–2613.

Andrew, L. D., Parks, D. J., Nelson, L. A., & Phi Delta Kappa Commission on

Teacher/Faculty Morale. (1985). *Administrator's handbook for improving faculty morale*. Phi Delta Kappa.

Anglum, J. C., & Park, A. (2021). Keeping up with the Joneses: District adoption of the 4-day school week in rural Missouri. *AERA Open, 7*, 23328584211002842.

Armitage, R., & Nellums, L. B. (2020). Considering inequalities in the school closure response to COVID-19. *Lancet Global Health, 8*(5), e644.

Asadullah, M. N., Bouhlila, D. S., Chan, S.-J., Draxler, A., Ha, W., Heyneman, S. P., . . . Yemini, M. (2023). A year of missed opportunity: Post-COVID learning loss—A renewed call to action. *International Journal of Educational Development, 99*, 102770.

Auger, K. A., Shah, S. S., Richardson, T., Hartley, D., Hall, M., Warniment, A., . . . Thomson, J. E. (2020). Association between statewide school closure and COVID-19 incidence and mortality in the US. *Journal of the American Medical Association, 324*(9), 859–870.

Bacher-Hicks, A., Chi, O. L., & Orellana, A. (2022). Two years later: How COVID-19 has shaped the teacher workforce (EdWorkingPaper No. 22–572). Retrieved from Annenberg Institute, Brown University. *www.edworkingpapers.com/ai22-572.*

Back to school and back to normal. Or at least close enough. (2022, October 6). *www.nytimes.com/2022/10/06/education/learning/students-schools-colleges-pandemic-life.html.*

Baker, C. N., Peele, H., Daniels, M., Saybe, M., Whalen, K., Overstreet, S., & the New Orleans Trauma-Informed Schools Learning Collaborative. (2021). The experience of COVID-19 and its impact on teachers' mental health, coping, and teaching. *School Psychology Review, 50*(4), 491–504.

Bandura, A. (1997). *Self-efficacy: The exercise of control.* Freeman.

Barnes, G., Crowe, E., & Schaefer, B. (2007). The cost of teacher turnover in five school districts: A pilot study (ED497167). National Commission on Teaching and America's Future. *https://eric.ed.gov/?id=ED497176.*

Baron, E. J., Goldstein, E. G., & Wallace, C. T. (2020). Suffering in silence: How COVID-19 school closures inhibit the reporting of child maltreatment. *Journal of Public Economics, 190*, 104258.

Bartek, N., Peck, J. L., Garzon, D., & Van Cleve, S. (2021). Addressing the clinical impact of COVID-19 on pediatric mental health. *Journal of Pediatric Health Care, 35*(4), 377–386.

Bartlett, L. (2022). Specifying hybrid models of teachers' work during COVID-19. *Educational Researcher, 51*(2), 152–155.

Bastian, K. C., & Fuller, S. C. (2022). Teacher and principal attrition during the COVID-19 pandemic in North Carolina: Updated analyses for the 2021–22 school year. Education Policy Initiative at Carolina. *https://epic.unc.edu/wp-content/uploads/sites/1268/2022/09/Teacher-and-Principal-Attrition-During-COVID-19.pdf.*

Bastian, K. C., & Fuller, S. C. (2023). Educator attrition and mobility during the COVID-19 pandemic. *Educational Researcher*, 0013189X231187890.

Beck, D. E., Maranto, R., & Lo, W.-J. (2014). Determinants of student and parent satisfaction at a cyber charter school. *Journal of Educational Research, 107*(3), 209–216.

Bhopal, S., Bagaria, J., & Bhopal, R. (2020). Children's mortality from COVID-19 compared with all-deaths and other relevant causes of death: Epidemiological information for decision-making by parents, teachers, clinicians, and policy-makers. *Public Health, 185*, 19–20.

Bignardi, G., Dalmaijer, E. S., Anwyl-Irvine, A. L., Smith, T. A., Siugzdaite, R., Uh, S., & Astle, D. E. (2021). Longitudinal increases in childhood depression symptoms during the COVID-19 lockdown. *Archives of Disease in Childhood, 106*, 791–797.

Billaudeau, N., Alexander, S., Magnard, L., Temam, S., & Vercambre, M. N. (2022). What levers to promote teachers' wellbeing during the COVID-19 pandemic and beyond: Lessons learned from a 2021 online study in six countries. *International Journal of Environmental Research and Public Health, 19*(15), 9151.

Borup, J., & Kennedy, K. (2017). The case for K–12 online learning. In R. A. Fox & N. K. Buchanan (Eds.), *The Wiley handbook of school choice* (pp. 403–420). Wiley.

Bottiani, J. H., Duran, C. A. K., Pas, E. T., & Bradshaw, C. P. (2019). Teacher stress and burnout in urban middle schools: Associations with job demands, resources, and effective classroom practices. *Journal of School Psychology, 77*, 36–51.

Bourne, R. A. (2021). *Economics in one virus: An introduction to economic reasoning through COVID-19.* Cato Institute.

Bower, M., Dalgarno, B., Kennedy, G. E., Lee, M. J. W., & Kenney, J. (2015). Design and implementation factors in blended synchronous learning environments: Outcomes from a cross-case analysis. *Computers and Education, 86*, 1–17.

Bowman, R. F. (1982). A "Pac-Man" theory of motivation: Tactical implications for classroom instruction. *Educational Technology, 22*(9), 14–16. *www.jstor.org/stable/44423699.*

Boyack, C., & DeAngelis, C. (2023). *Mediocrity: 40 ways government schools are failing today's students.* Libertas Press.

Braun, S. S., Roeser, R. W., & Mashburn, A. J. (2020). Results from a pre–post, uncontrolled pilot study of a mindfulness-based program for early elementary school teachers. *Pilot and Feasibility Studies, 6*(1), 178.

Brooks, S. K., Webster, R. K., Smith, L. E., Woodland, L., Wessely, S., Greenberg, N., & Rubin, G. J. (2020). The psychological impact of quarantine and how to reduce it: Rapid review of the evidence. *Lancet, 395*(10227), 912–920.

Bryant, J., Ram, S., Scott, D., & Williams, C. (2023, March 2). K–12 teachers are quitting. What would make them stay? *www.mckinsey.com/industries/education/our-insights/k-12-teachers-are-quitting-what-would-make-them-stay.*

Bullock's stay-at-home order lifted Monday with restrictions. (2020, April 22). *https://nbcmontana.com/news/coronavirus/bullocks-stay-at-home-order-lifted-monday-with-restrictions.*

Burke, M., & Kraut, R. E. (2016). The relationship between Facebook use and well-being depends on communication type and tie strength. *Journal of Computer-Mediated Communication, 21*(4), 265–281.

Camp, A. M., & Zamarro, G. (2022). Determinants of ethnic differences in school modality choices during the COVID-19 crisis. *Educational Researcher, 51*(1), 6–16.

Camp, A., Zamarro, G., & McGee, J. B. (2022). Changes in teachers' mobility and attrition in Arkansas during the first two years of the COVID-19 pandemic (EdWorking Paper No. 22-589). Retrieved from Annenberg Institute, Brown University. *www.edworkingpapers.com/sites/default/files/ai22-589.pdf.*

Camp, A., Zamarro, G., & McGee, J. B. (2023). Movers, switchers, and exiters: Teacher turnover during COVID-19 (EDRE Research Brief 2023-10). University of Arkansas College of Education and Health Professions. *https://edre.uark.edu/_resources/pdf/2022-23_turnover-research-brief.pdf.*

Cardullo, V., Wang, C.-h., Burton, M., & Dong, J. (2021). K–12 teachers' remote teaching self-efficacy during the pandemic. *Journal of Research in Innovative Teaching and Learning, 14*(1), 32–45.

Carpenter, D., & Dunn, J. (2020). We're all teachers now: Remote learning during COVID-19. *Journal of School Choice, 14*(4), 567–594.

Carpenter, D., & Dunn, J. (2022). Remote learning in rural America during COVID-19. In D. T. Marshall (Ed.), *COVID-19 and the classroom: How schools navigated the great disruption* (pp. 87–105). Lexington Books.

Carver-Thomas, D., Leung, M., & Burns, D. (2021, March). California teachers and COVID-19: How the pandemic is impacting the teacher workforce. *https://learningpolicyinstitute.org/sites/default/files/product-files/California_COVID_Teacher_Workforce_REPORT.pdf.*

Cash, C., Brinkmann, J., & Price, T. (2022). Superintendents' leadership during the pandemic. In D. T. Marshall (Ed.), *COVID-19 and the classroom: How schools navigated the great disruption* (pp. 123–143). Lexington Books.

CDC COVID-19 Response Team. (2020). Coronavirus disease 2019 in children—United States, February 12–April 2, 2020. *Morbidity and Mortality Weekly Report, 69*(14), 422–426.

Cena, L., Trainini, A., Zecca, S., Zappa, S. B., Cunegatti, F., & Buizza, C. (2022, March 8). Loneliness, affective disorders, suicidal ideation, and the use of psychoactive substances in a sample of adolescents during the COVID-19 pandemic: A cross-sectional study. *Journal of Child and Adolescent Psychiatric Nursing, 36*(3), 188–198.

Centers for Disease Control and Prevention (CDC). (2007). Interim pre-pandemic planning guidance: Community strategy for pandemic influenza mitigation in the United States—Early, targeted, layered use of nonpharmaceutical interventions. *www.cdc.gov/flu/pandemic-resources/pdf/community_mitigation-sm.pdf.*

Centers for Disease Control and Prevention (CDC). (2020, August 27). Previous U.S. COVID-19 case data. *www.cdc.gov/coronavirus/2019-ncov/covid-data/previouscases.html.*

Centers for Disease Control and Prevention (CDC). (2022, October 5). Operational guidance for K–12 schools and early care and education programs to support safe in-person learning. *https://cdc.gov/coronavirus/2019-ncov/community/schools-childcare/k-12-childcare-guidance.html.*

Centers for Disease Control and Prevention (CDC). (2023a). Youth Risk Behavior Survey data summary and trends report. *https://youth.gov/feature-article/2011-2021-yrbs-data-summary-and-trends-report.*

Centers for Disease Control and Prevention (CDC). (2023b, January 30). Technical notes: Provisional death counts for COVID-19. *https://cdc.gov/nchs/nvss/vsrr/covid19/tech_notes.htm.*

Centers for Disease Control and Prevention (CDC). (2023c, May 11). People with certain medical conditions. *www.cdc.gov/coronavirus/2019-ncov/need-extra-precautions/people-with-medical-conditions .*

Centers for Disease Control and Prevention (CDC). (2023d). COVID-19 diagnostic laboratory testing (PCR testing) time series. *https://healthdata.gov/dataset/COVID-19-Diagnostic-Laboratory-Testing-PCR-Testing/j8mb-icvb*

Center for New York City Affairs. (2023, May 10). Traditional schools are losing students. Here's the picture—and some prescriptions. *www.centernyc.org/urban-matters-2/traditional-schools-are-losing-students-the-picture-and-some-prescriptions.*

Chan, M.-k., Sharkey, J. D., Lawrie, S. I., Arch, D. A. N., & Nylund-Gibson, K. (2021). Elementary school teacher well-being and supportive measures amid COVID-19: An exploratory study. *School Psychology, 36*(6), 533–545.

Chen, F., Zheng, D., Liu, J. Gong, Y., Guan, Z., & Lou, D. (2020). Depression and anxiety among adolescents during COVID-19: A cross-sectional study. *Brain, Behavior, and Immunity, 88*, 36–38.

Cheng, G., Liu, J., Yang, Y., Wang, Y., Xiong, X., & Liu, G. (2021). Stressful events and adolescents' suicidal ideation during the COVID-19 epidemic: A moderated mediation model of depression and parental educational involvement. *Children and Youth Services Review, 127*, 106047.

Cherokee County School District. (2023). Digital learning days. *www.cherokeek12.net/divisions/curriculum-instruction/digital-learning-days-inclement-weather.*

Christakis, D. A. (2020). School reopening: The pandemic issue that is not getting its due. *JAMA Pediatrics, 174*(10), 928.

Christakis, D. A., Van Cleve, W., & Zimmerman, F. J. (2020). Estimation of US children's educational attainment and years of life lost associated with primary school closures during the coronavirus disease 2019 pandemic. *JAMA Network Open, 3*(11), e2028786.

Chu, L., & Lake, R. (2021, March). *The kids are (really) not alright: A synthesis of COVID-19 student surveys.* Arizona State University Center on Reinventing Public Education. *https://crpe.org/the-kids-are-really-not-alright-a-synthesis-of-covid-19-student-surveys*

Clark, S., McGrane, A., Boyle, N., Joksimovic, N., Burke, L., Rock, N., & O'Sullivan, K. (2021). "You're a teacher, you're a mother, you're a worker": Gender inequality during COVID-19 in Ireland. *Gender, Work and Organization, 28*(4), 1352–1362.

Coffey, M. (2023, May 4). *How lax grading policies make classrooms chaotic.* Thomas B. Fordham Institute. *https://fordhaminstitute.org/national/commentary/how-lax-grading-policies-make-classrooms-chaotic.*

Cohodes, S., Goldhaber, D., Hill, P., Ho, A., Kogan, V., Polikoff, M., . . . West, M. (2022). Student achievement gaps and the pandemic: A new review of evidence from 2021–2022. Arizona State University Center on Reinventing Public Education. *https://crpe.org/student-achievement-gaps-and-the-pandemic-a-new-review-of-evidence-from-2021-2022.*

Collie, R. J., Shapka, J. D., & Perry, N. E. (2012). School climate and social–emotional learning: Predicting teacher stress, job satisfaction, and teaching efficacy. *Journal of Educational Psychology, 104*(4), 1189–1204.

Collins, J. E. (2023). The politics of re-opening schools: Explaining public preferences reopening schools and public compliance with reopening orders during the COVID-19 pandemic. *American Politics Research, 51*(2).

Coughlan, R. J. (1970). Dimensions of teacher morale. *American Educational Research Journal, 7*(2), 221–234.

Cuban, L. (1986). *Teachers and machines: The classroom use of technology since 1920.* Teachers College Press.

Czeisler, M. E., Wiley, J. F., Facer-Childs, E. R., Robbins, R., Weaver, M. D., Barger, L. K., . . . Rajaratnam, S. M. W. (2021). Mental health, substance use, and suicidal ideation during a prolonged COVID-19-related lockdown in a region with low SARS-CoV-2 prevalence. *Journal of Psychiatric Research, 140*, 533–544.

Darling-Aduana, J., Woodyard, H. T., Sass, T. R., & Barry, S. S. (2022). Learning-mode choice, student engagement, and achievement growth during the COVID-19 pandemic. *AERA Open, 8*.

Dasgupta, S. (2022). School in the time of COVID. *Monash Bioethics Review, 40*, 120–144.

Davies, R. S., & West, R. E. (2014). Technology integration in schools. In J. M. Spector, M. D. Merrill, J. Elen, & M. J. Bishop (Eds.), *Handbook of research on educational communications and technology* (pp. 841–853). Springer.

Davis, C. R., Grooms, J., Ortega, A., Rubalcaba, J. A.-A., & Vargas, E. (2021). Distance learning and parental mental health during COVID-19. *Educational Researcher, 50*(1), 61–64.

DeAngelis, C. A., & Makridis, C. A. (2021). Are school reopening decisions related to union influence? *Social Science Quarterly, 102*(5), 2266–2284.

DeAngelis, C. A., & Makridis, C. A. (2022). Are school reopening decisions related to funding? Evidence from over 12,000 districts during the COVID-19 pandemic. *Journal of School Choice, 16*(3), 454–476.

Dee, T. S., Huffaker, E., Phillips, C., & Sagara, E. (2022). The revealed preferences for school reopening: Evidence from public-school disenrollment. *American Educational Research Journal, 60*(5), 916–940.

Dembo, M. H., & Gibson, S. (1985). Teachers' sense of efficacy: An important factor in school improvement. *Elementary School Journal, 86*(2), 173–184.

de Ree, J., Maggioni, M. A., Paulle, B., Rossignoli, D., Ruijs, N., & Walentek, D. (2023). Closing the income–achievement gap? Experimental evidence from high-dosage tutoring in Dutch primary education. *Economics of Education Review, 94*, 102383.

de Souza, T. H., Nada, J. A., Nogueira, R. J. N., Pereira, R. M., & Brandão, M. B. (2020). Clinical manifestations of children with COVID-19: A systematic review. *Pediatric Pulmonology, 55*(8), 1892–1899.

Dietrichson, J., Bøg, M., Filges, T., & Jørgensen, A. K. (2017). Academic interventions for elementary and middle school students with low socioeconomic status: A systematic review and meta-analysis. *Review of Educational Research, 87*(2), 243–282.

Digital Learning Collaborative (n.d.). *Alabama digital learning landscape. www.digitallearningcollab.com/state-profiles/alabama.* Diliberti, M. K., Schwartz, H. L., & Grant, D. (2021). Stress topped the reasons why public school teachers quit, even before COVID-19. *www.rand.org/pubs/research_reports/RRA1121-2.html.*

Dolighan, T., & Owen, M. (2021). Teaching efficacy for online teaching during the COVID-19 pandemic. *Brock Education Journal, 30*(1), 95–116.

Donohue, J. M., & Miller, E. (2020). COVID-19 and school closures. *Journal of the American Medical Association, 324*(9), 845–847.

Dooley, D. G., Simpson, J. N., & Beers, N. S. (2020). Returning to school in the era of COVID-19. *JAMA Pediatrics, 174*(11), 1028–1029.

Duckworth, A. L., Kautz, T., Defnet, A., Satlof-Bedrick, E., Talamas, S., Lira, B., & Steinberg, L. (2021). Students attending school remotely suffer socially, emotionally, and academically. *Educational Researcher, 50*(7), 479–482.

Durlak, J. A., Weissberg, R. P., Dymnicki, A. B., Taylor, R. D., & Schellinger, K. B. (2011). The impact of enhancing students' social and emotional learning: A meta-analysis of school-based universal interventions. *Child Development, 82*(1), 405–432.

Dylan, B. (1965). The times they are a-changin' [Song]. On *The times they are a-changin'*. Columbia Records.

Eckstine, H. (2023, June 13). Timeline: Everything we know about the shooting at Richneck and the aftermath. *www.wtkr.com/news/timeline-everything-we-know-about-the-shooting-at-richneck-and-its-aftermath.*

EdChoice. (2023a). Teens and their schooling preferences: A national polling report spring 2023. *https://edchoice.morningconsultintelligence.com/assets/221187.pdf.*

EdChoice. (2023b). Education savings accounts. *www.edchoice.org/school-choice/types-of-school-choice/education-savings-account.*

Edwards, D. S., Kraft, M. A., Christian, A., & Candelaria, C. A. (2022). *Teacher shortages: A unifying framework for understanding and predicting vacancies.* (EdWorking Paper No. 22–684). Retrieved from Annenberg Institute, Brown University.

EdWeek Research Center. (2022). 1st annual Merrimack College teacher survey: 2022 results. *www.edweek.org/research-center/reports/teaching-profession-in-crisis-national-teacher-survey.*

Elias, M. J., Zins, J. E., Weissberg, R. P., Frey, K. S., & Greenberg, M. T. (1997). *Promoting social and emotional learning: Guidelines for educators.* ASCD.

Ellis, W. E., Dumas, T. M., & Forbes, L. M. (2020). Physically isolated but socially connected: Psychological adjustment and stress among adolescents during the initial COVID-19 crisis. *Canadian Journal of Behavioural Science, 52*(3), 177–187.

Engzell, P., Frey, A., & Verhagen, M. D. (2021). Learning loss due to school closures during the COVID-19 pandemic. *Proceedings of the National Academy of Sciences, 118*(17), e2022376118.

Esposito, S., & Principi, N. (2020). School closure during the coronavirus disease 2019 (COVID-19) pandemic. *JAMA Pediatrics, 174*(10), 921–922.

European Centre for Disease Prevention and Control. (2020). Outbreak of novel coronavirus disease 2019 (COVID-19): Increased transmission globally—fifth update. *www.ecdc.europa.eu/sites/default/files/documents/RRA-outbreak-novel-coronavirus-disease-2019-increase-transmission-globally-COVID-19.pdf.*

Everington, K. (2022, April 1). 39 Taiwan schools declare closures due to COVID. *www.taiwannews.com.tw/en/news/4493640.*

Eykelbosh, A. (2021, November 17). A rapid review of the use of physical barriers in non-clinical settings and COVID-19 transmission. National Collaborating Centre for Environmental Health. *https://ncceh.ca/resources/evidence-reviews/rapid-review-use-physical-barriers-non-clinical-settings-and-covid-19.*

Fackler, S., & Malmberg, L.-E. (2016). Teachers' self-efficacy in 14 OECD countries: Teacher, student group, school and leadership effects. *Teaching and Teacher Education, 56*, 185–195.

Falk, A., Benda, A., Falk, P., Steffen, S., Wallace, Z., & Hoeg, T. B. (2021). COVID-19 cases and transmission in 17 K–12 schools—Wood County, Wisconsin, August 31–November 29, 2020. *Morbidity and Mortality Weekly Report, 70*(4), 136–140.

Feldman, D. L., Smith, A. T., & Waxman, B. L. (2017). *"Why we drop out": Understanding and disrupting student pathways to leaving school.* Teachers College Press.

Felfe, C., Saurer, J., Schneider, P., Vornberger, J., Erhart, M., Kaman, A., & Ravens-Sieberer, U. (2023). The youth mental health crisis: Quasi-experimental evidence on the role of school closures. *Science Advances,* 9(33), 1–12.

Ferdig, R. E., Baumgartner, E., Hartshorne, R., Kaplan-Rakowski, R., & Mouza, C. (Eds.) (2020). *Teaching, technology, and teacher education during the COVID-19 pandemic: Stories from the field.* Association for the Advancement of Computing in Education (AACE). *https://learntechlib.org/p/216903.*

Ferguson, K., Frost, L., & Hall, D. (2012). Predicting teacher anxiety, depression, and job satisfaction. *Journal of Teaching and Learning, 8*(1), 27–42.

Fine, M. (1991). *Framing dropouts: Notes on the politics of an urban public high school.* State University of New York Press.

Fisher, M. (2020, April 7). Flushing out the true cause of the global toilet paper shortage amid coronavirus pandemic. *www.washingtonpost.com/national/coronavirus-toilet-paper-shortage-panic/2020/04/07/1fd30e92-75b5-11ea-87da-77a8136c1a6d_story.html.*

Fitzpatrick, K. M., Harris, C., & Drawve, G. (2020). Fear of COVID-19 and the mental health consequences in America. *Psychological Trauma: Theory, Research, Practice, and Policy, 12*(Suppl. 1), s17–s21.

Flanders, W. (2021). Opting out: Enrollment trends in response to continued public school shutdowns. *Journal of School Choice, 15*(3), 331–343.

Fleming, C. M., Calvert, H. G., & Turner, L. (2023). Burnout among school staff: A longitudinal analysis of leadership, connectedness, and psychological safety. *School Mental Health, 15,* 900–912.

Fortin, J., & Fawcett, E. (2022, August 29). How bad is the teacher shortage? Depends where you live. *www.nytimes.com/2022/08/29/us/schools-teacher-shortages.html.*

Fraser, J. W., & Lefty, L. (2018). *Teaching teachers: Changing paths and enduring debates.* Johns Hopkins University Press.

Fray, L., Jaremus, F., Gore, J., Miller, A., & Harris, J. (2022). Under pressure and overlooked: The impact of COVID-19 on teachers in NSW public schools. *Australian Educational Researcher, 50,* 701–727.

Gais, T., Backstrom, B., Frank, J., & Wagner, A. (2019). The state of the Connecticut teacher workforce (ED605621). Nelson A. Rockefeller Institute of Government. *https://files.eric.ed.gov/fulltext/ED605621.pdf*.

Gallant, A., & Riley, P. (2014). Early career teacher attrition: New thoughts on an intractable problem. *Teacher Development, 18*(4), 562–580.

Gamonal-Limcaoco, S., Montero-Mateos, E., Lozano-López, M. T., Maciá-Casas, A., Matías-Fernández, J., & Roncero, C. (2022). Perceived stress in different countries at the beginning of the coronavirus pandemic. *International Journal of Psychiatry in Medicine, 57*(4), 309–322.

Gandhi, M., & Noble, J. (2021, June 10). The pandemic's toll on teen mental health. *www.wsj.com/articles/the-pandemics-toll-on-teen-mental-health-11623344542.*

Gastic, B. (2014). Closing the opportunity gap: Preparing the next generation of effective teachers. In F. M. Hess & M. Q. McShane (Eds.), *Teacher quality 2.0: Toward a new era in education reform* (pp. 91–108). Harvard Education Press.

Gendron, W. (2023, May 4). AI is going to offer every student a personalized tutor, founder of Khan Academy says. *www.businessinsider.com/ai-will-give-every-student-personalized-tutor-sal-khan-academy-2023-5.*

Gerstle, G., Rosenberg, E. S., & Rosenberg, N. L. (1999). *America transformed: A history of the United States since 1900.* Harcourt Brace College.

Golberstein, E., Wen, H., & Miller, B. F. (2020). Coronavirus disease 2019 (COVID-19) and mental health for children and adolescents. *JAMA Pediatrics, 174*(9), 819–820.

Goldhaber, D., Kane, T. J., McEachin, A., Morton, E., Patterson, T., & Staiger, D. O. (2022, May). The consequences of remote and hybrid instruction during the pandemic. Harvard University Center for Education Policy Research. *https://cepr.harvard.edu/files/cepr/files/5-4.pdf?m=1651690491.*

Goldhaber, D., & Theobald, R. (2022). Teacher attrition and mobility over time. *Educational Researcher, 51*(3), 235–237.

Goldstein, M., & Paulle, B. (2021, March). The narrow path to do it right: Lessons from vaccine making for high-dosage tutoring. *https://fordhaminstitute.org/national/research/narrow-path-do-it-right-lessons-vaccine-making-high-dosage-tutoring.*

Gore, J., Fray, L., Miller, A., Harris, J., & Taggart, W. (2021). The impact of COVID-19 on student learning in New South Wales primary schools: An empirical study. *Australian Educational Researcher, 48*(4), 605–637.

Gotlib, I. H., Miller, J. G., Borchers, L. R., Coury, S. M., Costello, L. A., Garcia, J. M., & Ho, T. C. (in press). Effects of the COVID-19 pandemic on mental health and brain maturation in adolescents: Implications for analyzing longitudinal data. *Biological Psychiatry Global Open Science.*

Greenberg, M. T., Domitrovich, C. E., Weissberg, R. P., & Durlak, J. A. (2017). Social and emotional learning as a public health approach to education. *The Future of Children, 27*(1), 13–32. *www.jstor.org/stable/44219019.*

Greenberg, M. T., Weissberg, R. P., O'Brien, M. U., Zins, J. E., Fredericks, L., Resnik, H., & Elias, M. J. (2003). Enhancing school-based prevention and youth development through coordinated social, emotional, and academic learning. *American Psychologist, 58*(6–7), 466–474.

Greene, J., & Paul, J. (2021, November 16). Political opinions of K–12 teachers: Results from a nationally representative survey. Heritage Foundation. *www.heritage.org/education/report/political-opinions-k-12-teachers-results-nationally-representative-survey.*

Gross, B., & Hamilton, L. (2023, February). Student mental health and well-being: A review of evidence and emerging solutions. Center on Reinventing Public Education. *https://crpe.org/student-mental-health-and-well-being-a-review-of-evidence-and-emerging-solutions.*

Grossman, M., Reckhow, S., Strunk, K. O., & Turner, M. (2021). All states close but red districts reopen: The politics of in-person schooling during the COVID-19 pandemic. *Educational Researcher, 50*(9), 637–648.

Guha, R., Hyler, M. E., & Darling-Hammond, L. (2016). The teacher residency: An innovative model for preparing teachers. *https://files.eric.ed.gov/fulltext/ED606443.pdf.*

Gwinnett County Public Schools. (2023). Digital learning days. *www.gcpsk12.org/Page/23593*

Haidt, J. (2022, May). Why the past 10 years of American life have been uniquely stupid: It's not just a phase. *www.theatlantic.com/magazine/archive/2022/05/social-media-democracy-trust-babel/629369.*

Haidt, J. (2023, February 8). The teen mental illness epidemic began around 2012. *www.persuasion.community/p/haidt-the-teen-mental-illness-epidemic.*

Haleemunnissa, S., Didel, S., Swami, M. K., Singh, K., & Vyas, V. (2021). Children and COVID-19: Understanding impact on the growth trajectory of an evolving generation. *Children and Youth Services Review, 120*, 105754.

Halloran, C., Hug, C. E., Jack, R., & Oster, E. (2023). Post COVID-19 test score recovery: Initial evidence from state testing data (Working Paper No. 31113). National Bureau of Economic Research. *www.nber.org/papers/w31113.*

Halloran, C., Jack, R., Okun, J. C., & Oster, E. (2021). *Pandemic schooling mode and student test scores: Evidence from US states* (Working Paper No. 29497). National Bureau of Economic Research.

Hamlin, D., Adams, C., & Adigun, B. (2023). Student performance in Oklahoma's virtual charter schools. *Oklahoma Education Journal, 1*(1), 12–18.

Hammerstein, S., König, C., Dreisörner, T., & Frey, A. (2021). Effects of COVID-19-related school closures on student achievement: A systematic review. *Frontiers in Psychology, 12*, 746289.

Hanel, J., & McGraw, J. (2023, March). *Using data to understand the state of teacher education in Virginia.* Paper presented at the annual conference of the Virginia Association of Colleges Teacher Educators.

Hanson, K. (2023, April 4). An Ohio school district is moving to a 4-day school week to curb burnout for teachers. *www.today.com/parents/family/4-day-school-week-rcna77276.*

Harris, D. N., Ziedan, E., & Hassig, S. (2021). The effects of school reopenings on COVID-19 hospitalizations. *www.reachcentered.org/publications/the-effects-of-school-reopenings-on-covid-19-hospitalizations.*

Hartney, M. T., & Finger, L. K. (2021). Politics, markets, and pandemics: Public education's response to COVID-19. *Perspectives on Politics, 20*(2), 457–473.

Hassan, M. M., Mirza, T., & Hussain, M. W. (2020). A critical review by teachers on the online teaching–learning during the COVID-19. *International Journal of Education and Management Engineering, 5*, 17–27.

Hawes, M. T., Szenczy, A. K., Olino, T. M., Nelson, B. D., & Klein, D. N. (2021). Trajectories of depression, anxiety and pandemic experiences: A longitudinal study of youth in New York during the Spring–Summer of 2020. *Psychiatry Research, 298*, 113778.

Hawrilenko, M., Kroshus, E., Tandon, P., & Christakis, D. (2021). The association between school closures and child mental health during COVID-19. *JAMA Network Open, 4*(9), e2124092.

Heinrich, C. J., Darling-Aduana, J., Good, A., & Cheng, H. (2019). A look inside online educational settings in high school: Promise and pitfalls for improving educational opportunities and outcomes. *American Educational Research Journal, 56*(6), 2147–2188.

Henderson, M. B., Peterson, P. E., & West, M. R. (2020). Pandemic parent survey finds perverse pattern: Students are more likely to be attending school in person where COVID is spreading more rapidly. *Education Next, 21*(2).

Hendricks, M. D. (2014). Does it pay to pay teachers more? Evidence from Texas. *Journal of Public Economics, 109*, 50–63.

Herman, K. C., Sebastian, J., Reinke, W. M., & Huang, F. L. (2021). Individual and school predictors of teacher stress, coping, and wellness during the COVID-19 pandemic. *School Psychology, 36*(6), 483–493.

Hess, F. (2023, May 10). AI tutoring has a lot to offer. But so does human mentoring. *www.forbes.com/sites/frederickhess/2023/05/10/ai-tutoring-has-a-lot-to-offer-but-so-does-human-mentoring/?sh=4750f50c5280.*

Hevia, F. J., Vergara-Lope, S., Velásquez-Durán, A., & Calderón, D. (2022). Estimation of the fundamental learning loss and learning poverty related to COVID-19 pandemic in Mexico. *International Journal of Educational Development, 88*,102515.

Heyward, G. (2021, September 13). From shutdown to reopening: Here's a look at N.Y.C. schools' trek through the pandemic. *https://nytimes.com/2021/09/13/world/reopening-timeline-nyc-schools.html.*

Hilger, K. J. E., Scheibe, S., Frenzel, A. C., & Keller, M. M. (2021). Exceptional circumstances: Changes in teachers' work characteristics and well-being during COVID-19 lockdown. *School Psychology, 36*(6), 516–532.

Hirshberg, M. J., Davidson, R. J., & Goldberg, S. B. (2023). Educators are not alright: Mental health during COVID-19. *Educational Researcher, 52*(1), 48–52.

Hodges, C., Moore, S., Lockee, B., Trust, T., & Bond, A. (2020, March 27). The difference between emergency remote teaching and online learning. *https://er.educause.edu/articles/2020/3/the-difference-between-emergency-remote-teaching-and-online-learning.*

Hoffman, J. A., & Miller, E. A. (2020). Addressing the consequences of school closure due to COVID-19 on children's physical and mental well-being. *World Medical and Health Policy, 12*(3), 300–310.

Holingue, C., Badillo-Goicoechea, E., Riehm, K. E., Veldhuis, C. B., Thrul, J., Johnson, R. M., . . . Kalb, L. G. (2020). Mental distress during the COVID-19 pandemic among US adults without a pre-existing mental health condition: Findings from American trend panel survey. *Preventive Medicine, 139*, 106231.

Honicke, T., & Broadbent, J. (2016). The influence of academic self-efficacy on academic performance: A systematic review. *Educational Research Review, 17*, 63–84.

Hope, S. T., Abrams, L. M., & Marshall, D. T. (2022). Coaching in teacher residency programs: A strategy for professional learning and development for in-service teachers. *International Journal of Mentoring and Coaching in Education, 11*(4), 434–451.

Horák, J., Lazaroiu, G., & Valášková, K. (2020). Scaring ourselves to death in the time of COVID-19: Pandemic awareness, virus anxiety, and contagious fear. *Linguistic and Philosophical Investigations, 19*, 114–120.

Horesh, D., & Brown, A. D. (2020). Traumatic stress in the age of COVID-19: A call to close critical gaps and adapt to new realities. *Psychological Trauma: Theory, Research, Practice, and Policy, 12*(4), 331–335.

Hou, T.-y., Mao, X.-f., Dong, W., Cai, W.-p., & Deng, G.-h. (2020). Prevalence of and factors associated with mental health problems and suicidality among senior high school students in rural China during the COVID-19 outbreak. *Asian Journal of Psychiatry, 54*, 102305.

Houchard, M. A. (2005). *Principal leadership, teacher morale, and student achievement in seven schools in Mitchell County, North Carolina* [Doctoral dissertation, East Tennessee State University]. Digital Commons at East Tennessee State. *https://dc.etsu.edu/etd/1081.*

Huck, C., & Zhang, J. (2021). Effects of the COVID-19 pandemic on K–12 education: A systematic literature review. *New Waves: Educational Research and Development Journal, 24*(1), 53–84.

Hull, M., & Duch, K. (2019). One-to-one technology and student outcomes: Evidence from Mooresville's digital conversion initiative. *Educational Evaluation and Policy Analysis, 41*(1), 79–97.

Hutchison, S. M., Watts, A., Gadermann, A., Oberle, E., Oberlander, T. F., Lavoie, P. M., & Mâsse, L. C. (2022). School staff and teachers during the second year of COVID-19: Higher anxiety symptoms, higher psychological distress, and poorer mental health compared to the general population. *Journal of Affective Disorders Reports*, 8, 100335.

Huysman, J. T. (2008). Rural teacher satisfaction: An analysis of beliefs and attitudes of rural teachers' job satisfaction. *Rural Educator*, 29(2), 31–38.

Idaho back to school framework 2020.(2020, July 9). *www.sde.idaho.gov/re-opening/files/Idaho-Back-to-School-Framework-2020.pdf.*

Ingersoll, R., Merrill, L., & May, H. (2014). *What are the effects of teacher education and preparation on beginning teacher attrition?* (Research report). Consortium for Policy Research in Education. *www.cpre.org/sites/default/files/researchreport/2018_prepeffects2014.pdf.*

Institute of Education Sciences. (2022). School pulse panel. *https://ies.ed.gov/schoolsurvey/spp.*

Iwata, K., Doi, A., & Miyakoshi, C. (2020). Was school closure effective in mitigating coronavirus disease (COVID-19)? Time series analysis using Bayesian inference. *International Journal of Infectious Diseases*, 99, 57–61.

Jakubowski, T. D., & Sitko-Dominik, M. M. (2021). Teachers' mental health during the first two waves of the COVID-19 pandemic in Poland. *PLoS One*, *16*(9), e0257252.

Jeffery, A. (2020, April 5). New Yorkers stop and give daily thanks and gratitude for coronavirus frontline workers. *www.cnbc.com/2020/04/05/new-yorkers-stop-and-give-daily-thanks-and-gratitude-for-coronavirus-frontline-workers.html.*

Jochim, A., Diliberti, M. K., Schwartz, H., Destler, K., & Hill, P. (2023, January). Navigating political tensions over schooling: Findings from the fall 2022 American School District Panel survey. Center for Reinventing Public Education. *https://crpe.org/asdp-2023-politics-brief.*

Joffe, A. R. (2021). COVID-19: Rethinking the lockdown groupthink. *Frontiers in Public Health*, 9, 625778.

Jones, S. E., Ethier, K. A., Hertz, M., DeGue, S., Le, V. D., Thornton, J., . . . Geda, S. (2022). Mental health, suicidality, and connectedness among high school students during the COVID-19 pandemic—Adolescent behaviors and experiences survey, United States, January–June 2021. *Mortality and Morbidity Weekly Report*, *71*(3), 16–21.

Jotkoff, E. (2022). NEA survey: Massive staff shortages in schools leading to educator burnout; alarming number of educators indicating they plan to leave profession [Press release]. *www.nea.org/about-nea/media-center/press-releases/nea-survey-massive-staff-shortages-schools-leading-educator.*

Kaden, U. (2020). COVID-19 school closure-related changes to the professional life of a K–12 teacher. *Education Sciences, 10*(6), 165.

Kaufman, J., & Diliberti, M. (2021). Teachers are not all right: How the COVID-19 pandemic is taking a toll on the nation's teachers. Evidence Project at CRPE. *https://crpe.org/wp-content/uploads/final-EP-teachers-synthesis.pdf.*

Keese, J., & McIntush, K. (2023, April 13–16). *The road back to normal? A longitudinal qualitative investigation of teacher experiences through COVID-19.* Paper presented at AERA Annual Meeting, Lives of Teachers SIG, Chicago

Keese, J., McIntush, K., & Waxman, H. (2022, April 21–26). *From the frying pan to the fire: Teacher experiences as schools emerge from COVID closures.* Paper presented at AERA Annual Meeting, Division K, San Diego, CA.

Kessler, R. C., Chiu, W. T., Hwang, I. H., Puac-Polanco, V., Sampson, N. A., Ziobrowski, H. N., & Zaslavsky, A. M. (2022). Changes in prevalence of mental illness among US adults during compared with before the COVID-19 pandemic. *Psychiatric Clinics of North America, 45*(1), 1–28.

Khoury, J. E., Kaur, H., & Gonzalez, A. (2021). Parental mental health and hostility are associated with longitudinal increases in child internalizing and externalizing problems during COVID-19. *Frontiers in Psychology, 12*, 706168.

Kilinçel, S., Kilinçel, O., Muratdaği, G., Aydin, A., & Usta, M. B. (2021). Factors affecting the anxiety levels of adolescents in home-quarantine during COVID-19 pandemic in Turkey. *Asia-Pacific Psychiatry, 13*(2), e12406.

Kim, H. J., Choi, J., & Lee, S. (2019). Teacher experience of integrating tablets in one-to-one environments: Implications for orchestrating learning. *Education Sciences,* 9(2), 87.

Kim, L. E., Oxley, L., & Asbury, K. (2022). "My brain feels like a browser with 100 tabs open": A longitudinal study of teachers' mental health and well-being during the COVID-19 pandemic. *British Journal of Educational Psychology,* 92(1), 299–318.

Kinder, M. (2020, May). *Meet the COVID-19 frontline heroes. www.brookings.edu/articles/meet-the-covid-19-frontline-heroes.*

Kingsbury, I. (2021). Online learning: How do brick and mortar schools stack up to virtual schools? *Education and Information Technologies, 26*, 6567–6588.

Kingsbury, I., & Marshall, D. T. (2023). Assessing access to online course choice among brick-and-mortar K–12 students. *Journal of Online Learning Research,* 9(1), 83–100. *www.learntechlib.org/primary/p/221255.*

Kishida, K., Tsuda, M., Waite, P., Creswell, C., & Ishikawa, S.-i. (2021). Relationships between local school closures due to the COVID-19 and mental health problems of children, adolescents, and parents in Japan. *Psychiatry Research, 306*, 114276.

Klein, A. (2022, September 12). New York City schools cancel snow days in disturbing new trend. *www.nbcnews.com/think/opinion/new-york-city-schools-cancel-snow-days-disturbing-new-trend-rcna47046.*

König, J., Jäger-Biela, D. J., & Glutsch, N. (2020). Adapting to online teaching during COVID-19 school closure: Teacher education and teacher competence effects among early career teachers in Germany. *European Journal of Teacher Education, 43*(4), 608–622.

Kotowski, S. E., Davis, K. G., & Barratt, C. L. (2022). Teachers feeling the burden of COVID-19: Impact on well-being, stress, and burnout. *Work, 71*(2), 407–415.

Kraft, M. A., Bolves, A. J., & Hurd, N. M. (2023, May). How informal mentoring by teachers, counselors, and coaches supports students' long-run academic success (Working Paper No. 31257). *www.nber.org/papers/w31257.*

Kraft, M. A., List, J. A., Livingston, J. A., & Sadoff, S. (2022). *Online tutoring by college volunteers: Experimental evidence from a pilot program* (EdWorking Paper No. 22-568). Retrieved from Annenberg Institute, Brown University.

Kraft, M. A., & Lyon, M. A. (2022). *The rise and fall of the teaching profession: Prestige, interest, preparation, and satisfaction over the last half century* (EdWorking Paper No. 22-679). Retrieved from Annenberg Institute, Brown University.

Kraft, M. A., Simon, N. S., & Lyon, M. A. (2021). Sustaining a sense of success: The protective role of teacher working conditions during the COVID-19 pandemic. *Journal of Research on Educational Effectiveness, 14*(4), 727–769.

Kuhfeld, M., Soland, J., & Lewis, K. (2022). Test score patterns across three COVID-19–impacted school years. *Educational Researcher, 51*(7), 500–506.

Kulldorf, M., Gupta, S., & Bhattacharya, J. (2020, October 4). The Great Barrington Declaration. *https://gbdeclaration.org.*

Kurtz, H. (2022, April 14). A profession in crisis: Findings from a national teacher survey. *Education Week. www.edweek.org/research-center/reports/teaching-profession-in-crisis-national-teacher-survey.*

Kush, J. M., Badillo-Goicoechea, E., Musci, R. J., & Stuart, E. A. (2022). Teachers' mental health during the COVID-19 pandemic. *Educational Researcher, 51*(9), 593–597.

LaBelle, B. (2019). Positive outcomes of a social–emotional learning program to promote student resiliency and address mental health. *Contemporary School Psychology, 27,* 1–7.

Ladd, H. F. (2011). Teachers' perceptions of their working conditions: How predictive of planned and actual teacher movement? *Educational Evaluation and Policy Analysis, 33*(2), 235–261.

Lee, P.-I., Hu, Y.-L., Chen, P.-Y., Huang, Y.-C., & Hsueh, P.-R. (2020). Are children less susceptible to COVID-19? *Journal of Microbiology, Immunology, and Infection, 53*(3), 371–372.

Leeb, R., Bitsko, R., Radhakrishnan, L., Martinez, P., Njai, R., & Holland, K. M. (2020). Mental health-related emergency department visits among children aged < 18 years during the COVID-19 pandemic: United States, January 1–October 17, 2020. *Morbidity and Mortality Weekly Report, 69,* 1675–1680. *www.cdc.gov/mmwr/volumes/69/wr/mm6945a3.*

Leidman, E. L., Duca, L. M., Omura, J. D., Proia, K., Stephens, J. W., & Sauber-Schatz, E. K. (2021). COVID-19 trends among persons aged 0–24 years—United States, March 1–December 12, 2020. *Morbidity and Mortality Weekly Report, 70*(3), 88–94.

Lewis, K., & Kuhfeld, M. (2021). Learning during COVID-19: An update on student achievement and growth at the start of the 2021–22 school year. *www.nwea.org/research/publication/learning-during-covid-19-an-update-on-student-achievement-and-growth-at-the-start-of-the-2021-22-school-year.*

Lin, C.-H., Kwon, J. B., & Zhang, Y. (2019). Online self-paced high school class size and student achievement. *Educational Technology Research and Development, 67*(2), 317–336.

Liu, Y., Yue, S., Hu, X., Zhu, J., Wu, Z., Wang, J., & Wu, Y. (2021). Associations between feelings/behaviors during COVID-19 pandemic lockdown and depression/anxiety after lockdown in a sample of Chinese children and adolescents. *Journal of Affective Disorders, 284*, 98–103.

Loades, M. E., Chatburn, E., Higson-Sweeney, N., Reynolds, S., Shafran, R., Brigden, A., . . . Crawley, E. (2020). Rapid systematic review: The impact of social isolation and loneliness on the mental health of children and adolescents in the context of COVID-19. *Journal of the American Academy of Child and Adolescent Psychiatry, 59*(11), 1218–1239.

Lochner, B., Conrad, R.-M., & Graham, E. (2015). Secondary teachers' concerns in adopting learning management systems: A U.S. perspective. *Tech Trends, 59*, 62–70.

Love, S. M., & Marshall, D. T. (2022). Teacher experiences during COVID-19. In D. T. Marshall (Ed.), *COVID-19 and the classroom: How schools navigated the great disruption* (pp. 21–65). Lexington Books.

Lovison, V. S., & Mo, C. H. (2022). *Investing in the teacher workforce: Experimental evidence on teachers' preferences* (EdWorking Paper No. 22-528). Retrieved from Annenberg Institute, Brown University.

Lu, R., & Overbaugh, R. C. (2009). School environment and technology implementation in K–12 classrooms. *Computers in the Schools, 26*(2), 89–106.

Lücker, P., Kästner, A., Hannich, A., Schmeyers, L., Lücker, J., & Hoffman, W. (2022). Stress, coping, and considerations of leaving the profession: A cross-sectional online survey of teachers and school principals after two years of the pandemic. *International Journal of Environmental Research and Public Health, 19*(23), 16122.

Lukianoff, G., & Haidt, J. (2018). *The coddling of the American mind: How good intentions and bad ideas are setting up a generation for failure.* Penguin Press.

Lumsden, L. (1998). Teacher morale (ED422601). *https://eric.ed.gov/?id=ED422601.*

Ma, K., Chutiyami, M., Zhang, Y., & Nicoll, S. (2021). Online teaching self-efficacy during COVID-19: Changes, its associated factors and moderators. *Education and Information Technologies, 26*(6), 6675–6697.

Maas, J., Schoch, S., Scholz, U., Rackow, P., Schüler, J., Wegner, M., & Keller, R. (2022). School principals' social support and teachers' basic need satisfaction: The mediating role of job demands and job resources. *Social Psychology of Education, 25*(6), 1545–1562.

Mackenzie, N. (2007). Teacher morale: More complex than we think? *Australian Educational Researcher, 34*(1), 89–104.

Madigan, S., Eirich, R., Pador, P., McArthur, B. A., & Neville, R. D. (2022). Assessment of changes in child and adolescent screen time during the COVID-19 pandemic: A systematic review and meta-analysis. *JAMA Pediatrics, 176*(12), 1188–1198.

Magis-Weinberg, L., Gys, C. L., Berger, E. L., Domoff, S. E., & Dahl, R. E. (2021). Positive and negative online experiences and loneliness in Peruvian adolescents during the COVID-19 lockdown. *Journal of Research on Adolescence, 31*(3), 717–733.

Magson, N. R., Freeman, J. Y. A., Rapee, R. M., Richardson, C. E., Oar, E. L., & Fardouly, J. (2021). Risk and protective factors for prospective changes in adolescent mental health during the COVID-19 pandemic. *Journal of Youth and Adolescence, 50*(1), 44–57.

Maine Department of Education. (2020a). Coronavirus update: Coronavirus (COVID-19) resources for schools. *www.maine.gov/doe/index.php/covid-19.*

Maine Department of Education. (2020b). Coronavirus update: Framework for reopening schools and returning to in-person instruction. *www.maine.gov/doe/framework.*

Malkus, N., Marsicano, C. Schurz, J., Audet, A., Wahl, D., & Martin, R. (2022). A failure to respond: Public school mask mandates in the 2021–22 school year. *https://returntolearntracker.net.*

Mansfield, K. L., Newby, D., Soneson, E., Vaci, N., Jindra, C., Geulayov, G., . . . Fazel, M. (2021). COVID-19 partial school closures and mental health problems: A cross-sectional survey of 11,000 adolescents to determine those most at risk. *JCPP Advances, 1*(2), e12021.

Maranto, R. (2020a, October 13). It's the tradeoffs, stupid: Six thoughts on COVID-19 and reopening schools. *www.discoursemagazine.com/economics/2020/10/13/its-the-tradeoffs-stupid.*

Maranto, R. (2020b). Corona's curse in the U.S.: How online schooling will decrease academic quality and equity. *International Journal for Educational Law and Policy, 16,* 151–160.

Maranto, R., & Marshall, D. T. (2023). *COVID-19 and schools: Policy, stakeholders, and school choice.* Routledge.

Maranto, R., Marshall, D. T., & Bradley-Dorsey, M. (2020, September 21). Football aside, politics isn't influencing school pandemic plans. *www.ajc.com/education/get-schooled-blog/opinion-football-aside-politics-isn't-influencing-school-pandemic-plans/PO7QFZUKRJGX5FXJKOSQERKFG4.*

Maranto, R., & Shuls, J. V. (2013). How do we get them on the farm? Efforts to improve rural teacher recruitment and retention in Arkansas. *Rural Educator, 34*(1).

Marciano, L., Ostroumova, M., Schulz, P. J., & Camerini, A.-L. (2022). Digital media use and adolescents' mental health during the COVID-19 pandemic: A systematic review and meta-analysis. *Frontiers of Public Health,* 9, 793868.

Margolis, J., & Nagel, L. (2006). Education reform and the role of administrators in mediating teacher stress. *Teacher Education Quarterly, 33*(4), 143–159.

Marianno, B. D. (2021, March 25). Teachers' unions: Scapegoats or bad-faith actors in COVID-19 school reopening decisions? *www.brookings.edu/blog/brown-center-chalkboard/2021/03/25/teachers-unions-scapegoats-or-bad-faith-actors-in-covid-19-school-reopening-decisions.*

Marietta, G., & Marietta, S. (2020). *Rural education in America: What works for our students, teachers, and communities.* Harvard Education Press.

Marshall, D. T. (2009, Fall). Game-facilitated knowledge-building communities. *Teacher Educators' Journal, 16,* 11–14.

Marshall, D. T. (2017). Equity and access in charter schools: Identifying issues and solutions. *Education Policy Analysis Archives, 25,* 83.

Marshall, D. T. (Ed.). (2022a). *COVID-19 and the classroom: How schools navigated the great disruption.* Lexington Books.

Marshall, D. T. (2022b). School closures and their deleterious effects on students. *Teachers College Record. https://journals.sagepub.com/pb-assets/cmscontent/TCZ/Commentaries%20Collection/2022%20Commentaries/School%20Closures%20and%20their%20Deleterious%20Effects%20on%20Students-1650325611.pdf.*

Marshall, D. T. (2022c). Course grades as actionable early warning indicators: Predicting high school graduation in an urban school district. *Preventing School Failure, 66*(3), 206–213.

Marshall, D. T. (2023). COVID-19 and school closures: A narrative review of pediatric mental health impacts. *Journal of School Choice. www.tandfonline.com/doi/abs/ 10.1080/15582159.2023.2201734?journalCode=wjsc20.*

Marshall, D. T. (in press). What changes remain? Teacher perspectives on changes made to U.S. schools during the COVID-19 pandemic. *International Journal of Education Reform.*

Marshall, D. T., & Bradley-Dorsey, M. (2020). Reopening America's schools: A descriptive look at how states and large school districts are navigating Fall 2020. *Journal of School Choice, 14*(4), 534–566.

Marshall, D. T., & Bradley-Dorsey, M. (2022). Reopening schools in the United States. In D. T. Marshall (Ed.), *COVID-19 and the classroom: How schools navigated the great disruption* (pp. 147–164). Lexington Books.

Marshall, D. T., Love, S. M., Neugebauer, N. M., & Smith, N. E. (2023). How additional professional time benefitted teachers during COVID-19. In S. M. McCarther & D. M. Davis (Eds.), *Breakthrough: From pandemic panic to promising practice* (pp. 61–72). Information Age.

Marshall, D. T., Love, S. M., Shannon, D. M., & Neugebauer, N. M. (2023). Burnout, workload, and morale: Describing teacher experiences at the conclusion of a pandemic year. *SocArXiv. https://osf.io/preprints/socarxiv/cnxp6.*

Marshall, D. T., & Neugebauer, N. M. (2022). How charter school leaders navigated COVID-19. In D. T. Marshall (Ed.), *COVID-19 and the classroom: How schools navigated the great disruption* (pp. 107–122). Lexington Books.

Marshall, D. T., & Neugebauer, N. M. (2023). Charter schools and crisis leadership during COVID-19. In D. J. Fowler & M. B. Raehll (Eds.), *On leadership: An interdisciplinary approach* (pp. 311–328). Information Age.

Marshall, D. T., Neugebauer, N. M., Pressley, T., & Brown-Aliffi, K. (2023). Teacher morale, job satisfaction, and burnout in schools of choice following the COVID-19 pandemic. *Journal of School Choice. www.tandfonline.com/doi/abs/ 10.1080/15582159.2023.2201737?src=&journalCode=wjsc20.*

Marshall, D. T., & Pressley, T. (2023, May 13). Mississippi teachers fared better by some metrics. *www.djournal.com/opinion/columnists/mississippi-teachers-fare-better-by-some-metrics/article_63966fd6-8624-5a1d-bc50-58c38ee585ea.html.*

Marshall, D. T., Pressley, T., & Love, S. M. (2022). The times they are a-changin': Teaching and learning beyond COVID-19. *Journal of Educational Change, 23*, 549–557.

Marshall, D. T., Pressley, T., Neugebauer, N. M., & Shannon, D. M. (2022). Why teachers are leaving and what we can do about it. *Phi Delta Kappan, 104*(1), 6–11.

Marshall, D. T., Pressley, T., & Shannon, D. M. (2023, November 8–10). *The impact of mental health interventions and administrative support on teacher well-being following the COVID-19 pandemic* [Poster presentation]. Mid-South Educational Research Association, Pensacola, Florida.

Marshall, D. T., Scott, M. R., & Wan, G. (2021). Through failure and reflection: Conceptualizations of a successful teacher residency experience. *Action in Teacher Education, 43*(2), 160–175.

Marshall, D. T., Shannon, D. M., & Love, S. M. (2020). How teachers experienced the COVID-19 transition to remote instruction. *Phi Delta Kappan, 102*(3), 46–50.

Marshall, D. T., Shannon, D. M., & Love, S. M. (2022). Teaching during the transition to remote instruction. In D. T. Marshall (Ed.), *COVID-19 and the classroom: How schools navigated the great disruption* (pp. 9–20). Lexington Books.

Marshall, D. T., Shannon, D. M., Love, S. M., & Neugebauer, N. M. (2023). Factors related to teacher resilience during COVID-19. *International Journal of Education Policy and Leadership, 19*(1), 1–18.

Marshall, D. T., Shannon, D. M., Love, S. M., & Norris, L. (in press). Teacher sense of efficacy and capturing the initial transition to remote instruction. *Journal of Education.*

Marshall, D. T., Smith, N. E., Love, S. M., Neugebauer, N. M., & Shannon, D. M. (in press). "At some point we're going to reach our limit": Understanding COVID-19's impact on teacher burnout and subjective mental health. *Psychology in the Schools.*

Marshall, D. T., Varier, D., Hope, S. T., & Abrams, L. M. (2020). The role of mentor–resident match in a teacher residency program: A comparison of three cases. *Journal of Research in Education, 29*(2), 88–117.

Marshall, D. T., & Witte, J. (2023, May 26). Guest opinion: Aerospace, aviation-themed charter school concludes successful first year. *www.al.com/opinion/2023/05/guest-opinion-aerospace-aviation-themed-charter-school-concludes-successful-first-year.html.*

Mathews, R. A., Streit, J. M. K., & Smith, C. E. (2020). Teaching in the time of COVID-19: Executive summary. University of Alabama Human Resources Institute. *www.researchgate.net/publication/344243803_Teaching_in_the_Time_of_COVID-19_Executive_Summary.*

McCarthy, C. J., Lambert, R., Lineback, S., Fitchett, P. G., & Baddouh, P. G. (2016). Assessing teacher appraisals and stress in the classroom: Review of the classroom appraisal of resources and demands. *Educational Psychology Review, 28*(3), 577–603.

McClelland, H., Evans, J. J., Nowland, R., Ferguson, E., & O'Connor, R. C. (2020). Loneliness as a predictor of suicidal ideation and behaviour: A systematic review and meta-analysis of prospective studies. *Journal of Affective Disorders, 274*, 880–896.

McCluskey, N. (2021, November 22). Private schooling status update: Things keep looking up. Cato Institute. *www.cato.org/blog/private-schooling-status-update-things-keep-looking.*

McCluskey, N. (2022). Assessing the pandemic's toll on private schools. In D. T. Marshall (Ed.), *COVID-19 and the classroom: How schools navigated the great disruption* (pp. 183–196). Lexington Books.

McCrae, N., Gettings, S., & Purssell, E. (2017). Social media and depressive symptoms in childhood and adolescence: A systematic review. *Adolescent Research Review, 2*, 315–330.

McDougald, V. (2023, May 25). Dire straits: Taking stock of and addressing pandemic-related learning loss. *https://fordhaminstitute.org/national/commentary/dire-straits-taking-stock-and-addressing-pandemic-related-learning-loss.*

McKnight, K., Hope, S., Marrs, S., & Pitre-Martin, M. (2022). Lessons learned from an urban teacher residency. In D. T. Marshall (Ed.), *COVID-19 and the classroom: How schools navigated the great disruption* (pp. 247–262). Lexington Books.

McMakin, D., Ballin, A., & Fullerton, D. (2023). Secondary trauma, burnout, and teacher self-care during COVID-19: A mixed-methods case study. *Psychology in the Schools, 60*(5), 1442–1458.

McShane, M. Q. (2021). *Hybrid homeschooling: A guide to the future of education.* Rowman & Littlefield.

McShane, M. Q. (2022, July). How do teachers spend their time? Reporting findings from a national survey of educators in district, charter, and private schools. *www.edchoice.org/engage/new-report-how-do-teachers-spend-their-time.*

McShane, M. (2023, May 24). Democratizing school choice. *www.forbes.com/sites/mikemcshane/2023/05/24/democratizing-school-choice/?sh=48d8f6e0608e.*

Meeter, M. (2021). Primary school mathematics during COVID-19: No evidence of learning gaps in adaptive practicing results. *Trends in Neuroscience and Education, 25*, 100163.

Merriam-Webster. (2020). Word of the year: Pandemic. *www.merriam-webster.com/words-at-play/word-of-the-year-2020-pandemic/pandemic.*

Michelson, K. A., & Samuels-Kalow, M. E. (2022). Association of elementary school reopening status and county COVID-19 incidence. *Academic Pediatrics, 22*(4), 667–670.

Milam, L., Butler, A., & Vanderhaar, J. (2022). School climate and emotional wellbeing. *SocArXiv. https://osf.io/preprints/socarxiv/b4rfj.*

Milanowski, A. T., & Odden, A. R. (2007). A new approach to the cost of teacher turnover. School Finance Redesign Project, Center on Reinventing Public Education. (Working Paper No. 13). *https://crpe.org/wp-content/uploads/wp_sfrp13_milanowskiodden_aug08_0.pdf.*

Miller, A. N., Sellnow, D. D., & Strawser, M. G. (2021). Pandemic pedagogy challenges and opportunities: Instruction communication in remote, hyflex, and blendflex courses. *Communication Education, 70*(2), 202–204.

Milman, N. B. (2020, March 25). Pandemic pedagogy. *Phi Delta Kappan. https://kappanonline.org/pandemic-pedagogy-covid-19-online-milman.*

Moe, T. M. (2011). *Special interest: Teachers unions and America's public schools.* Brookings Institution Press.

Moe, T. M., & Chubb, J. E. (2009). *Liberating learning: Technology, politics, and the future of American education.* Jossey Bass.

Molnár, G., & Hermann, Z. (2023). Short- and long-term effects of COVID-related kindergarten and school closures on first- to eighth-grade students' school readiness skills and mathematics, reading and science learning. *Learning and Instruction, 83*, 101706.

Munro, A., Buonsenso, D., González-Dambrauskas, S., Hughes, R. C., Bhopal, S. S., Vásquez-Hoyos, P., . . . Roland, D. (2023). In-person schooling is essential even during periods of high transmission of COVID-19. *BMJ Evidence-Based Medicine, 28*(3), 175–179.

Murray, J. (2022, October 3). Teacher compensation compared to other professions. *https://fordhaminstitute.org/ohio/commentary/teacher-compensation-compared-other-professions.*

Musaddiq, T., Stange, K., Bacher-Hicks, A., & Goodman, J. (2022). The pandemic's effect on demand for public schools, homeschooling, and private schools. *Journal of Public Economics, 212*, 104710.

Naff, D., Williams, S., Furman-Darby, J., & Yeung, M. (2022). The mental health impacts of COVID-19 on PK–12 students: A systematic review of emerging literature. *AERA Open, 8*(1), 1–40.

Näslund-Hadley, E., Alonzo, H., Villanueva, N., Gideon, R., & Flowers, Y. (2023, April). *The effects of the COVID-19 pandemic on education outcomes in Belize.* Inter-American Development Bank.

Natanson, H., & Jouvenal, J. (2023, February 10). How Richneck Elementary failed to stop a 6-year-old from shooting his teacher. *www.washingtonpost.com/dc-md-va/2023/02/10/richneck-elementary-school-shooting-timeline-warnings.*

National Academies of Sciences, Engineering, and Medicine. (2020). *Reopening K–12 schools during the COVID-19 pandemic: Prioritizing health, equity, and communities.* National Academies Press.

National Assessment of Educational Progress. (2022a). Scores decline in NAEP reading at grades 4 and 8 compared to 2019. *www.nationsreportcard.gov/highlights/reading/2022.*

National Assessment of Educational Progress. (2022b). Largest score declines in NAEP mathematics at grades 4 and 8 since initial assessments in 1990. *www.nationsreportcard.gov/highlights/mathematics/2022.*

National Assessment of Educational Progress. (2022c). Explore results for the 2022 NAEP civics assessment. *www.nationsreportcard.gov/civics.*

National Association of Pediatric Nurse Practitioners, Developmental Behavioral Mental Health Special Interest Group, Fry, L., Lusk, P., Van Cleve, S., Heighway, S., & Johnson-Smith, A. (2020). NAPNAP position statement on the integration of mental health care in pediatric primary care settings. *www.jpedhc.org/article/S0891-5245(20)30128-0/pdf.*

National Center for Education Statistics. (2016). *Teacher turnover: Stayers, movers, and leavers. The condition of education.* U.S. Department of Education, Institute of Education Sciences. *https://nces.ed.gov/programs/coe/pdf/coe_slc.pdf.*

National Center for Education Statistics. (2022a). Racial/ethnic enrollment in public schools. U.S. Department of Education, Institute of Education Sciences. *https://nces.ed.gov/programs/coe/indicator/cge.*

National Center for Education Statistics. (2022b). Private school enrollment. U.S. Department of Education, Institute of Education Sciences. *https://nces.ed.gov/programs/coe/indicator/cgc.*

National Center for Education Statistics. (2023). *PIRLS 2021 U.S. Highlights Web Report* (NCES 2023-054). U.S. Department of Education. *https://nces.ed.gov/surveys/pirls/pirls2021/index.asp.*

National Center for Education Statistics. (n.d.). *School choice in the United States: 2019.* U.S. Department of Education, Institute of Education Sciences. *https://nces.ed.gov/programs/schoolchoice/ind_02.asp.*

National Center for Health Statistics. (2023). *Deaths by selected demographic and geographic characteristics.* Centers for Disease Control and Prevention. *www.cdc.gov/nchs/nvss/vsrr/covid_weekly/index.htm.*

Nebraska Department of Education. (2022). *E-learning days. www.education.ne.gov/educational-technology/e-learning-days.*

Nerlino, E. (2023). "From heroes to scapegoats": Teacher perceptions of the media and public's portrayal of teachers during COVID-19. *Educational Forum, 87*(4), 282–303.

Newberry, M., & Hinchcliff, E. (2023). Changed for the better: Positive teacher experiences with COVID-19 driven changes. *Teachers and Teaching, 29*(3), 329–343.

Ng, K., Cosma, A., Svacina, K., Boniel-Nissim, M., & Badura, P. (2021). Czech adolescents' remote school and health experiences during the spring 2020 COVID-19 lockdown. *Preventive Medicine Reports, 22*, 101386.

Nguyen, L. H. (2021). Calculating the impact of COVID-19 pandemic on child abuse and neglect in the U.S. *Child Abuse and Neglect, 118*, 105136.

Nickow, A., Oreopoulos, P., & Quan, V. (2020). *The impressive effects of tutoring on PreK–12 learning: A systematic review and meta-analysis of the experimental evidence* (Working Paper No. 27476). National Bureau of Economic Research.

Noonoo, S. (2022, May 2). The mental health crisis causing teachers to quit. *www.edsurge.com/news/2022-05-02-the-mental-health-crisis-causing-teachers-to-quit*.

North Carolina State Board of Education Department of Public Instruction. (2023). Report to the North Carolina General Assembly. One year later: A recovery analysis of student learning during the COVID-19 pandemic. *www.dpi.nc.gov/documents/files/2021-22-recovery-analysis-report/download?attachment.*

Oosterhoff, B., Palmer, C. A., Wilson, J., & Shook, N. (2020). Adolescents' motivations to engage in social distancing during the COVID-19 pandemic: Associations with mental and social health. *Journal of Adolescent Health, 67*(2), 179–185.

Opalka, A., & Talkington, B. (2020, May). Avoiding long-term harm from "do no harm" grading policies. Center for Reinventing Public Education. *www.crpe.org/thelens/avoiding-long-term-harm-do-no-harm-grading-policies.*

Orgilés, M., Morales, A., Delvecchio, E., Mazzeschi, C., & Espada, J. P. (2020). Immediate psychological effects of the COVID-19 quarantine in youth from Italy and Spain. *Frontiers in Psychology, 11*, 579038.

Oster, E., Jack, R., Halloran, C., Schoof, J., & McLeod, D. (2021). COVID-19 mitigation practices and COVID-19 rates in schools: Report on data from Florida, New York, and Massachusetts. *MedRxiv. www.medrxiv.org/content/10.1101/2021.05.19.21257467v1.*

Oster, E., Jack, R., Halloran, C., Schoof, J., McLeod, D., Yang, H., Roche, J., & Roche, D. (2021). Disparities in learning mode access among K–12 students during the COVID-19 pandemic, by race/ethnicity, geography, and grade level: United States, September 2020–April 2021. *Morbidity and Mortality Weekly Report, 70*(26), 953–958.

Papay, J. P., Bacher-Hicks, A., Page, L. C., & Marinell, W. (2017). The challenge of teacher retention in urban schools: Evidence of variation from a cross-site analysis. *Educational Researcher, 46*(8), 434–448.

Papay, J. P., West, M. R., Fullerton, J. B., & Kane, T. J. (2012). Does an urban teacher residency increase student achievement? Early evidence from Boston. *Educational Evaluation and Policy Analysis, 34*(4), 413–434.

Papert, S. (1993). *The children's machine: Rethinking school in the age of the computer.* BasicBooks.

Park, J. H., Choi, J., & Kim, B. (2022). COVID-19 pandemic and mental health problems of adults in the United States: Mediating roles of cognitive concerns and behavioral changes. *Social Psychiatry and Psychiatric Epidemiology, 57*(8), 1557–1570.

Patrick, S. K., Grissom, J. A., Woods, S. C., & Newsome, U. W. (2021). Broadband access, district policy, and student opportunities for remote learning during COVID-19 school closures. *AERA Open, 7*(1).

Patrinos, H. A. (2022). Learning loss and learning recovery. *Decision, 49*(2), 183–188.

Patrinos, H. A. (2023). The longer students were out of school, the less they learned. *Journal of School Choice, 17*(2), 161–175.

Payne, C. M. (2008). *So much reform, so little change: The persistence of failure in urban schools.* Harvard Education Press.

Payton, J., Weissberg, R. P., Durlak, J. A., Dymnicki, A. B., Taylor, R. D., Schellinger, K. B., & Pachan, M. (2008). *The positive impact of social and emotional learning for kindergarten to eighth-grade students: Findings from three scientific reviews* (Technical report). Collaborative for Academic, Social, and Emotional Learning.

Pearson, L. C., & Moomaw, W. (2005). The relationship between teacher autonomy and stress, work satisfaction, empowerment, and professionalism. *Educational Research Quarterly, 29*(1), 38–54.

Pellerone, M. (2021). Self-perceived instructional competence, self-efficacy and burnout during the COVID-19 pandemic: A study of a group of Italian school teachers. *European Journal of Investigation in Health, Psychology and Education, 11*(2), 496–512.

Pendola, A. (2022a). Behaviors and future intentions of dissatisfied teachers. *SocArXiv. https://osf.io/preprints/socarxiv/zjpur.*

Pendola, A. (2022b). We can keep them here: Value conflicts and teacher retention strategies. *SocArXiv. https://osf.io/preprints/socarxiv/yt3cx.*

Pendola, A., & Fuller, E. J. (2018). Principal stability and the rural divide. *Journal of Research in Rural Education, 34*(1), 1–20.

Pendola, A., Marshall, D. T., Pressley, T., & Trammell, D. L. (2023). A silver lining: There is no shortage of teacher dedication. *Phi Delta Kappan, 105*(1), 51–55.

Penner, F., Ortiz, J. H., & Sharp, C. (2021). Change in youth mental health during the COVID-19 pandemic in a majority Hispanic/Latinx U.S. sample. *Journal of the American Academy of Child and Adolescent Psychiatry, 60*(4), 513–523.

Peréz, J., & Kapos, S. (2022, January 10). Chicago schools, teachers reach tentative deal to end classroom shutdown. *www.politico.com/news/2022/01/10/chicago-schools-teachers-deal-stalemate-526868.*

Peterson, P. E. (2020). The price students pay when schools are closed. *www.educationnext.org/price-students-pay-when-schools-are-closed.*

Phi Delta Kappan. (2022). PDK poll of the public's attitudes toward the public schools. *https://pdkpoll.org.*

Pier, L., Christian, M., Tymeson, H., & Meyer, R. H. (2021, June). *COVID-19 impacts on student learning: Evidence from interim assessments in California. https://edpolicyinca.org/sites/default/files/2021-06/r_pier_jun2021.pdf.*

Pisano, S., Catone, G., Gritti, A., Almerico, L., Pezzella, A., Santangelo, P., . . . Senese, V. P. (2021). Emotional symptoms and their related factors in adolescents during the acute phase of COVID-19 outbreak in South Italy. *Italian Journal of Pediatrics, 47*(86).

Plato. (2000). *The Republic* (B. Jowett, Trans.). Dover. (Original work published ca. 380 b.c.).

Pondiscio, R. (2023, March 23). *Conservatives' blunder: Making enemies of public school teachers. https://fordhaminstitute.org/national/commentary/conservatives-blunder-making-enemies-public-school-teachers.*

Pressley, M., Mohan, L., Raphael, L. M., & Fingeret, L. (2007). How does Bennett Woods Elementary School produce such high reading and writing achievement? *Journal of Educational Psychology, 99*(2), 221–240.

Pressley, T. (2021a). Factors contributing to teacher burnout during COVID-19. *Educational Researcher, 50*(5), 325–327.

Pressley, T. (2021b). Elementary hybrid and virtual teacher stress during COVID-19. *Journal of Research in Education, 30*(3), 97–116.

Pressley, T. (2021c). Returning to teaching during COVID-19: An empirical study on elementary teachers' self-efficacy. *Psychology in the Schools, 58*(8), 1611–1623.

Pressley, T., Croyle, H., & Edgar, M. (2020). Different approaches to classroom environments based on teacher experience and effectiveness. *Psychology in the Schools, 57*(4), 606–626.

Pressley, T., & Ha, C. (2021). Teaching during a pandemic: United States teachers' self-efficacy during the COVID-19 pandemic. *Teaching and Teacher Education, 106*, 103465.

Pressley, T., & Ha, C. (2022). Teacher exhaustion during COVID-19: Exploring the role of administrators, self-efficacy, and anxiety, *Teacher Educator, 57*(1), 61–78.

Pressley, T., Ha, C., & Learn, E. (2021). Teacher stress and anxiety during COVID-19: An empirical study. *School Psychology, 36*(5), 367–376.

Pressley, T., Kidd, M., & Wheatley, S. (2023, April). *"We were kept in the dark": Teacher perspectives on returning to learning plans.* Paper presented at the annual meeting of the American Educational Research Association, Chicago.

Pressley, T., Marshall, D. T., Love, S. M., & Neugebauer, N. M. (2022). Teacher morale and mental health following the COVID-19 pandemic. *SocArXiv. https://osf.io/preprints/socarxiv/9yxaq.*

Pressley, T., Marshall, D. T., & Moore, T. (in press). Understanding teacher burnout following COVID-19. *Teacher Development.*

Pressley, T., & Rangel, R. (2023). Elementary teacher self-efficacy after a year of teaching during COVID-19. *Psychology in the Schools, 60*(9), 3284–3297.

Psacharopoulos, G., Collis, V., Patrinos, H. A., & Vegas, E. (2021). The COVID-19 cost of school closures in earnings and income across the world. *Comparative Education Review, 65*(2), 271–287.

Rabaglietti, E., Lattke, L. S., Tesauri, B., Settanni, M., & De Lorenzo, A. (2021). A balancing act during COVID-19: Teachers' self-efficacy, perception of stress in the distance learning experience. *Frontiers in Psychology, 12,* 644108.

Radwan, E., Radwan, A., & Radwan, W. (2020). The role of social media in spreading panic among primary and secondary school students during the COVID-19 pandemic: An online questionnaire study from the Gaza Strip, Palestine. *Heliyon, 6*(12), e05807.

Ravens-Sieberer, U., Erhart, M., Devine, J., Gilbert, M., Reiss, F., Barkmann, C., . . . Kaman, A. (2022). Child and adolescent mental health during the COVID-19 pandemic: Results from the three-wave longitudinal COPSY study. *Journal of Adolescent Health, 71*(5), 570–578.

Reyes, M. R., Brackett, M. A., Rivers, S. E., White, M., & Salovey, P. (2012). Classroom emotional climate, student engagement, and academic achievement. *Journal of Educational Psychology, 104*(3), 700–712.

Rodriguez-Quintana, N., Meyer, A. E., Bilek, E., Flumenbaum, R., Miner, K., Scoville, L., . . . Koschmann, E. (2021). Development of a brief group CBT intervention to reduce COVID-19 related distress among school-age youth. *Cognitive and Behavioral Practice, 28*(4), 642–652.

Roehrig, A. D., Turner, J. E., Arrastia, M. C., Christesen, E., McElhaney, S., & Jakiel, L. M. (2012). Effective teachers and teaching: Characteristics and practices related to positive student outcomes. In K. R. Harris, S. Graham, T. Urdan, S. Graham, J. M. Royer, & M. Zeidner (Eds.), *APA educational psychology handbook, Vol. 2: Individual differences and cultural and contextual factors* (pp. 501–527). American Psychological Association.

Rogers, A. A., Ha, T., & Ockey, S. (2021). Adolescents' perceived socio-emotional impact of COVID-19 and implications for mental health: Results from a U.S.-based mixed-methods study. *Journal of Adolescent Health, 68*(1), 43–52.

Ronfeldt, M., Loeb, S., & Wyckoff, J. (2013). How teacher turnover harms student achievement. *American Educational Research Journal, 50*(1), 4–36.

Rosenberg, D., & Anderson, T. (2021). Teacher turnover before, during, and after COVID. *https://files.eric.ed.gov/fulltext/ED614496.pdf.*

Rousseau, C., & Miconi, D. (2020). Protecting youth mental health during the COVID-19 pandemic: A challenging engagement and learning process. *Journal of the American Academy of Child andAdolescent Psychiatry,* 59(11), 1203–1207.

Rumberger, R. W. (2011). *Dropping out: Why students drop out of high school and what can be done about it.* Harvard University Press.

Ryan, S. V., von der Embse, N. P., Pendergast, L. L., Saeki, E., Segool, N., & Schwing, S. (2017). Leaving the teaching profession: The role of teacher stress and educational accountability policies on turnover intent. *Teaching and Teacher Education, 66,* 1–11.

Sahin, A., & Matteson, S. M. (2022). Impact of online learning and students' personal factors on students' NWEA scores. *European Journal of Education and Pedagogy, 3*(5), 134–146.

Salzano, G., Passanisi, S., Pira, F., Sorrenti, L., La Monica, G., Pajno, G. B., . . . Lombardo, F. (2021). Quarantine due to the COVID-19 pandemic from the perspective of adolescents: The crucial role of technology. *Italian Journal of Pediatrics, 47,* 40.

Savaş, A. C., Bozgeyik, Y., & Eser, İ. (2014). A study on the relationship between teacher self-efficacy and burnout. *European Journal of Educational Research, 3*(4), 159–166.

Sawchuk, S. (2020, April 1). Grading students during the coronavirus crisis: What's the right call? *Education Week. www.edweek.org/teaching-learning/grading-students-during-the-coronavirus-crisis-whats-the-right-call/2020/04.*

Sawchuk, S. (2022, April 6). Millions toward tutoring: Funders bank on the recovery strategy despite big challenges. *www.edweek.org/leadership/millions-toward-tutoring-funders-bank-on-the-recovery-strategy-despite-big-challenges/2022/04.*

Scafidi, B., Tutterow, R., & Kavanagh, D. (2021). This time really is different: The effect of COVID-19 on independent K–12 school enrollments. *Journal of School Choice, 15*(3), 305–330.

Scardamalia, M., & Bereiter, C. (1994). Computer support for knowledge-building communities. *Journal of the Learning Sciences, 3*(3), 265–283.

Schiller, K. S., Wilcox, K. C., Leo, A., Khan, M. I., & Ávila, J. A. M. (2023). "I was on an island": COVID-19 impacts on educator collegiality. *Journal of Educational Change, 24,* 1099–1110.

School districts' reopening plans: A snapshot 2020. (2020). *www.edweek.org/ew/section/multimedia/school-districts-reopening-plans-a-snapshot.html.*

Schult, J., Mahler, N., Fauth, B., & Lindner, M. A. (2022). Did students learn less during the COVID-19 pandemic? Reading and mathematics competencies before and after the first pandemic wave. *School Effectiveness and School Improvement, 33*(4), 544–563.

Senst, L., Baimoukhametova, D., Sterley, T.-L., & Bains, J. S. (2016). Sexually dimorphic neuronal responses to social isolation. *eLife, 5,* e18726.

Shapiro, E. (2020, November 29). New York City will reopen elementary schools and reduce hybrid learning. *www.nytimes.com/2020/11/29/nyregion/schools-reopening-partially.html.*

Shapiro, E., & Rubenstein, D. (2020, November 15). Did it hit 3%? Why parents and teachers are fixated on one number. *www.nytimes.com/2020/11/15/nyregion/coronavirus-nyc-schools-shutdown.html.*

Sharpe, S. W., Marshall, D. T., & Shetty, P. (2022). Clinical experiences and program outcomes in alternative licensure pathways. In D. Polly & E. Garin (Eds.), *Preparing quality teachers: Advances in clinical practice* (pp. 311–334). Information Age.

Shaw, P. A., & Shaw, A. (2021). COVID-19 and remote learning: Experiences of parents supporting children with special needs and disability during the pandemic. *Education 3–13, 51*(3), 371–385.

Siciliano, M. D. (2016). It's the quality not the quantity of ties that matters: Social networks and self-efficacy beliefs. *American Educational Research Journal, 53*(2), 227–262.

Silberstein, K., & Roza, M. (2023, April 4). The massive ESSER experiment: Here's what we're learning. *www.educationnext.org/the-massive-esser-experiment-heres-what-were-learning.*

Sims, V. J., Lord, K., Megos, M., & Mitchell, U. (2023). Teacher residency: Growing and diversifying the profession. *Phi Delta Kappan, 104*(8), 6–11.

Singh, A., Romero, M., & Muralidharan, K. (2022). *COVID-19 learning loss and recovery: Panel data evidence from India* (Working Paper No. 30552). Washington, DC: National Bureau of Economic Research. *www.nber.org/papers/w30552.*

Skaalvik, E. M., & Skaalvik, S. (2011). Teacher job satisfaction and motivation to leave the teaching profession: Relations with school context, feeling of belonging, and emotional exhaustion. *Teaching and Teacher Education, 27*(6), 1029–1038.

Skaalvik, E. M., & Skaalvik, S. (2015). Job satisfaction, stress and coping strategies in the teaching profession: What do teachers say? *International Education Studies, 8*(3), 181–192.

Smith, M., & Ballard, J. (2021, February 8). *Scientists and doctors are the most respected professions worldwide. https://today.yougov.com/topics/economy/articles-reports/2021/02/08/international-profession-perception-poll-data.*

Sokal, L., Trudel, L. E., & Babb, J. (2020a). Canadian teachers' attitudes toward change, efficacy, and burnout during the COVID-19 pandemic. *International Journal of Educational Research Open, 1*, 100016.

Sokal, L. J., Trudel, L. E., & Babb, J. C. (2020b). Supporting teachers in times of change: The job demands–resources model and teacher burnout during the COVID-19 pandemic. *International Journal of Contemporary Education, 3*(2), 67–74.

Sokal, L., Trudel, L. E., & Babb, J. (2021). I've had it! Factors associated with burnout and low organizational commitment in Canadian teachers during the second wave of the COVID-19 pandemic. *International Journal of Educational Research Open, 2*(2), 1–9.

Sonnenschein, S., & Stites, M. L. (2021). The effects of COVID-19 on young children's and their parents' activities at home. *Early Education and Development, 32*(6), 789–793.

Sorensen, L., Frank, J., Gais, T., & Sun, H. (2018). *Virginia is for teachers? An analysis of the state's teacher demand and supply.* Nelson A. Rockefeller Institute of Government. *https://files.eric.ed.gov/fulltext/ED605639.pdf*

Sorensen, L. C., & Ladd, H. F. (2020). The hidden costs of teacher turnover. *Aera Open, 6*(1).

Spitzer, M., & Musslick, S. (2021). Academic performance of K–12 students in an online-learning environment for mathematics increased during the shutdown of schools in wake of the COVID-19 pandemic. *PLoS ONE, 16*(8), e0255629.

Sprang, G., & Silman, M. (2013). Posttraumatic stress disorder in parents and youth after health-related disasters. *Disaster Medicine and Public Health Preparedness, 7*(1), 105–110.

Stang-Rabrig, J., Brüggemann, T., Lorenz, R., & McElvany, N. (2022). Teachers' occupational well-being during the COVID-19 pandemic: The role of resources and demands. *Teaching and Teacher Education, 117*, 103803.

Steiner, E. D., & Woo, A. (2021). Job-related stress threatens the teacher supply. *www.rand.org/content/dam/rand/pubs/research_reports/RRA1100/RRA1108-1/RAND_RRA1108-1.pdf.*

Stewart, S. L., Vasudeva, A. S., Van Dyke, J. N., & Poss, J. W. (2022). Child and youth mental health needs and service utilization during COVID-19. *Traumatology, 28*(3), 311–324.

Storey, N., & Slavin, R. E. (2020). The US educational response to the COVID-19 pandemic. *Best Evidence in Chinese Education*, 5(2), 617–633.

Stronge, J. H. (2018). *Qualities of effective teachers.* Association for Supervision and Curriculum Development.

Tan, W. (2021). School closures were over-weighted against the mitigation of COVID-19 transmission. *Medicine, 100*(30), e26709.

Tang, S., Xiang, M., Cheung, T., & Xiang, Y.-T. (2021). Mental health and its correlates among children and adolescents during COVID-19 school closure: The importance of parent–child discussion. *Journal of Affective Disorders, 279*, 353–360.

Thompson, A., Darwich, L., & Bartlett, L. (2020). Not remotely familiar: How COVID-19 is reshaping teachers' work and the implications for teacher education. *Northwest Journal of Teacher Education, 15*(2), Article 2.

Tinubu Ali, T., & Herrera, M. (2020). Distance learning during COVID-19: 7 Equity considerations for schools and districts (Issue brief). *Southern Education Foundation. https://southerneducation.org/wp-content/uploads/documents/southern-education-foundation_covid19-distance-learning-equity-brief.pdf.*

Trinidad, J. E. (2021). Teacher satisfaction and burnout during COVID-19: What organizational factors help? *International Journal of Leadership in Education*, 1–19.

Tschannen-Moran, M., & Hoy, A. W. (2001). Teacher efficacy: Capturing an elusive construct. *Teaching and Teacher Education*, *17*(7), 783–805.

Tschannen-Moran, M., Hoy, A. W., & Hoy, W. K. (1998). Teacher efficacy: Its meaning and measure. *Review of Educational Research*, *68*(2), 202–248.

Twenge, J. M. (2017). *iGen: Why today's super-connected kids are growing up less rebellious, more tolerant, less happy—and completely unprepared for adulthood.* Atria Books.

Tyack, D., & Cuban, L. (1995). *Tinkering toward utopia: A century of public school reform.* Harvard University Press.

UNESCO. (2020). UN Secretary-General warns of education catastrophe, pointing to UNESCO estimate of 24 million learners at risk of dropping out. *www.unesco.org/en/articles/un-secretary-general-warns-education-catastrophe-pointing-unesco-estimate-24-million-learners-risk.*

UNICEF. (2022, June). The state of global learning poverty: 2022 update. *www.unicef.org/reports/state-global-learning-poverty-2022.*

U.S. Department of Education. (2019). Department of Education: Salaries and expenses overview. *www2.ed.gov/about/overview/budget/budget19/justifications/w-seoverview.pdf.*

U.S. Department of Education Office of Elementary and Secondary Education. (2023). Elementary and secondary school emergency relief fund. *https://oese.ed.gov/offices/education-stabilization-fund/elementary-secondary-school-emergency-relief-fund.*

Vahle, C., de Araujo, Z., Han, J., & Otten, S. (2023). Teachers' instructional responses to the COVID-19 pandemic. *Teaching and Teacher Education, 124*, 104040.

van der Velde, M., Sense, F., Spijkers, R., Meeter, M., & van Rijn, H. (2021). Lockdown learning: Changes in online foreign-language study activity and performance of Dutch secondary school students during the COVID-19 pandemic. *Frontiers in Education, 6*, 712987.

Van Lancker, W., & Parolin, Z. (2020). COVID-19, school closures, and child poverty: A social crisis in the making. *Lancet Public Health*, 5(5), e243–e244.

Vanourek, G. (2020, August). Schooling COVID-19: Lessons from leading charter networks from their transition to remote learning. *https://fordhaminstitute.org/sites/default/files/publication/pdfs/2020825-schooling-covid-19-lessons-leading-charter-networks-their-transition-remote-learning.pdf.*

Varma, J. K., Thamkittikasem, J., Whittemore, K., Alexander, M., Stephens, D. H., Arslanian, K., . . . Long, T. G. (2021). COVID-19 infections among students and staff in New York City public schools. *Pediatrics, 147*(5), e2021050605.

Veney, D. (2023, August). *Listen to your teacher! An analysis of teacher sentiment on the state of public education.* National Alliance for Public Charter Schools.

Veney, D., & Jacobs, D. (2021, September). Voting with their feet: A state-level analysis of public charter school and district public school trends. National Alliance for Public Charter Schools. *www.publiccharters.org/sites/default/files/documents/2021-09/napcs_voting_feet_rd6.pdf.*

Viano, S., Pham, L. D., Henry, G. T., Kho, A., & Zimmer, R. (2021). What teachers want: School factors predicting teachers' decisions to work in low-performing schools. *American Educational Research Journal*, 58(1), 201–233.

Viner, R. M., Bonell, C., Drake, L., Jourdan, D., Davies, N., Baltag, V., . . . Darzi, A. (2021). Reopening schools during the COVID-19 pandemic: Governments must balance the uncertainty and risks of reopening schools against the clear harms associated with prolonged closure. *Archives of Disease in Childhood, 106*(2), 111–113.

Viner, R., Russell, S., Saulle, R., Croker, H., Stansfield, C., Packer, J., . . . Minozzi, S. (2022). School closures during social lockdown and mental health, health behaviors, and well-being among children and adolescents during the first COVID-19 wave: A systematic review. *JAMA Pediatrics, 176*(4), 400–409.

Vivinetto, G. (2022, August 8). Nationwide teacher shortage prompts "scramble" ahead of the school year. *www.today.com/news/news/nationwide-teacher-shortage-2022-2023-school-year-rcna42057.*

Waldrop, T. (2020, July 16). *Teachers are so worried about returning to school that they're preparing wills.* CNN. *www.cnn.com/2020/07/16/us/coronavirus-teachers-preparing-wills/index.html.*

Wall, P. (2023, February 9). COVID exodus: Where did 1 million public school students go? New data sheds some light. *www.chalkbeat.org/2023/2/9/23591903/school-enrollment-data-decline-covid-attendance.*

Walsh, N. R., Ginger, K., & Akhavan, N. (2020). Benefits of instructional coaching for teacher efficacy: A mixed methods study with PreK–6 teachers in California. *Issues in Educational Research, 30*(3), 1143–1161.

Walsh, S., Chowdhury, A., Braithwaite, V., Russell, S., Birch, J. M., Ward, J. L., . . . Mytton, O. T. (2021). Do school closures and school reopenings affect community transmission of COVID-19? A systematic review of observational studies. *BMJ Open, 11*(8), e053371.

Walter, H. L., & Fox, H. B. (2021). Understanding teacher well-being during the COVID-19 pandemic over time: A qualitative longitudinal study. *Journal of Occupational and Organizational Psychology, 21*(25), 36–50.

Wang, L., Berger, N. A., Kaelber, D. C., Davis, P. B., Volkow, N. D., & Xu, R. (2022). COVID infection rates, clinical outcomes, and racial/ethnic and gender disparities before and after Omicron emerged in the US. *medRxiv. https://pubmed.ncbi.nlm.nih.gov/35233579*

Watson, A. R. (2022). Pandemic pods and alternative modes of education. In D. T. Marshall (Ed.), *COVID-19 and the classroom: How schools navigated the great disruption* (pp. 197–210). Lexington Books.

Weare, K., & Nind, M. (2011). Mental health promotion and problem prevention in schools: What does the evidence say? *Health Promotion International, 26*(Suppl. 1), i29–i69.

Weissberg, R. P., Durlak, J. A., Domitrovich, C. E., & Gullotta, T. P. (2015). Social and emotional learning: Past, present, and future. In J. A. Durlak, C. E. Domitrovich, R. P. Weissberg, & T. P. Gullotta (Eds.), *Handbook of social and emotional learning: Research and practice* (pp. 3–19). Guilford Press.

Westphal, A., Kalinowski, E., Hoferichter, C. J., & Vock, M. (2022). K–12 teachers' stress and burnout during the COVID-19 pandemic: A systematic review. *Frontiers in Psychology, 13*.

Will, M. (2022, April 14). Teacher job satisfaction hits an all-time low. *Education Week, 41*(31).

Willett, J. B., & Singer, J. D. (1991). From whether to when: New methods for studying student dropout and teacher attrition. *Review of Educational Research, 61*(4), 407–450.

Wisconsin Department of Public Instruction. (n.d.). Virtual learning time for public schools. *https://dpi.wi.gov/cal/innovation/virtual-learning-time.*

Wolters, C. A., & Daugherty, S. G. (2007). Goal structures and teachers' sense of efficacy: Their relation and association to teaching experience and academic level. *Journal of Educational Psychology, 99*(1), 181–193.

Wong, C., & Faherty, L. (2020, July 16). Back to school: Working parents will need help from employers. *www.usatoday.com/story/opinion/2020/07/16/covid-19-back-school-complications-employers-and-working-parents-column/5429833002.*

Woodruff-Borden, J., Morrow, C., Bourland, S., & Cambron, S. (2002). The behavior of anxious parents: Examining mechanisms of transmission of anxiety from parent to child. *Journal of Clinical Child and Adolescent Psychology, 31*(3), 364–374.

World Bank. (2022, October 12). Ending learning poverty. *www.worldbank.org/en/topic/education/brief/ending-learning-poverty.*

Wright, B. (2023, June 27). *More NAEP losses for high achievers–and how to reverse them.* Thomas B. Fordham Institute. *https://fordhaminstitute.org/national/commentary/more-naep-losses-high-achievers-and-how-reverse-them.*

Wright, D. S., Weinberg, A. E., Sample McMeeking, L. B., Lin Hunter, D. E., & Balgopal, M. M. (2022). I will survive: Teachers reflect on motivations to remain in education amidst a global pandemic. *Journal of Research in Science Teaching, 60*(6), 1266–1291.

Wyoming schools to remain closed through May 15th. (2020, April 28). *https://oil-city.news/wyoming/2020/04/28/wyoming-schools-to-remain-closed-through-may-15th.*

Wyse, A. E., Stickney, E. M, Butz, D., Beckler, A., & Close, C. N. (2020). The potential impact of COVID-19 on student learning and how schools can respond. *Educational Measurement: Issues and Practice, 39*(3), 60–64.

Xu, W., Li, X., Dozier, M., He, Y., Kirolos, A., Lang, Z., . . . Theodoratou, E. (2020). What is the evidence for transmission of COVID-19 by children in schools? *Journal of Global Health, 10*(2), 021104.

Yard, E., Radhakrishnan, L., Ballesteros, M. F., Sheppard, M., Gates, A., Stein, Z., . . . Stone, D. M. (2021). Emergency department visits for suspected suicide attempts among persons aged 12–25 years before and during the COVID-19 pandemic: United States, January 2019–May 2021. *Morbidity and Mortality Weekly Report, 70*(24), 888–894.

Yoo, J. H. (2016). The effect of professional development on teacher efficacy and teachers' self-analysis of their efficacy change. *Journal of Teacher Education for Sustainability, 18*(1), 84–94.

Yun, C., & DeMoss, K. (2020). Sustainable strategies for funding teacher residencies: Lessons from California. Learning Policy Institute. *https://files.eric.ed.gov/fulltext/ED610885.pdf.*

Zamarro, G., Camp, A., Fuchsman, D., & McGee, J. B. (2022). Understanding how COVID-19 has changed teachers' chances of remaining in the classroom. University of Arkansas Education Reform Faculty and Graduate Students Publications. *https://scholarworks.uark.edu/edrepub/132.*

Zeichner, K. M. (2018). *The struggle for the soul of teacher education.* Routledge.

Zhao, Y., & Watterston, J. (2021). The changes we need: Education post COVID-19. *Journal of Educational Change, 22,* 3–12.

Zhou, P., Yang, X.-L., Wang, X.-G., Hu, B., Zhang, L., Zhang, W., . . . Shi, Z.-L. (2020). A pneumonia outbreak associated with a new coronavirus of probable bat origin. *Nature, 579*(7798), 270–273.

Zimmer, R., Gill, B., Booker, K., Lavertu, S., Sass, T. R., & Witte, J. (2009). Charter schools in eight states: Effects on achievement, attainment, integration, and competition. *www.rand.org/content/dam/rand/pubs/monographs/2009/RAND_MG869.sum.pdf.*

Zimmerman, B. J., Bandura, A., & Martinez-Pons, M. (1992). Self-motivation for academic attainment: The role of self-efficacy beliefs and personal goal setting. *American Educational Research Journal, 29*(3), 663–676.

Zins, J. E., Bloodworth, M. R., Weissberg, R. P., & Walberg, H. J. (2004). The scientific base linking social and emotional learning to school success. In J. E. Zins, R. P. Weisberg, M. C. Wang, & H. J. Walberg (Eds.), *Building academic success on social and emotional learning: What does the research say?* (pp. 3–22). Teachers College Press.

Index

P

R

S

T

U

V

W